Need to Lead

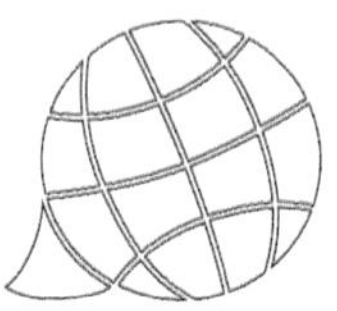

CCBS Press

Cross Cultural Business Skills Minor

Need to Lead

Mapping cross-cultural differences in leadership practices

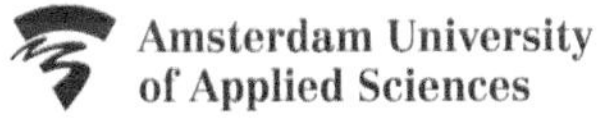

CCBS-Press
First edition 2022, ISBN: 978-90-79646-54-8, NUR: 812
Editorial managers: Christopher Higgins, Aynur Doğan, Sander Schroevers
Bibliographic and citations editor: Aynur Doğan
CCBS is an elective course (highest evaluated) at the Amsterdam University of Applied Sciences (HvA)
Inner and cover design: SH69T Studio, Amsterdam, Netherlands
Logo design: Erica Frank, Designer Gráfico, Vitória, Espirito Santo, Brazil
Cover graphic: Golden Dayz

Table of Contents

Preface

Welcome to the latest edition of our ongoing empirical cross-cultural analyses of global leadership styles and practices. This book is the result of collaborative research by 125 students on the 'Cross-Cultural Business Skills' elective (minor), which is hosted by the University of Applied Sciences Amsterdam. Over the course of a single semester, these students have empirically investigated leadership styles and practices across multiple countries, through employing a combination of research methods. More specifically, the students performed desk-based literature reviews of local scholarship, in conjunction with generating both quantitative and qualitative data through conducting a survey and interviews with thousands of local business professionals and cross-cultural scholars and practitioners. This achievement is made even more notable by the fact that their investigations were still conducted online amidst the attendant lockdown policies of governments across the globe. The quality of the contributions in this edited collection are thus, above all, a testament to the perseverance and collaborative work ethic of everyone involved, and, moreover, provide rich and colourful insights into countries that we may still not be able to visit for some time.

First and foremost, we would like to take this opportunity to thank all the individual co-authors for their flexibility and determination to complete their respective analyses during such difficult times. Moreover, we also wish to extend our upmost gratitude to all the survey respondents and interviewees for being gracious enough to provide insight into the prevailing leadership styles and practices in their country. To the reader, we hope this book finds you well and perhaps, dare we say it, sitting in a convenient airport lounge waiting to board a flight to one of the countries explored in this book, with locally-informed insights into cross-cultural leadership, eager to apply them in practice.

Christopher Higgins, Sander Schroevers & Aynur Dogan

About CCBS

Since 2010, Cross-Cultural Business Skills (CCBS) has sought to educate bachelor students in both the fundamentals of cross-cultural business skills and specific research methods. CCBS is an elective course ('minor') established and taught by prof. Sander Schroevers, alongside Christopher Higgins MA and Aynur Doğan MA at the Amsterdam University of Applied Sciences (the Netherlands).

Educational approach

At CCBS we believe that effective learning takes place through sharing and engaging with first-hand experiences. For this reason, we challenge our students to produce new knowledge from a localised perspective. Often this involves conducting research in an unknown language, alphabet or cultural milieu, which, in turn, helps out students develop fundamental skills for the contemporary interconnected world. Our main objective is to co-create country-specific bodies of knowledge, which we generate through carrying out both expert-interviews (video and audio) with native professionals and scholars and in-depth analyses of local academic and trade literature. In order to create a truly international classroom experience, we try to host students from across the globe. Moreover, we attempt to connect our students with a broad range of representatives from the business, media and diplomatic sectors, through hosting professional symposia in the school. All CCBS-learning materials (print, digital and video) are 100% bespoke. We are honoured by the fact that we have consistently received the university's highest evaluation scores over the last seven years.

About CCBS global leadership research

CCBS global leadership is our ongoing academic research project for the Amsterdam University of Applied Sciences, which directly informs the cross-cultural business material taught on the minor. Every six months, CCBS researchers survey C-level executives around the world. Our analytical gaze is focused on five main areas: management, meetings, leadership, recruitment and expatriates. Since conducting the inaugural international poll in 2012, the CCBS global-fact-tank has conducted interviews in 128 trade nations, with more than twenty-one-thousand professionals. Thank you!

Methodological approach

Three modes of data collection were employed to generate the insights published in this book. Firstly, insights into the cultural aspects of leadership were gathered through country-specific literature searches, in both peer-reviewed academic journals and in-country books, which served as the foundation for the subsequent research. Secondly, a global online survey on leadership was conducted with qualified respondents from each country (CCBS Survey, year). Expert sampling was used to identify the survey respondents, in conjunction with snowballing techniques, which were subsequently introduced to target a population who are often difficult to reach. In total, over 21,000 respondents participated in the CCBS survey; however almost one-third of these surveys were not used, because they were not fully completed, or their background or sometimes IP-addresses did not match our target group. The survey was created in English and subsequently translated by competent bilinguals, who were either research collaborators or supervised by them. The present study made use of translations into Arabic, Chinese, French, Hungarian, Kazakh, Latvian, Polish, Romanian, Russian, Spanish, Uzbek and surely: English. Evaluations of translation accuracy were completed by using back-translation or parallel translations, where possible. The Spanish version was rolled out in five countries, the English version in four. The questionnaire comprised 27 items, both multiple-choice and open-ended questions, which provided descriptive information on national-based views on leadership.
The respondents answered the psychometric multiple-choice questions on five or six-point Likert scales, which were anchored by terms ranging from 'not at all' to 'a lot'. All the qualitative data provided comprehensive knowledge into the topic of local leadership styles and practices. The multinational survey and interviewing were conducted between 28 September and 16 December 2022. The findings that emerged out of this research have not been presented prior to the publication of this book. Thirdly, in addition to the survey respondents, a selection of 37 leadership experts were also interviewed for the present study. These audio and video recorded interviews lasted between 20-40 minutes on average, and were transcribed verbatim (a selection of these will be published on the YouTube and Spotify channels of the CCBS minor).

Country profiles

Sander Schroevers

Empirical studies have revealed that the relationship between certain kinds of motivating leadership behaviour and work outcomes systematically varies from culture to culture. As noted by the Global Leadership and Organizational Behavior Effectiveness (GLOBE) Research Program: "to date, 90 percent of leadership literature reflects US-based research and theory". The American-centric nature of extant literature is a profound problem, insofar as it fails to account for how leadership theories, styles and practices operate across national frontiers. This is important, because as the number of countries expand, so do the differences.
It is for this reason that I have always been fond of Peter Drucker's quote: "Management is doing things right; leadership is doing the right things".
That is to say, leadership encompasses the human element of business, whereas management is often about systems and processes. For the purposes of writing this paragraph, I conducted a quick check on Amazon.com for the number of books with the word 'leader' in their title, which produced an incredible 60,000 results. Similarly, a quick search on ProQuest (one of the databases we recommend to students for accessing scholarly journals) resulted in almost a million hits for 'leadership'. Evidently, there is extensive research informing us of how leaders' communication styles are profoundly influenced by the geographical region in which they are operating. Regrettably, some business leaders overlook local managerial and cultural practices, and instead acquiesce to management-styles that are grounded in Western concepts, which, in turn, undermines the performance of their organisation. Given that ineffective managers risk costing organisations notably large sums of money, there is an emergent trend among both human resource professionals and senior executives to adopt more localised leadership styles and practices.

Chapter makeup

This book consists of country-specific chapters, which each describe at length the leadership styles and practices within their respective country. All country profiles have been written in a standard format, in order to allow for a clearer identification of points of similarity and divergence across the different business cultures. Most of the country profiles in this book contain the following sections:

- Country introduction,
- How the indigene characterise leaders,
- Survey results and what local respondents say,
- An in-country YouTube review,
- A transcribed telephone interview with a local leadership scholar,
- A summarised video interview with a local cross-cultural trainer,
- A description of an in-country best-selling book on leadership,
- Understanding hierarchy in the chapter's country,
- How to achieve leadership empathy in that particular culture.

I will briefly introduce each of these sections in turn below.

Local leadership analysis

The more I work abroad, the more I realise that it takes more than just a survey to examine and classify national cultures. More specifically, there is too much cultural heterogeneity and nuance, which substantially impacts upon how one effectively operates in a particular country, but yet simply does not fit within prevailing academic constructs on this topic. Notwithstanding the many good Western-centric books on a variety of countries, what is invariably obfuscated in these texts is the local perspective. The need to address this lacuna in the field by prioritising localised perspectives became pivotal to our approach to investigating country-specific leadership styles and practices. This approach comprises gathering data from indigenous sources, including: (i) survey-results and what local respondents say, (ii) a local leadership scholar, (iii) a local cross-cultural trainer, (iv) and an in-country best-selling book on leadership. While having to conduct research sometimes in other languages and even scripts has proven to be incredibly challenging for some of our students, it has undoubtedly produced rich local-based data that provides insight into how leadership styles and practices are enacted in these selected markets.

Understanding hierarchy in a country

Most of the trends in Western leadership across the twentieth century were centred on moving away from hierarchical command-and-control processes. To this end, both management literature and business school education began to introduce a more egalitarian and facilitative style of leadership. For example, we started to see open-plan office architecture and 360-degree feedback. However, it is important to note that there are profound cross-cultural differences with respect to how authority is viewed. In India, for example, the teaching staff are addressed by Madam or Sir, while I also observed on occasion students standing up when their 'senior-lecturer' entered the classroom. Conversely, on my own Dutch course (CCBS - the authors of this book) local students address me by my first name, and at times feel free to contradict me in front of the class.

Relational hierarchy

Eight out of ten Swiss survey respondents (CCBS Survey, 2021) reported that employees greeted their leaders by their first name. This low-level of hierarchy results in equal and harmonious relationships between superiors and their employees, which are based on mutual trust. Being acutely aware of someone's relative level of authority is of critical importance in a country such as South Korea. This is because it determines how colleagues interact with each other, including choosing between the many different linguistic levels of politeness. For example, organisations tend to have far more levels of management compared to some other countries, each of which have their own corresponding forms of address. Hence, the informal way in which business is conducted in Australia, for example, would likely completely confuse the average Korean employee. This would especially be the case for those Korean workers who have attained senior positions within their organisations, and are wholly accustomed to VIP treatment.

Power Distance

The words Hierarchy and Power Distance are often used interchangeably. The latter can be defined as "the degree to which members of an organisation or society expect and agree that power should be stratified and concentrated at higher levels of an organisation or government" (House & Javidan, 2004, p. 12). Countries that have scored high Power Distance values in either Hofstede or Trompenaars' respective research, believe that power dispenses agreement, social order, and role stability, and, hence, should be concentrated within those in the upper echelon of organisations. In high power distance cultures, leader-subordinate relationships are characterised by paternalism, whereby a leader assumes a parental role and feels obligated to provide support and protection to subordinates under their care (Yan & Hunt, 2005). Many of the country profiles in this book reference their country's Power Distance Index score (PDI), as measured by Dutch cultural scientist Geert Hofstede. However, the value score in and of itself cannot fully explain how hierarchy operates within a particular culture. For example, despite Greece and South Korea both having equally high PDI values (60), leadership is enacted in a fundamentally different way in both countries. Therefore, in this book we attempt to account for such cultural contingencies by conducting culture-specific qualitative research, including interviewing local cultural experts.

How to achieve leadership empathy

This section addresses a specific people-oriented leadership requirement: empathic soft skills. Here, empathy is defined as a leader's capacity to relate to the feelings and experiences of their employees. Empathy is an altogether broader category than sympathy, and, in fact, several researchers consider empathy to be both a key part of emotional intelligence and a critical element of being an effective leader (Bar-On & Parker, 2000). Of course, the ability to successfully build and maintain relationships has long been regarded as a fundamental managerial skill; however, in accordance with the Center for Creative Leadership, the point being made here is that, in some cultures, empathy is more important to job performance than other aspects of leadership (Gentry, Weber, & Sadri, 2016). In addition to this, the way empathic understanding is expressed varies dramatically from country-to-country. Above all, empathy touches upon a leader's understanding of role requirement. To understand its importance across different cultures, several questions in our online survey (CCBS Survey, 2020) pertained to the specific expectations that local leaders had towards empathy. Furthermore, each team attempted to interview local experts, scholars and cross-cultural trainers on the country-specific ways in which empathy is effectively utilised. To cite an example: whereas in Nordic countries empathy is partly established through low-key and modest behaviour, Latin countries prefer a warm, personal and 'simpatico' approach, while, conversely, South Koreans value a courteous leader who, above all, attempts to save face (Kibun). It is well-established that how we connect with people is dependent on our cultural background, and, as such, the ability to be empathetic is especially important for leaders working across cultural boundaries (Alon & Higgins, 2005). The results of our CCBS survey (2020) reflect this, insofar as a large majority of the respondents from the different cultures examined in this book agreed with the statement that a manager should actively spend time on the personal wellbeing of their team members. When one compares the actual country scores (Dell, Eriks, 2018), South Korea and Ukraine score significantly lower on empathy than countries such as Uruguay and Portugal, due, in part, to the fact that Ukrainian and South Korean leaders generally prefer to keep more personal distance from their employees. However, it is important to stress that having empathy for others is not the same as demonstrating empathy; this is because staff expectations may vary considerably across culture in terms of: (i) the amount of verbal attention employees require; (ii) the praise and encouragement expected by staff; or (iii) the daily routine of managers. When managers increase their awareness of the cultural context in which empathy takes place, it often has a direct impact on employee performance, the organisational climate, and the quality of the productive working relations between leaders and employees.

Concluding Remarks

It was Darwin who first showed us the supreme value inherent to diversity. With this in mind, both the increased cultural heterogeneity of today's workforce and the increasingly global footprint of contemporary organisations transforms the styles and practices through which we lead teams. This calls for leaders with an ability to decode cultural differences and adjust their leadership-style to fit the cultural milieu in which they are operating. In summary, I hope that our findings contribute to increasing the richness of extant leadership literature, alongside aiding professional leaders to recalibrate their skills and mindsets in a manner advantageous to themselves, their employees, and, above all, the organisations they serve.

de Baas

ප්‍රධාන විධායක නිලධාරී

தலைமை நிர்வாக அதிகாரி

Big-man

प्रबन्धक

Chief Executive Officer

Gerente general

Manajer umum

Generálny Riaditeľ

المدير التنفيذي

総監督

Président Directeur Géneral

Consejero Delegado

генеральний директор

MAIN DUDE

Basque country

Sara Huegun, Ander Roteta, Anastasija Spirovska, Raffaele Tartaglione, ,Jon Villafranca

Euskal Herria (the Basque Country) is an Atlantic peripheral region of southern Europe, located on the north coast of Spain, in the Bay of Bizkaia, with around 3 million inhabitants (Lopez-Rodriguez et al., 2010). Situated on both sides of the Pyrenees, it is divided into two parts called *Iparralde* (North), the French side where the provinces of Lapurdi, Zuberoa and Nafarroa Behera are located, and *Hegoalde* (South), the Spanish side, which comprises Gipuzkoa, Bizkaia, Araba and Nafarroa. The officially recognised languages are *Euskara* (Basque), French and Spanish. *Euskara* is a specific heritage of the Basques that sets them apart from the rest of the country's autonomous communities. Of the entire Basque population, around one-quarter are Basque speakers, most of whom live in the Spanish Basque Country (David Lasagabaster et al., 2007). With respect to Basque folklore and traditions, some notable examples are *herri kirolak* (typical Basque games that take place in village festivals) and *bertsolaritza* (the art of improvised singing in verse for conversation or speeches) or the festivity of *Santa Ageda* (a feast in the name of the virgin and martyr of the Third century, according to Christian tradition) (Eusko Ikaskuntza, 2007). The country's economy has undergone significant changes in recent years. Specifically, the economy has shifted from a largely commercial sector, consisting mainly of agriculture, livestock and/or fishing, to an industrial and service-based sector. Some of the many things they excel in are iron and steel, processed products, shipbuilding, capital goods, machine tools, the chemical industry, and paper mills (Zallo et al., 2009). The Basque Country has a strong sense of social and national identity. A person in a position of power within a company must have a strong personality, so that they can more effectively influence the team and determine the objectives to be followed by the group (Pittaway et al., 2005). Precisely how this passionate sense of social and national identity impacts upon leadership styles and practices in the Basque Country will be explored in detail in this chapter.

How the Basque characterise leaders?

Basque leaders are considered to be enterprising people, which is reflected in the strong commitment to innovation and entrepreneurship within the Basque Country (Ferreira, 2022). They are also noble and affectionate people who empathise with and care about the needs of others. These social and behavioural norms also translate into the preferred traits and qualities of leaders in the Basque business sector. For instance, in the Basque Country leaders are expected to be noble in character, which is defined as being attentive to all employees and striving to recognise and celebrate the merits of others within the organisation (Balderas, 2022). These aforesaid characteristics, broadly speaking, are emblematic of a transformational leadership style, which according to House at al. (2004) is the preferred and most effective style of leadership at the middle management level in the Basque Country, outperforming transactional and laissez-faire leaders in terms of effectiveness. Basque leaders who adopt this leadership style seek to motivate and encourage the positive development of their subordinates (López, 2022). In order to foster learning and the development of their subordinates, it is important that leaders embody good moral principles, and cultivate an ethical work environment characterised by clear values, priorities and rules (Balderas, 13 October 2022). The importance placed upon clear priorities and values is reflected in the fact that Basque leaders are highly committed to achieving targets by the assigned date, otherwise they are considered to have failed (CCBS Survey, 2022). Alongside this, Ugalde (2022) underscores two additional main strengths of Basque leaders, namely their capacity for work and their competence. According to the the CCBS Survey (2022) that was administered to Basque business leaders, we can conclude that, generally speaking, leaders are very close to their employees. This is evidenced by the fact that they operate in an ethical manner, which encourages trust from employees in return on leaders, allow employees to call them by their first name, and show concern regarding the well-being of their team-members. Moreover, despite being a more individualistic society, which, in turn, poses challenges with respect to team building, it is important that leaders strive to mobilise people by convincing them and facilitating the overcoming of obstacles (CCBS Survey, 2022). With respect to whether it is still preferred for males to be leaders in organisations or whether there has been a change over time in the Basque Country, the results of the survey show that many of the repondents believe that today women have the same opportunities and ability as men to attain senior-level positions within organisations in the Basque Country (CCBS Survey, 2022).

Survey results and what local respondents say

The CCBS Survey (2022) exploring Basque Country leadership styles and practices was completed by over forty local and experienced leadership professionals in the country. While the results show clear differences of opinion with respect to leadership styles and practices, there are nevertheless sufficiiently similar perspectives to be able to draw generalisations regarding leadership in the Basque country. Firstly, a marginal majority of the respondents reported that leaders are prepared to change thei rmind once a decision has been made (CCBS Survey, 2022). Secondly, there were recurrent themes with respect to the preferred leadership styles of Basque leaders. Specifically, three-quarters of the respondents noted that leaders should actively spend time on the personal well-being of their staff. Similarly, half of the respondents noted that leaders did not have to keep a level of personal distance, in order to maintain the right level of respect (CCBS Survey, 2022). This is in line with Madinabeitia's (2021) research, which shows that Basque leaders empathise with their employees, rather than expecting them to perform up to expected standards without any exemptions. This emphasises the importance that Basque leaders attach to the relational aspect of leadership, as opposed to hierarchical structures. The relational nature of Basque leadership was also evidenced in the survey, insofar as despite the fact that the majority of managers reported that leaders prefer to hear criticism in a direct manner during meetings, they stated that criticism of employees should be done in private (CCBS Survey, 2022). Alongside the importance placed on the relational dimension of leadership, the respondents also noted that Basque employees expect their leaders to be powerful decision-makers, good listeners, good consensus seekers and visionary thinkers (CCBS Survey, 2022). The respondents were also broadly in agreement over which qualities employees look up to in managers, namely organisational experience, technical competence and being a market expert. Interestingly, most of the respondents disagreed with the statement that an academic title on a business card or in an email signature is important (CCBS Survey, 2022). This was also the same with respect to addressing leaders by their title, as the vast majority of the respondents stated that employees are allowed to address their leaders by their first name (CCBS Survey, 2022). Thirdly, in response to questions over the level of gender (in)equality in Basque organisations, more than half of the respondents either 'strongly' or 'somewhat agreed' that men and women have equal opportunity to attain sernior-level positions within companies. Finally, the respondents reported typical characteristics of Basque leadership culture, which includes closeness with employees (*cercanía*), team spirit, flexibility and hard work. One respondent also pointed out an important and formally revered aspect of Basque organisations across Spain that had changed in recent years. Formally, *"The given word was kept and fulfilled... we were serious and hard-working. Today, the Basque Country has the highest rate of non-attendance to work in the whole country"* (CCBS Survey, 2022).

Local leadership analysis

Esteban Vicente: a Basque leadership scholar

Esteban Vicente is a business consultant who has been advising companies on people management for more than 35 years. He also teaches at several universities, but mainly at the University of Deusto in San Sebastian. He is a specialist in the selection, training, diagnosis and management of people and teams. During our interview, Vicente emphasised that Basque business leaders are different from their spanish counterparts (8 November 2022). Basque leaders lead more by example, due to the simple fact that they are very close to the day-to-day running of the business. This closeness, in turn, enables them to be more innovative in their approach. To illustrate this, Vicente cited the example of how the Basques make very good steel, but they do not mix steel with other substances in search of other things. In this respect, Vicente proceeded to add that the Basques perhaps have a more export-oriented, universal mentality than other countries. He uttered a phrase that struck him about Basque leaders: *"Here, we know what money costs, and that is noticeable when making investments"* (Vicente, 8 November 2022). In contrast, Vicente argued, Spanish leaders are financiers who are always striving to generate a quick profit. Another notable difference between Basque leaders and their Spanish counterparts is that Basque leaders' primary objective is not to make money; rather, for them, money is simply a consequence of doing a job well (Vicente, 8 November 2022). Furthermore, he emphasised that entrepreneurs always win in the end, because they have a project in which they have absolute faith as well as a team around them that they believe in. Vicente argued that it is vital to have faith in a project, and to bring together people who are worthwhile and who do not always agree with you. Indeed, the biggest mistake that a leaders can make, according to Vicente, is to surround yourself only with people who agree with you.

Adela Balderas: a Basque cross-cultural trainer

Adela Balderas, a successful entrepreneur and cross-cultural trainer, was interviewed in order to learn more about her experiences and gain further insight into leadership skills and practices in Basque country. She is currently working as a lecturer at the Duesto Business School in San Sebastian, running training sessions o leadership and team management, alongside being an active researcher at the University of Oxford. She describes her professional career as always revolving around managing people and leadership issues. Over the course of our interview, Adela described the perfect Basque leader as someone who is trustworthy and hard working (13 October 2022). As the interview proceeded, she continued to explain how important it is for herself specifically and Basque leaders generally to keep their word. To illustrate this, Balderas cited the example of how she works in two different parts of the Basque country, San Sebastian and Bilbao, and described how trust is the number one issue within both companies (Balderas, 13 October 2022). Indeed, making a promise and sticking to it is vitally important across the entire *Euskal Herria*. In response to a question about what distinguishes Basque leadership from leadership in other parts of the world, Adela reported that previously there was not a notable difference, but that over the past five years, in part, due to the global pandemic, much of the young and bright talent had left the country, and Basque leaders did not know how to keep or attract them (13 October 2022). Balderas continued to discuss how that has led to companies and leaders having to adopt a more open mind and attempt to find deeper value within the companies and their leadership styles, in order to stop the brain drain and make young people want to remain with the companies they are working for (13 October 2022). Balderas ended the interview by pointing out: *"People have discovered that we also want to live, in addition to working and trying to be happy in our work"* (13 October 2022). This latter point is critical for understanding how both Basque leaders and those training them in leadership think; they are not perfect, however they are cognisant of their situation and surroundings and doing their best to adapt and improve their leadership skills and practices (Balderas, 13 October 2022).

In-country leadership bestseller

Déjame trabajar por tus sueños (Let Me Work for your Dreams) is one of the best selling books on leadership and management in Northern Spain (Lideditorial, n. d.) The author of the book is Jose Manuel Gil Vegas, who was born in Aranda de Duero (Burgos) in 1959. He holds a PhD in Industrial Psychology and is a lecturer at Deusto Business School. Besides being an author of several publications, he is also a senior-level management coach. *Let me work for your dreams*, is, as its subtitle suggests, a manual for building and leading teams and people in contemporary Spanish organisations (Lideditorial, n. d.). The manual explores how Basque companies today are not aware of the value that both properly trained leaders

and effective management of people can bring to organisations.
As aforementioned, team formation and team work is extremely difficult for Basque people due to the prevailing individualism, and Jose Manuel touches explores this issue further by discussing how stable teams are rare and difficult to uphold. The author provides tips to deal with this issue; for example, one strategy would be to eliminate all jobs that require less than three people working below them. The book also provides other fundamental recommendations regarding how to build and lead solid teams in the Basque region, such as, amongst other things, ensuring that meeting schedules, decision-making mechanisms, and commitment tracking systems are executed in a more professional manner, which not only provides competitive advantages, but also shows that leaders are patient and willing to work together with their employees.

Local leadership book	
Title	*Déjame trabajar por tus sueños*
Subtitle	-
Author	Jose Manuel Gil Vegas
Publisher	Europa Ediciones
Year	2021
ISBN	9791220110716

Basque leadership YouTube review

Besdies academic research, survey data and interviews, YouTube is also an important source of information for learning more about local approaches to leadership. In the first video entitled *"Cómo motivar a los profesionales de tu empresa en 10 minutos"* (How to motivate your employees in 10 minutes), Alfonso Alcantara, who, amongst other things, is a motivational speaker for professionals and teams as well as offering services such as conferences and sessions on people management in the fields of HR, education, employment and professional reinvention, speaks as part of the TEDx platform (TEDx Talks, 2018). In the vide, Alfonso talks about how motivation affects the performance and mood of employees in companies and gives advice on how to manage it. He says that if you are struggling with a goal, and you are not motivated, then the consequence of this is that you will always see the glass as being half empty; you need to choose a smaller glass (Alcántara, 2018). In his words: *"Motivation is not something you have or bring from home: it is a result"* (Alcántara, 2018, 4:25) of the interaction between each professional and the culture, context, incentives and methods of the organisation and its teams. He then proceeds to talk about the *"'comfort zone' [as being] not as a place where you are more comfortable, but more motivated"* (Alcántara, 2018, 12:53). Hence, the solution is not to get out of one's comfort zone necessarily, but rather to enlarge it. The next video to be discussed, *"Cómo ser un buen líder gestionando equipos en la empresa"* (How to be a good leader in managing teams in the company), posted by the YouTube channel *Máster de Emprendedores*, is from a conference organised by Sergio Fernandez, who is the Director and founder of the Master of Entrepreneurship as well as a lecturer and trainer who specialises in personal development and entrepreneurship in the Basque Country. During his speech, he focuses on the vital steps that good Basque leaders should take in order to effectively manage teams inside their company. Fernandez states that the first critical step in becoming a good leader in the Basque country is to understand that *"a team is well managed when it has a purpose"* (Fernandez, 2019, 01:18). He then proceeds to state that it is fundamental to define the organisational culture, along with its mission, vision, values, objectives and policy, with the express aim of employing or hiring people who are aligned with the company's values (Fernandez, 2019). Moreover, the spokesman explains the importance of promoting both formal and informal effective communication. Finally, Fernandez stresses the importance of leaders in the Basque Country fostering team synergy, in light of the fact that it is better for the company if everyone is placed in the area where they shine the most (Fernandez, 2019). The last video to be summarised is *"Aprendizajes de vida: valores, éxito y liderazgo"* (Life lessons: values, success and leadership). Carlos Torres Vila, current Chairman of BBVA Bank, answers questions as part of an audience Q&A, with respect to the video for the Aprendemos Juntos 2030 platform. Through this platform, BBVA aims to '*Put the opportunities of this new era within everyone's reach*', promoting education through sustainability to help people build a greener and more inclusive future (Acerca, 2022). For him, the first and most important responsibility of a leader in the Basque country is to know how to manage oneself as a person *"because to lead is to go first, it is to lead the way"* (Torres, 2020, 20:20). Ultimately, it is the leader's actions, words, behaviours and values that lead the way. Torres concluded the session by citing the following quote that although he read it eslewhere, he fully agrees with: *"leading means allowing those you lead to lead"*, thus indicating the importance of knowing how to delegate within Basque organisations (Torres, 2020, 21:02).

Understanding hierarchy in the Basque Country

When looking at Spain more broadly, research has shown that companies historically have been vertically hierarchically structured (Nurhidayat et al., 2022). This is supported by Back (2012), who argues that in Spanish businesses, the prevailing norm is that leaders operate relatively independently from their employees, amd that the way thet dress, act and speak serves to differentiate them from their subordinates. However, there have been changes over the course of the last decade. This shift has been driven, on the one hand, by the the new generation of business leaders who have emerged in recent years, who are more influenced by American leadership styles and practices, which, generally speaking, are characterised by more participatory methods, and, on the other hand, the new wave of expats entering the country who have forced organisations to adapt to a less structured and more relaxed approach (De Jong, 2018). To further discern the differences between Spain generally and the Basque country specifically, it is instructive to utilise Hofstede's power distance index. Hofstede (2013) defines power distance as the extent to which less powerful members of organisations accept that power is distributed unequally across society. According to Hofstede's dimensions model, Spain scores moderately high on the dimension of power distance, thus indicating that they are defined by a corporate structure in which individuals or groups are placed above one another according to their respective status or power in the organisation (Gurbanli, 2020). Indeed, hierarchical structures are evident in most Spanish businesses as well as government controlled sectors, insofar as one can can still espie traditional aspects of hierarchy, such as, for example, profound respect for superiors (Kooyers, 2015). Interestingly, this proposentity for showing respect to one's superiors is also intrinsic to the Spanish language itself, insoafar as it has a form of conjugation *'usted'* that is specifically used when speaking directly to authority figures (Chhokar et al., 2008). This sense of differentiation and distance between leaders and their subordinates can be traced back to distinct socio-cultural features of the Basque Country, most notably the fact that, as aforementioned, the country itself is relatively individualistic, and team work is not strongly favoured within organisations (Nurhidayat et al., 2022). This aspect of Basque culture and organisational life was corroborated by one of our interviewees, Balderas, who stressed that teamwork in the Basque Country can be challenging due to the individualistic nature of the country, which also explains, at least in part, the continued preferenced for traditional rigid hierarchical structures (13 October 2022). As aforesaid, authors like Nurhidayat et al. (2022) and De Jong (2018) both draw attention to the fact that there has been a shift in the country in recent years as a result of the younger generation of leaders entering the business sector and the influx of expats into Spain as a whole. This shift perhaps helps explain the findings of the CCBS Survey (2022) which painst a slightly different story with respect to hierarchy within organisations in the Basque Country. For example, the majority of the respodents reported that Basque leaders do not prefer to be addressed by their titles, but rather prefer to have employees refer to them by their first name (CCBS Survey, 2022). Moreover, according to the respondents, achieveing a high status within an organisation is no longer the goal of Basque leaders, as reflected in the fact that they are not accorded certain benefits from their position in the upper echeleons of the organisation, such as, parking spaces or private offices, for example. These findings thus appear to show that leaders are increasingly looking to close the physical, professional and emotional distance between themselves and those that they lead, as suggested by Nurhidayat et al. (2022) and De Jong (2018).

How the Basque achieve leadership empathy

As aforementioned, although the various regions of the Iberian Peninsula may not be similar to each other in various aspects, when it comes to empathy there is a strong degree of alignment (Lewis, 2010). Therefore, in order to understand how Basque leaders achieve empathic understanding with their employees, we will also draw upon research that discusses Spanish managers more broadly. A study conducted by Mittal and Dorfman (2012) demonstrates that the endorsement of empathy by leaders in Latin European organisations is low. In fact, Latin Europe, of which Spain is part, has the lowest score out of all the researched regions (Mittal & Dorfman, 2012). One reason for this is that Spanish leaders place greater emphasis on reason and intellect than emotional values, which, in turn, has contributed to the lower endorsement of empathy (CCBS, 2018). However, one of our interviewees noted that there had been a profound shift in the behaviour of leaders in the Basque country, as a result of the fact that organisations have failed to retain many of their younger and brighter employees over the last five years who opted to move elsewhere (Balderas, 13 October, 2022). In response to this trend, Basque leaders have invested more time and energy into trying to understand their employees and thinking about how best to utilise their individual skillsets in order to benefit the company. Specifically, Balderas stressed that Basque leaders have focused more on listening to their employees, and that this is indeed the best way for managers to show more affective empathy towards their employees. This shift towards a more relational style of leadership is also reflected in the results of the CCBS Survey (2022), where the respondents stated how important it is for leaders to spend time ensuring the personal well-being of their team members. Furthermore, in the CCBS Survey (2022) it was also noted that the hierarchical distance between managers and employees has lessened in recent years, insofar as the majority of the respondents stated that they no longer sought to retain personal distance from their employees. Furthermore, as stated by Madinabeitia (2021), Basque leaders today are more likely to empathise with their employees, rather than expecting them to perform up to expected standards without any exemptions. Notwithstanding these more recent changes towards a more relational style of leadership, it is also important to highlight that some aspects of the old manage were conducive to empathic attitudes towards employees. Most notably, honour has and continues to play a key role in Basque society and organisations. It is thus important not to say anything that might be interpreted as impinging upon an employee's personal dignity. Indeed, for many Spaniards, *pundonor* (point of honour) is the most important word in their language (Lewis, 2010). Similar to certain Asian cultures, such as China and Japan, losing face is the worst thing that can happen in the workplace. This helps to explain why Basque leaders prefer to address problems privately with their employees in order to avoid any public embarrassment on their behalf (CCBS Survey, 2022). According to Balderas, engaging in private conversations in this way with employees, and simply asking them how they are feeling can lead to an open conversation: *"From there empathy begins and emotions begin to be understood"* (Balderas, 13 October 2022).

Belize

Thimo Hoorn, Tjebbiene Botter, Chanel Pinas, Rayen Jaggoe, Moaz Elrokh, Jessy Mitrasing

Belize, or British Honduras as it was formally known, is a scuba diving paradise located in Latin America. The name Belize is believed to derive from the Mayan word *''belix''*, which means muddy water (Mwakikagile, 2014). On the flag of Belize, one can see a mestizo and a man of colour, which pays homage to the multi-ethnic composition of the population in Belize. Beneath this lies the nation's motto *"Sub Umgra Floreo"* (under the shade I flourish) (Hannerz & Gingrich, 2017). This is a reference to both the forests in Belize and its time under colonial rule. Belize is around half the size of the Netherlands, which testifies to the country's small size. Their official language is English, but there are at least another ten languages spoken in Belize, including, amongst others, Spanish, Mayan, and Creole. The reason why Belize is the only English-speaking country in Latin and South America is because it is a former British colony and remains part of the Commonwealth (Salmon, 2018). The majority of Belizeans are descendants of immigrants from various countries, which contributes to the diversity and richness of the culture. Food is an important part of their culture. The national dish is rice and beans. The importance placed on food is exemplified in the saying *"empty crocus bag kant stan up"* which is creole for 'you cannot do proper work if you are hungry' (Wilk & Barbosa, 2013). Belize's economy is underdeveloped as result of their former colonisation. It is heavily dependent on agriculture and tourism. Belize's economy is comparable to countries like San Marino (Li & Carballo, 2019). One of the main attractions for tourists is the Belize Carnival, which is held every September to celebrate their independence. It is comparable to the Brazilian carnival with lots of colours and dancing parades. In terms of the business sector, Belize has a relatively small market, which means that it is characterised by a lack of large global chains and a preponderance of smaller businesses that tend to communicate with each other on a more personal level (Li & Carballo, 2019). These smaller businesses have distinct business customs and leadership styles and practices. As this chapter will shed light on, negotiation skills and good etiquette form an important part of the organisational culture in Belize, and, in fact, failure to adhere to these practices will lead to a loss of respect from leaders there.

How the Belizeans characterise leaders

The people of Belize characterise their leaders as open and involved. This explains, in part, why the most preferred traits of leaders in the country are charisma and genuineness (CCBS Survey, 2022). As aforementioned, Belize is a multi-active culture, which is to say they are a highly dialogue-oriented culture. Because of this, leaders are certainly happy to hear criticism from their employees and to engage in dialogue with them over these issues, provided this is done in an indirect manner, such as, for example, outside of staff meetings (CCBS Survey, 2022). In Belize, everything is extremely laid back, including, at least to some extent, within the business sector. For example, things take a considerable amount of time to be completed because they run on something called "Belize Time". This is a local joke which refers to the fact that Belizians do things at their own easy-going pace, in such a way that lends itself to the least level of stress possible. This life philosophy is a consequence of their close ties with the Caribbean, and the fact that the idyllic, island-life philosophy has stuck with them (CCBS Survey, 2022). This is also reflected in the prevailing leadership skills and practices in the country, insofar as being charismatic and making those around you laugh and feel at ease are accorded tremendous significance (CCBS Survey, 2022). Indeed, the results of the CCBS Survey (2022) demonstrate that Belizeans like to joke about everything, so it is important for even senior-level executives to quickly learn that they should not take life so seriously, as this makes them appear more down-to-earth and relatable to their employees (CCBS Survey, 2022). Besides this, it is also crucially important that Belizean leaders know absolutely everything about both their competitors and customers (Li and Carballo, 2018). Related to this, both possessing and exhibiting an appreciation for gender equality is also vital for effective organisational leadership in Belize. Indeed, over half of the respondents in the CCBS Survey (2022) agreed that men and woman have equal opportunities to attain senior-level leadership positions. Finally, Belizeans also value their leaders on the basis of other specific factors, such as, for example, their family background, appearance, age and level of market experience (CCBS Survey, 2022). This is summarised in the following quotation from one of our respondents: "*Leadership styles are typically top-down as it is influenced by the fact that most businesses are family owned. It is also influenced by the fact that government is one of the largest employers*" (CCBS Survey, 2022). However, above all, the most important attribute for Belizean leaders is their organisational experience and technical competence (CCBS Survey, 2022).

Survey results and what local respondent say

To gain further insight into Belizean leadership, local C-level executives were asked to participate in the Cross-Cultural Business skills (CCBS) Survey (2022). Only the most notable results are discussed in this section. Firstly, the majority of the respondents reported that Belizean leaders do not mind hearing criticism in a direct manner (CCBS Survey, 2022); however, one-quarter of the respondents agreed with the statement that criticism should take place in an indirect manner outside of staff meetings (CCBS Survey, 2022). Another finding pertains to the fact that more than half of the respondents agreed that Belizean leaders should spend time actively ensuring the personal well-being of their team members (CCBS Survey, 2022). This testifies to the fact that it is important for Belizean leaders to display empathy towards their staff. This was confirmed by one of our respondents, Miranda, who noted: *"Belizean leaders try to create an environment where employees feel that they are valued and that their opinion matters"* (CCBS Survey, 2022). Whereas manners are critically important for leaders in Belize, on the other hand, employees find good treatment to be more important. With respect to what Belizean employees expect from their leaders, the survey demonstrated that they want different things from leaders. For example, the majority of the respondents stated that employees prefer a leader who is a powerful decision maker (CCBS Survey, 2022). Most of the respondents also stated that it was important for Belizean leaders to have strong political connections, insofar as having access to the right networks goes a long way in a country where political power is decisive (CCBS Survey, 2022). This was elaborated on by one of our respondents, Boscardi, who stated: *"Our leadership styles are very antiquated and based heavily on connections rather than qualifications"* (CCBS Survey, 2022). The latter was supported by the fact that under half of the respondents opined that being highly educated is important for leaders in Belize. Conversely, around half of the respondents stated that a leader must have a strong charismatic personality and be resourceful (CCBS Survey, 2022). With respect to what qualities employees look up to in their leaders, the majority of the respondents noted that employees look up to their leaders on the basis of their organisational experience, technical competence and respectable age (CCBS Survey, 2022). This shows both what employees expect from and how they act towards their leaders. To reflect the status of leaders in Belizean companies, they are provided with their own office space and transportation. Indeed, status is very important to leaders in Belize. To have an academic title on your business card or in your email signature also benefits leaders' status (CCBS Survey, 2022). This is also reflected in the fact that the respondents agreed that it is important for subordinates to address leaders by their titles or positions within the organisation (CCBS Survey, 2022). Deanna Gomez, a lead consultant, stated: "*The leadership style is predominantly old-school, however, with younger people with higher levels of education taking over more leadership positions there is a move to more democratic leadership styles.*" (CCBS Survey, 2022). Regarding the level of gender (in)equality in Belizean organisations, two-thirds of the respondents agreed with the statement that men and women have equal access to senior-level positions in companies. However, this does mean that one-third of the respondents believed that there was still a disparity between the opportunities of men and women to attain these positions (CCBS Survey, 2022).

Local leadership analysis

Michelle Vanzie: a Belizean cross cultural trainer

The first interviewed expert is Michelle Vanzie. She is currently doing an MBA in digital marketing. She recently worked for the government of Belize in the role of Deputy Ambassador for Belize, Mexico and Jamaica. She was also a Country-specific Executive and Senior Advisor to the Chief Executive Officer at the Ministry of Foreign Affairs for more than eighteen years. She is the founder of Michelle Vanzie Ltd, which is a company that trains, coaches and guides entrepreneurs to realize their entrepreneurial goals. During the interview, Mrs Vanzie stated that at the beginning of her career she was the National Director for Policy Analysis and Planning at the Ministry of Health in Belize (Vanzie, 23 November 2022). In fact, Vanzie posited that she was then and remains now the first and only health economist in Belize. In the interview, Mrs Vanzie described that Belize shares a lot of characteristics of British culture, which means they are very polite and diplomatic in their interactions with others (Vanzie, 23 November 2022). It also became evident during our interview that people in Belize refer to each other as Mr and Ms, both within and outside the workplace. One explanation for why people address others by their titles is because Belize has an extremely strong sense of authority. During our interview, Ms Vanzie also talked about education in Belize. She stated that most Belizeans study abroad, and do not return back to their home country. This explains why there is both a low population in Belize and a relatively small business sector (Vanzie, 23 November 2022). According to Ms Vanzie, a large population of Belize is highly educated, but the reason why Belize has such a low literacy rate is that there are foreigners with a low-level of education that migrate to Belize. Furthermore she also discussed the nature of the societal and organisational hierarchy in Belize, "*like I said, its a pyramid, right? And it is the line of authority you respect. Even when we write something official, you cannot skip over this and write directly to someone else"* (Vanzie, 23 November 2022). This testifiies to the fact that Belize has a clear division of roles inside the organisational culture and hierarchy. albeit she did state that Belizean society more generally is characterised by a strong sense of equality.

Accalia Boscardi: a Belizean director

The second expert we interviewed is Accalia Boscardi, who has a master's degree in Business Administration and a bachelor's degree in Psychology and Sociology. Accalia Boscardi has five years of experience working as the Human Resource Director for the Belizean collection, who have around six different properties across the country related to residencies, resorts and one corporate office in the capital city (Boscardi, 10 November 2022). During our interview, she explained that Belizean leaders are highly charismatic, which, in turn, helps them build a sense of trust and connections with both their employees and wider networks. As she herself put it: *"You have to put yourself out there and have to be willing to be comfortable socialising, and being a positive role model is I think very important as well. And setting a good example for those around you"* (Boscardi, 10 November 2022). Ms Boscardi proceeded to discuss how she feels that there is a shift currently taking place within the country with respect to the business sector generally and leadership skills and practices specifically, which is that the younger generation is placing far greater emphasis upon and putting more effort and commitment into their roles and responsibilities as leaders (10 November 2022). She stressed that the younger generation is cognisant of the fact that leadership is no longer simply about giving direction and delegating task and responsibilities to one's subordinates. Rather, she proceeded to explain, the younger generation of leaders in the country are more influenced by Western best-practices when it comes to the manner of communication and leadership styles they employ (Boscardi, 10 November 2022).

In-country leadership bestseller

The best-selling book on leadership in Belize is *Help them Glow: 9 simple steps to improve your leadership!*, which was written in 2017 by Dr. Dionne Regina Chamberlain. She has completed multiple specialised training programs including Leadership at the Centre for Applied Sciences in Geneva Switzerland, which gives her excellent knowledge and insight into this topic. Chamberlain also has a master's degree in Global Management from the University of Phoenix, and runs a leadership consulting company in Belize that helps local businesses to perform more effectively. In this book, Chamberlain writes about how important it is to be a good leader instead of a manager in Belize. She also explains how good leadership ultimately helps to engage more employees, which, in turn, results in a better company. Overall, there are eight real steps delineated in the book, with the ninth step serving as more of a summary of the previous steps. These steps are: *Commmit to your people, Get to know them, create your unique culture, lead with integrity, be positive, be persistent, learn to listen and hold them accountable.* The steps are very employee-driven, with the express purpose being to ensure that employees feel acknowledged and listened to by their leaders. Alongside these steps, Chamberlain also explains that there are four diferent types of generations in the Belizian workforce who all prefer a different type of communication. In the step *"get to know them"*, she explains how important it is to know your employees so that you are aware of their capabilties. In the chapter *"Hold them accountable"*, Chamberlain writes about the consuqences of responsibility. Specifically, she notes that it is important for a leader to be critical, but it is equally important for them to praise someone who did a good job. Overall, the book focuses on teaching a new style of leadership that is grounded in becoming a more inclusive leader. This inclusive leader is more focused on their employees and their well-being, which, in turn, results in a better work environment according to Chamberlain.

Local leadership book	
Title	*Help them Glow*
Subtitle	*9 simple steps to improve your leadership!*
Author	Dr. Dionne Regina Chamberlain
Publisher	Independently published
Year	2017
ISBN	978-1521075630

Belize leadership YouTube review

Channel 5 Belize is a Belizean YouTube channel that primarily talks about different aspects of leadership and management in Belize. In one of their recent videos, they talk about the annual global leadership summit (GLS). The GLS is a yearly event where different speakers unite to educate Belizeans on leadership. In the video, they interviewed the chairman, Kerm Thimbrel, and the executive member, Claudio Leal of the GLS. They are being interviewed about the impact the event has on Belize. *"In GLS, we teach that it really matters who trains you* [as a leader] *because your trainer has the ability to transform you."* (Thimbrel, 2022, 3:33). It is this rationale that underpins why they have selected only the best speakers for this event. Leal and Thimbrel want to make sure that the people attending this event receive the proper education on leadership skills and practices in Belize. The next video to be summarised is a talk with Dr. Jenn Saunders, who discusses that the educational level of teachers in Belize is not to the required standard. In the video, Saunders explains that very few people in Belize have a Ph.D in language skills and culture. Although there are people who do the work, they lack both the specialisation and real expertise needed to understand research, best-practices or the theory that supports good teaching. This is a problem that must be solved from the top down, Saunders argues. She started a program at Oklahoma state university, which is designed to build the capacity and enhance the leadership skills by training teachers in Belize. She notes: *"We kept coming up with the question of how to create a sustainable capacity within Belize, so that Belizeans have the expertise within the country and are not reliant on, you know, professors from other educational programs and institutions"* (Saunders, 2022, 3:38).

Understanding hierarchy in Belize

Latin American countries rank high in power distance, but, interestingly, Belize differs from its neighbouring countries in several key respects. In fact, Belize is more comparable to the Caribbean region, such as Jamaica, for example, in addition to being profoundly shaped by its colonisation by the United Kingdom (Boscardi, 10 November 2022). According to one of our interviews, Vanzie, who served in the Belizean government for eighteen years, Belizeans like to be ranked by importance, and the hierarchical system is akin to a pyramid structure, insofar as everyone is divided into their own classes based on their respective position in the company (23 November 2022). If you want to get in touch with the leader of the organisation, then one cannot skip the different levels of the pyramid to speak to them. Similarly, the senior-level executive directly above your middle-level manager is not supposed to contact you directly either, so, in this respect, the hierarchical system also serves to function as a shield (Vanzie, 23 November 2022). The level of hierarchy in Belizean organisations is also reflected in the fact that it is common to address everyone above you in the hierarchical structure as either Miss. and Mr. followed by their last name, which applies to everyone right up until the owners of the company (Boscardi, 10 November 2022). Interestingly, however, in our interview with Michelle Vanzie, she stated that *"Outside of the office we are a very equal society. For example, the Prime Minister's children go to school with very poor children."* (Vanzie, 23 November 2022). Moreover, Belize also scores high on Hofstede's masculine dimension, which means that the business sector is characterised by a high level of competitiveness. Although Belizean businesses remain male-dominated, women's participation in businesses is continuing to increase (Li & Carballo, 2018). This was corroborated by the CCBS Survey (2022), insofar as more than half of the respondents stated that men and women have equal access to senior-level positions in Belizean companies.

How the Belizeans achieve leadership empathy

The way leaders empathise with their employees in the business sector is very consistent and unique to Belize. This was shown in the results of the CCBS Survey (2022), where the majority of the respondents stated that Belizean leaders do not prefer to retain a personal distance from their employees, because they feel like cultivating a more personal relationship with them will increase the level of respect between both parties. Furthermore, according to the majority of the respondents, a separation in the workspace between leaders and employees is not preferred, which is why most of the leaders like to participate in the same work area as their employees (CCBS Survey, 2022). Although, as aforesaid, Belizean leaders are expected to make powerful decisions, they are also acutely aware of the importance of letting their subordinates contribute to making these decisions. According to one of our survey respondents, Belizeans are very laid back in the field of leadership because things take a considerable amount of time to get done. From this perspective, Belizeans can be said to operate on something called "Belize Time", which is a local joke that refers to the fact that Belizeans do things at an easy-going pace (CCBS Survey, 2022). Hence, it can be said that the Belizean leaders take the so called 'Belize Time" into consideration when it comes to their relations with their employees, insofar as they are not strictly focused on utilising their employees for productivity and profit, but rather spend time with them to cultivate a personal as opposed to merely a business relationship with them. In return, this relational leadership style encourages healthy relations, and, in most cases, enables empathy to further develop between both parties. Finally, as part of displaying more empathy with their employees, leaders like to grant equal opportunity to men and women when it comes to attaining senior-level leadership positions (CCBS Survey, 2022).

Cameroon

Brandy Masamba, Chanel Bosc, Di-annah Seck, Nikayla Koeiman, Shaniss Nyamoto & Wanda Needham

"*Africa in miniature*" has become a moniker synonymous with Cameroon, due to its geographical and cultural diversity (BBC News, 2018). Located in west-central Africa, it is officially known as *République du Cameroun* (Republic of Cameroon); while its capital city is Yaoundé, the economic centre is Douala. The country is twice the size of Great Britain and has a population of around 28 million (Statista, 2022). The country is home to over 200 ethnic groups, which explains why it has been described as an "*ethnic crossroads*" (Ojong, 2018, p. 1). Furthermore, Cameroon has as many as 275 local languages, making it one of the most linguistically diverse countries in the world (Doyiso, 2022). English and French are the two official languages, with French being the most widely spoken in eight out of the ten regions. The bilingualism in Cameroon is a legacy of the country's colonial past when both the French and the British ruled separate regions of what is now Cameroon (Coleman, 2013). In 2021, the country's GDP amounted to $45 billion (World Bank, 2021), with the major industries, which are oil and gas, aluminium, timber, mining, agriculture, and the service sector, all playing significant roles in contributing to the economic diversity (Miamo & Achuo, 2021). Alongside this, two-thirds of the population practice Christianity, with one-fifth being Muslim, while a minority practice traditional religions (La Croix Africa, 2020). Sigismond and Fotso (2021) state that religion is of critical importance, insofar as it functions as a tool through which to measure trustworthiness and social cohesion in Cameroonian society. They also observed that religion plays a significant role with respect to the prevailing leadership styles and practices in Cameroonian organisations, namely in terms of the values, attributes, and behaviours that leaders are required to possess to operate effectively (Sigismond & Fotso, 2021).

How Cameroon characterises leaders?

According to Wirba (2015), being trustworthy, humble, and respectful are considered fundamental qualities when it comes to defining what constitutes a good leader in Cameroon. However, these characteristics, interestingly, do not negate leaders' ability to assert their authority, which is seldomly challenged in Cameroon. Indeed, employees expect little to no flexibility or involvement in their work routine, daily agendas, and the formation of final decisions and policies (Wirba, 2015). This interrelationship between leaders and their subordinates is deemed to be effective due to Cameroonian people's overriding cultural reverence for elders and respect for authority (Biaka, 2020). While the high esteem in which leaders are held is undeniable, and rarely contested, it is also of utmost importance that leaders show respect to all members of their organisation. This is influenced by the collectivistic social values that underpin Cameroonian society, which serves to promote an egalitarian work environment, irrespective of the leader's superiority (Littrell, 2011). This was corroborated by one of our interviewees, who opined that a good leader in Cameroon is someone who exhibits an interest in getting to know their subordinates, has a vested interest in their concerns and can approach employees to address them (Vonk, 7 November 2022). Further support for this comes from Cherfan and Allen (2021), who found that Cameroonian employees value a humble leader who can relate to their subordinates. Leaders can showcase this through their ability to not only set examples for their employees, but to put them into practice, which, in turn, further reinforces how knowledgeable the leader is. Their knowledge and intellect is not something that should encourage arrogance or self-praise, but rather should cultivate a sense of relatability between leaders and their subordinates (Cherfan & Allen, 2021). Finally, and most important of all, Wirba (2015) emphasises that leaders can display that they are trustworthy via their ability to simultaneously manage one's family life and professional responsibilities, which serves as an example of how they will manage, organise, and care for their workforce. However, Batouan, in our interview with them, pointed out that though this link between family and the professional environment exists, it does not detract from how assertive leaders can be (7 November 2022). The reason for this is that Cameroonians prefer paternalistic leaders; therefore, in their role as the leader, they will be viewed as the *"head of the family"*, with the *"family"* being the company. As well as the aforementioned, it is imperative to emphasise the nuance that several ethnic groups, geographical locations, and cultural contexts bring to how a leader is characterised in Cameroon (Djamen et al., 2020; Vonk, 7 November 2022). First, some characterisations are directed by the importance of honouring traditional, cultural values for a leader. *Kefor* (leadership) in Kenyang, a language from the Cross River region, is in essence about community leadership (Eyong, 2016). This humane leadership style, fervently noted by a deputy chairman in Eyong's (2019) research, honours the ways of Cameroon's forefathers. These paternal figures were cognisant of the significance of being loved by the people, and for the leader to love them in return. Within this approach, the appointed leader is seen as the central figure of the community, however, the people within the community can also have influence over decision-making. To cite another example, the symbolism and mythology distinct to some ethnic groups also inform the attributes of a leader. For example, the Manyu people, an ethnic group in the Southwest region of Cameroon, hold the leopard as the symbol of leadership (Eyong, 2016). Deriving from the belief in a myth that the leopard possesses a myriad of spiritual powers, this symbol has endured over time. Hence, in this region business leaders must showcase spiritual strength, intelligence, prowess, and physical ability in their management style, like a leopard (Eyong, 2016). In conclusion, being trustworthy, relatable, and fulfilling their duty as a *"father figure"* to the organisation are the most preferred attributes in a good leader in Cameroon.

Survey results and what local respondents say

In order to gain greater insight into the organisational culture, leadership styles and practices in Cameroon, the CCBS Survey (2022) was completed by a group of managers who are currently working or have previously worked in Cameroon. The survey focuses on leadership styles, skills, and practices. The most important findings that emerged from the survey are summarised below. The first interesting result is that most respondents agreed that they, as leaders, are provided with office space and transportation which reflects their status in the company (CCBS Survey, 2022). This confirms that the Cameroonians care about the status and experience of their leaders, because most of the respondents also reported that in their country employees look up to their leaders based on their organisational experience, market expertise and technical competence (CCBS Survey, 2022). Therefore, according to the survey respondents, it is not a matter of age, appearance, or family background, but rather one's experiences and qualities that ultimately define what constitutes an effective leader in Cameroon (CCBS Survey, 2022). Secondly, it is interesting to note that most of the respondents reported that managers encourage some degree of competition within their teams, in order to achieve better results in the end. This is supported by the fact that the majority of the respondents stated that managers are prepared to confront subordinates during staff meetings, in order to obtain the desired results (CCBS Survey, 2022). Another interesting finding emerging from the survey pertained to the extent to which different cultural systems within Cameroonian society impact upon the prevailing leadership styles within certain companies. As one respondent noted: "*[leadership] Practices are adjustable according to cultural habits: religion, customs, opinions, etc."* (CCBS Survey, 2022). Similarly, a General Director from Diamond Business Technologies, stated: *"YES, Understand the local culture and exercise leadership in a culturally sensitive manner"* (CCBS Survey, 2022). Despite the influence of culture, the survey also underscored that the individual personalities of leaders themselves also play a major role in terms of shaping the company's culture. Yves Azugue, a General Services Officer at the General Society in Cameroon stated: *"Leadership is only an extension of the personality of the man (the Manager). It therefore varies according to the individual. If a distinction had to be made, I would say that our leadership straddles the line between participative and authoritarian leadership"* (CCBS Survey, 2022). As a leader in Cameroon, it is not only important that you have a lot of experience in the field you are a leader in, but it is also important that you possess good character traits and qualities, so that a good working atmosphere is built up and employees can work and learn well in it and be inspired. As Jules Ndam, CEO and co-founder of Afribobo in Doula, Cameroon, opined: *"Below are some qualities that some of my managers have inspired me in my small experience: inspiring, competent, transparent, ethical, motivating, good communicator, encouraging, good listener, empowered, personifies the company's values, humble, willing to learn"* (CCBS Survey, 2022).

Local leadership analysis

Joseph-Alain Batouan: a Cameroonian leadership scholar

Joseph-Alain Batouan is a Cameroonian leadership scholar as well as a professional coach and lecturer in transformational leadership. For the past two years he has been working as a consultant at Maxwell Leadership Francophonie. According to Batouan, leaders in Cameroon are expected to deliver results, and therefore they are very goal oriented. Once you are someone who has competence and skill in a leadership position you gain respect, regardless of your age and gender—although, elders will always be respected (7 November 2022). Batouan observed that today in comparison with the past leaders in Cameroon are exposed to international best practices and have access extensive training on management, entrepreneurship, and leadership. Batouan concluded that these factors ensure that extant knowledge and leadership practices in Cameroon are in alignment with the current demands of the business environment (7 November 2022). Furthermore, when asked about the influence of religion on leadership in Cameroon, he stated that *"in general it is not religion that affects a management style or a leadership style. It just happens at some companies"* (7 November 2022).

Batouan is convinced that there are some leaders who practice religions that impact upon their leadership behaviour. To illustrate this point, he noted that he knows of some industries and some businesses that only work with members of the same religion. When asked about the level of hierarchy in Cameroonian companies, he conceded that in a professional environment there exists what can be considered as "classic leadership", which is autocratic in nature. In these companies, there is a significant degree of power distance; however, as leadership styles have evolved over time, it appears as if the nature of the relationship between leaders and employees is shifting in many organisations. He proceeded to suggest that implementing a transformational leadership approach and good communication is the most expedient way to both connect with people and build trust and respect as a leader in Cameroon (7 November 2022). As aforementioned, Cameroon is a multi-lingual country, which, broadly speaking, can be divided into a French speaking and English-speaking part. When asked if leaders were treated differently depending on their cultural and regional background, Batouan answered that because of his experience he believes that French speakers are more formal than their English-speaking counterparts, who generally try to connect more with their employees, which, in turn, impacts upon the way leaders are viewed and treated by their subordinates. In conclusion, Batouan stated: *"I can say that there is an evolution in the leadership practices in Cameroon, as far as I can see"* (7 November 2022).

Alette Vonk: a cross-cultural trainer

To gain additional qualitative insights into leadership practices in Cameroon, we interviewed a scholar and leadership consultant, Alette Vonk (Dutch), who has worked and lived in Cameroon for a considerable amount of time. Alette Vonk is an intercultural management lecturer at Leiden University and an independent intercultural management and organizational change consultant at Hofstede insights. When asked during the interview what constitutes a typical Cameroonian leader, Vonk described that it is difficult to give a general description about a typical business leader in Cameroon (7 November 2022). According to Vonk, this depends on someone's age and the city they are working in. However, Vonk did add that, in general, most Cameroonian business leaders are sharper than their Western counterparts, both in terms of how they act and the way they dress (7 November 2022). Indeed, appearance and the way a leader looks are critically important in the Cameroonian business world, insofar as it influences the level of respect one is accorded. This is especially the case amongst younger employees who need to show respect to older leaders, by, amongst other things, dressing well and being well-groomed. In so doing, younger people show respect to both themselves and their superiors. Here, the idea of 'keeping face' and 'giving face' is strongly observed (7 November 2022). The reason for this can be traced back to the high level of power distance in the Cameroonian business world. In response to whether the level of power distance had changed in recent decades, Vonk described that there had been a slight discernible change, in part, because of the increased number of Cameroonians entering higher education (7 November 2022). The consequence of this is that younger people are more prepared to speak up to someone who is their superior than in the past, albeit while still showing the necessary deference and respect (7 November 2022). It is important to stress here that the word 'respect' in African countries is mostly translated in a vertical sense: a person with lower power shows more respect to a person with more power (7 November 2022). A good example of this is that Cameroonians do not really speak up openly/publicly to someone with more power when in the presence of others. Besides the level of power distance, showing one's authority as a leader also plays a key role in the Cameroonian business world. Indeed, leaders like to show their authority indirectly. They do this by speaking eloquently (using nice words), the way they carry themselves and putting on display material things like expensive cars, large houses, or nice clothes. Despite the distance between leader and their subordinates, there is nevertheless good personal relationship between the two parties, Vonk noted (7 November 2022). For instance, it is important for Cameroonian leaders to take good care of their employees, both inside and outside of the organisation, as this helps leaders build trust and empathy with their subordinates, and, in so doing, indirectly also maintain their authority (7 November 2022). Finally, Vonk noted that there are three important points to consider as a foreigner when doing business in Cameroon: building good relationships, showing interest in another person's life and sometimes *"biting your tongue," not speaking your mind too quickly* and listening first." (7 November 2022).

In-country leadership bestseller

Management par le Kongossa (Management by *Kongossa*) by James Soh is one of Cameroon's best-selling books about leadership. James Soh is a Senior Accountant and Certified Internal Auditor Candidate. Soh (2018) reveals the realities that business professionals in Cameroonian companies may face through recourse to personal reflections and anecdotes from over two hundred business leaders in an effort to provide wisdom and guidance. Moreover, Soh (2018) gives practical advice on how to cope in a business environment where management by *Kongossa* reigns. According to Joseph, a senior lecturer at a Cameroonian university, a leader is more of a manager than a leader in Cameroon due to the cultural system in place (7 November 2022). There are many challenges that will arise for business professionals in Cameroon, from companies being managed in a familial way, the rights of employees being rarely respected, not to mention the inability to evolve in an environment conducive to their professional development. Therefore, in situations where quitting or losing one's job is not an option, it is necessary to heed the sage advice of this book and have the courage to face the difficulties in order to move forward. It is for that reason that Emmanuel Ndukong, a CEO, founder, and lead software engineer, cited Soh's book as being popular in Cameroon amongst leaders and employees (CCBS Survey, 2022). When asked to summarise four key messages that he learned about leadership from this book, Ndukong first explained what *Kongossa* means: *"Kongossa in Cameroon simply means gossip, complicity. We gossip with people we are close to"* (Personal Communication, 25 November 2022). He then proceeded to explain four key points he took away from the book. First, *"the book illustrates management as building a relationship of complicity with each of your subordinates and teams"*. Second, *"It reflects on how healthy gossip can bind the team together rather than split them apart"*. Third, *"Competitors and clients should be the subject of our gossip. Business strategy and innovation should be conversed not only in official meetings but in the most relaxing situations possible"*. The final key point he took from the book was as follows: *"In internal conflict resolutions, gossip should not be one-sided; rather, by bringing all parties involved to the same table and creating a new enemy - a competitor or a client for them to focus their energy on"* (Personal Communication, 25 November 2022). This is in line with our survey respondents, who agreed that managers are prepared to confront subordinates during staff meetings as well as encourage competition within teams, in order to achieve better results. We can than conclude that *Kongossa*, competition and conflict in Cameroon are encouraged, in a healthy way, in other to achieve better results.

Local leadership book	
Title	*Management par le Kongossa*
Subtitle	-
Author	James Soh
Publisher	Living Books Publishing
Year	2018
ISBN	B07DT3GD16

Cameroonian leadership YouTube review

In a video, Yves Bollanga, a recipient of the 2012 Distinguished Honour Award in Cameroon and the founder and CEO of Afrotainment, the television channel, gives a keynote speech about leadership and the values he has learnt from his own experience of being a leader. He states early in his speech that a leader must be trusted by their subordinates. He goes on to note that a leader should expect people to come for advice and be prepared to provide vision and direction. According to Bollanga, *"a leader is someone who can create a vision and is able to execute that vision"* (Bollanga, 2012, 21:11). He proceeds to discuss that organisational structure does not achieve anything in a business and is not efficient. He also emphasises that titles do not necessarily guarantee achievement in Cameroonian organisations. Rather, to achieve efficiency, respect, and trust, a leader needs to be a team player and show they can work well together with their colleagues. In the next video to be discussed, Joel Nana Kontchou, who is the CEO of Sonel, one of the largest companies in Cameroon, talks about his experience as a leader. Like Bollanga, he stresses that leadership is closely related to teamwork. That is to say, being a leader is ultimately about building a team and relying on the resources that you have in front of you. Kontchou also emphasises how powerful it is as a leader to know your subordinates and have a personal connection with them, which, in turn, results in employees being more motivated to perform their work well. He notes that prior to starting a business, it is important to have your own definition of success and to have a proper business structure. Furthermore, patience is a key virtue for a good leader to possess in Cameroon. The chief reason for this is that, in Africa, businesses run very differently in comparison to, for example, America, where everything moves fast. The relationship Cameroonians have with time is completely different in this respect. Towards the end of the interview, he opined that it is in Cameroonians' nature to be judgmental, negative, and complain, but that it is important to encourage and facilitate positivity within organisations. In his own word, *"I want to emphasise the power of a positive attitude. It has to come from top-down from bottom-up from inside-out"* (Kontchou, 23:52). In conclusion, Kontchou explains, *"leadership is not about what you do, it is about what you make other people do"* (31:39). Leadership is not about oneself but much more about the result that can be produced by a team of people who are well managed and led.

Understanding hierarchy in Cameroon

According to Djamen et al. (2020), Cameroon scores in the middle, but indicates a slight tendency to the advanced side of power distance index (PDI). The authors cite the example that directors in Cameroon believe that hierarchy should be adhered to and that inequalities amongst people are respectable. The different distribution of power justifies the fact that power holders have further benefits than those lower down the societal hierarchy. In Cameroon, it is important to show respect to elders; indeed, children take pride in being able to care for their senior parents. This mindset also translates to the workspace: in companies, there is one leader who takes complete responsibility over decision-making. Status symbols of power (expensive clothes and cars) are important indicators of one's standing within the company (Djamen et al., 2010). This high-power distance in Cameroon was also affirmed by one of our interviewees, a cross cultural trainer, Alette Vonk, who said that, historically, there has been a high-power distance in Cameroon, but that this has decreased slightly in recent years, because of the younger generation being more educated and willing to express their opinions to their managers, albeit while showing the necessary respect (7 November 2022). Furthermore, according to Djamen et al. (2020), society fosters strong relationships where everyone takes responsibility for fellow members of their group. With a moderately low score of 42 on the individualism scale, managers in Cameroon partly share and implement this collectivist orientation. One of the ways in which this collectivistic mindset manifests amongst managers pertains to both their opinion of, and sense of obligation towards, the extended family. Notwithstanding this, Djamen et al. (2022) argue that more modern, individualistic traits are also coming to the fore, particularly amongst managers who are exposed to the competitive world of business and educated in business schools in Europe or the United States. This point was corroborated by Vonk, who argued: *"I don't see it [high power distance in Cameroonian businesses] disappear very quickly, research also shows that if education goes up in a society, people will, you know, start to really think for themselves and start to challenge a leader who is talking nonsense. Of course, they will not directly challenge a leader. They will go along but education is the key to the hierarchy gap not being as big."* (7 November 2022). According to Woods Jr. et al. (2021), it also appears that the level of education has a significant effect on long-term orientation and uncertainty avoidance. The higher the level of education, the higher the long-term orientation and the lower the level of uncertainty avoidance. Batouan, a Cameroonian leadership scholar, noted in our interview that English speaking managers tend to be more open and operate with a smaller power distance than their French counterparts, in an effort to connect with their employees on a more human level, whereas French-speaking leaders retained a more formal and distant stance towards their subordinates. A further element of hierarchy within Cameroonian organisations pertains to the level of gender inequality with respect to senior-level management positions. In this respect, a study by Njimanted and Mukete (2016) employed a time series approach over a period of almost four decades and found that fertility is not a direct obstacle to female performance in the labour market or in terms of gaining positions within the upper echelons of the organisational hierarchy within Cameroonian organisations, which is the case in a lot of other West African countries (Kuepie et al., 2013).

How Cameroon achieves leadership empathy

Due to the socio-cultural importance accorded to traditional customs and values, a protective and paternal empathetic leader prevails in Cameroon—irrespective of their gender (Lewis, 2005; Mirabell, 2016). This is because of the way fathers are seen as the head of the household culturally, and, as such, act as the pillar that serves to look after the general well-being of the environment, which also extends to the business sector in Cameroon. Cameroonian leaders achieve empathetic leadership through adopting a paternalistic leadership style, which encompasses effective communication, being trustworthy and displaying a vested interest in and concern over employees' well-being (Lewis, 2005). The CCBS Survey (2022) confirmed this aspect of Cameroonian leadership, insofar as the majority of the respondents reported that leaders actively spend time ensuring the well-being of their team. Cherfan and Allen (2021) lend further support to this by underscoring that a paternalistic leader is someone that strikes the required balance between friendship and respect. Cameroonian leaders express this in the way they can encourage and guide employees towards achieving business objectives, which is akin to the relationship between a father and child. Similar to a family unit, the authors found that when leaders spoke to their employees in terms such, "'we can do this' or 'we have done this'" (Cherfan & Allen, 2021, p.143), this testifies to the collectivistic devotion and support they have for their team, while, simultaneously, communicating their appreciation for their employees' output, which, in turn, effectively motivates them. Since leaders are seen as father figures in Cameroonian organisations, even outside of the work environment, showing a healthy concern about their team's social and psychological well-being is crucial. Day-to-day examples of this can include the leader taking time to greet workers, asking about their family, listening to matters in their personal lives as well as providing support and sympathising with their personal issues (Littrell, 2011).

This is in accordance with Vonk, who expressed in her interview how some leaders support their employees by helping to pay their hospital bills and actively supporting them to make funeral arrangements (7 November 2022). Both Vonk (7 November 2002) and Batouan (7 November 2022) emphasised that leaders must go out and seek to connect and build relationships with their subordinates and convey empathy consistently. Mary and Ozturen (2019) affirm that all these levels of attentiveness and care to subordinates empower employees of their value, encourages commitment from them, in addition to increasing productivity and performance. The CCBS Survey (2022) also supports the empathic nature of leaders, insofar as it was found that the majority of the respondents reported that leaders no not retain distance from their employees in order to maintain the right level of respect. An additional way through which paternalistic leaders show interest in the well-being of their employees in the workplace is by effectively communicating the reasons behind their decision making, and attentively addressing any questions subordinates may have regarding them (Pendati & Mirabell, 2016). This involvement of workers in the decision-making process fosters trust and loyalty (Mary & Ozturen, 2019). Our survey respondents noted that leaders are generally flexible regarding changing decisions once they have been made, which also affirms other findings in the survey that highlight that being a good compromiser and a powerful decision-maker should go hand-in-hand for Cameroonian leaders (CCBS Survey, 2022).

China PRC

Adil Fkyerat, Esmee Wong(王绕霖), Yoon Fong Chong (钟永丰), Hoang Nguyen, Hieu Nguyen, Zev van der Geest, Zhaohan Zhang (张兆涵)

China, locally known as *Zhōnghuá* (中华, central beauty), is the most populated country in the world with almost a fifth of the world's population residing there (Zhou, 2019). China is also one of the most multilingual countries in the world. According to the Ministry of Education of China (n.d.), there are more than 80 spoken languages in China, albeit Mandarin Chinese, or rather *Pǔtōnghuà* (普通话), is the most predominant, with over 955 million speakers out of China's total population of 1.4 billion people. China is known for its architectural wonders, beautiful landscape, martial arts, and its long history of inventions (Cao, 2006; Mun, 2013). Since ancient times, China has promoted respect towards multiple religious denominations and beliefs. In 1949, the Chinese Communist Party took power on the mainland, and the newly founded *Zhōnghuá Rénmín Gònghéguó* (中华人民共和国), or People's Republic of China (PRC) was established. The two most crucial traditional cultural Chinese values are *Zhōng* (忠, loyalty) and *Xiào* (孝, filial piety), which are based on *Rújiā* (儒家, Confucianism) (Huangfu et al., 2013). While the traditional cultural values are still discernible in China, the economic reforms in the late 1970s resulted in a more attractive business model through which to achieve growth as part of global trade. Since then, both the level of foreign investment and export numbers have increased rapidly, which, in turn, has resulted in the contemporary economic climate that is slowly transitioning from a manufacturing economy to a knowledge economy (Ramesh, 2012). This chapter will examine the ways in which traditional Chinese culture and the prevailing economic and political context impacts upon business leadership styles and practices in China, by drawing upon academic research, and empirical interview and survey data from Chinese professionals and experts.

How the Chinese characterise leaders

Rújiā (儒家), also known as Confucian values, have influenced Chinese society for the past three millennia, thus making them the foundation of the preferred business leadership styles and practices in the country. Because of these values, traditional Chinese business leaders, or *Lǐngdǎo* (领导, leader), tend to exhibit extremely high degrees of authoritarianism, while, simultaneously, displaying *Rén* (仁, benevolence) towards subordinates and demonstrating a strong level of moral character in their actions and decisions (Wang et al., 2004). According to Cheng et al. (2004), such forms of authoritarian leadership result in greater dependence and compliance from employees, while, conversely, benevolent leadership induces a greater sense of gratitude and repayment amongst one's employees. Cheng et al. (2004) posit that Chinese leaders have the most positive effect on subordinates when there is a strong balance between high authority and high benevolence. This approach can be described as a paternalistic leadership approach, which Cheng et al. (2004) argue is the most prevalent leadership style in Chinese organisations. High benevolence means that leaders treat their employees like family members, showing care towards them and taking an interest in their personal lives (Cheng et al., 2013; Wang, 2019). However, Chinese leaders take personal control over most matters, insofar as they make unilateral decisions and take individual action, and, as such, are highly authoritative. This suggests that Confucian values do indeed continue to underpin the desired leadership behaviour in China (Wang et al., 2004). Chen et al.'s (2011) research demonstrates that benevolence, morality, and authority do indeed have positive effects on employees' in-role performance. However, they also showed that highly authoritative behaviours negatively impact upon extra-role performance, while, conversely, benevolence and morality enhanced the extra-role performance of subordinates (Chen et al., 2011). It is important to stress here that there are additional forces besides Confucian values that have moulded the behaviour of Chinese leaders, most notably, the economic reforms in 19878 that fundamentally transformed the country. Prior to the reforms, all enterprises were owned by the state, but now these enterprises can also be privately owned or receive foreign investment (Song et al., 2012). Research has shown that there is a difference in the behaviours of CEOs in *Sīrén gōngsī* (私人公司, POE) compared to State-Owned Enterprises (SOEs), or *Guóyǒu qǐyè* (国有企业, SOE). Firstly, the executives in POEs tend to be younger, are less controlled by higher authorities, and are generally more willing to take risks and experiment with innovative ideas than their counterparts in SOEs (Li et al., 2014). According to Li et al (2014), most of the CEOs in POEs adopt an advanced leadership style, which is to say that they focus less on being authoritative and more on articulating their vision, are creative and take risks as well as focusing on communication and the relation with their employees. For example, they are often more willing to try out new projects and ideas, and clearly communicate their vision about the future of the company (Wang et al.,

2004). Hongwei Bi 毕宏伟, the Director of the patent department in a Chinese business, states that a Chinese leader must have the mindset of being a life-long learner who strives to keep their knowledge up to date. Moreover, they should prioritise the relational aspect and pay attention to the wellbeing of their employees (Hongwei, 2016). In contrast, the CEOs in SOEs tend to be more focused on monitoring operations and being authoritative, and, in so doing, remain closer to the traditional Confucian values and principles. This is in line with the results of the CCBS Survey (2017), which showed that senior leaders in particular are very sensitive when it comes to their authority. Generally speaking, however, the authoritative behaviour of Chinese CEOs is deemed to be perfectly legitimate (Li & Sun, 2015). Hence, employees often choose to remain silent about organisational problems and are ordinarily reluctant to voice their thoughts to others, especially colleagues higher up the corporate ladder (Li & Sun, 2015). Changning Xu (徐昌宁), a Sector Manager for the international trade department, captured this nicely: *"In China, most employees always follow the rules, if they want to change something, they will ask first"* (CCBS Survey, 2017).

Survey results and what local respondents say

Almost sixty Chinese executives shared their experience and knowledge by completing the CCBS Survey (2017), which provided comprehensive insight into the various leadership styles and practices adopted in China. The most significant findings from the survey with C-level professionals in China will be discussed in turn in this section. To start with, the findings show that it is difficult to change management decisions without having a discussion beforehand, insofar as managers try to both avoid uncertainty and maintain their authority. This phenomenon can also be observed in the fact that 60% of the respondents reported that Chinese leaders prefer to hear criticism in an indirect manner outside of staff meetings. Moreover, it was noted that senior leaders in particular are incredibly sensitive when it comes to their authority (CCBS Survey, 2017). Secondly, more than 75% of the respondents agreed with the statement that employees should always, or most of the time, follow established procedures and rules to ensure that the organisation operates smoothly (CCBS Survey, 2017).
If an employee does not follow the established rules and procedures, then the employee is considered to be either incompetent or insufficiently serious about their duties. When asked to state their opinion on Chinese leaders' attitudes towards employees missing deadlines, 65% of the respondents defined missing deadlines as being synonymous with failure and utterly unacceptable (CCBS

Survey, 2017). With respect to the leeway that employees in Chinese organisations have regarding bending the rules, Changning Xu (徐昌宁), a Sector Manager for the international trade department in a Chinese company, stated: *"In China, most employees always follow the rules, if they want to change something, they will ask first"* (CCBS Survey, 2017). However, over 60% of the respondents reported that they would accept their employees bending the rules if this were to culminate in better results or enhanced performance. This is interesting, insofar as it indicates that Chinese organisations may not quite be as inflexible as they are often portrayed as being. Thirdly, regarding the level of gender equality within contemporary Chinese organisations, namely whether men and women have equal access to senior-level leadership positions, the results indicate that this is strongly dependent on the type of organisation. According to our respondents, the main difference between male and female Chinese leaders is that men tend to be more powerful, while women are more approachable, friendly and display greater patience than their male counterparts (CCBS Survey 2017). Yuyo Tsen (岑喻嵘), a Branch Manager for a logistics company located in China, who participated in the CCBS Survey (2017), described the differences between male and female leaders as follows: *"A man can decide, and the team follows. A woman can also decide, and we follow, though sometimes more questions for clarification will be asked."*

Local leadership analysis

Jinkai Zhu: a Chinese leadership scholar

Jinkai Zhu (朱金凯) is a native scholar, Master graduate and lecturer in leadership at a university in Shanghai district. In addition to his rich background in teaching and researching leadership in China, he has extensive work experience at different companies in Australia as well as publishing multiple books on business and management. During the interview with Zhu, it quickly became evident that he does not entirely share the belief that there is *"one single Chinese leadership style"* (24 November 2022). He elaborated on this further by saying: *"I think the Chinese leadership styles is rooted in history. It came out of history and eventually became a unique characteristic style of China. Furthermore, the most prominent thing is the integration of several cultures, which includes the Western leadership styles, Confucianism, Daoism, and others. For example, Rodin believes that 'the leadership of the East and West is like martial arts and boxing, the differences can be seen at a glance.' However, from the perspective of the picture, they are the same thing"* (Zhu, 24 November 2022). On the other hand, he also explained, *"In my opinion, Chinese business leaders can be summed up in one word. "planners".*

Chinese leaders are good at "strategic planning". From the first emperor in Chinese history to present, leadership has been nurtured in this cultural context with intrigue. This kind of power involves the right time, place, and people" (Zhu, 24 November 2022). Zhu also explained that it is fundamentally important for leaders to have a strong knowledge and understanding of Eastern culture, which is generally less direct in terms of communication, insofar as it can provide tangible benefits business relationships. To illustrated this, he cited the following example: *"The difficulties encountered by foreigners when coming to China are generally due to two points: communication and the way of thinking. Because the Chinese communication style is not the same as in the West. Chinese also think differently than people from the West. As a result, in many cases there will be a certain misunderstanding"* (Zhu, 24 November 2022). Zhu concluded the interview by elucidating that *"first, it must be professional ability, which can play a decisive role in some issues. Secondly, only by trusting your subordinates, will your subordinates trust you in turn. Make achievements and let them know your ability and value. Last but not least, understanding employees and solving problems from the perspective of employees is the most important thing"* (24 November 2022).

Chinese Social Media review

A later section of this chapter explores how YouTube can be an expedient resource for learning about how people or businesses in China communicate about leadership. This section expands on this further by extending the research to all social media channels in China that are specifically used to communicate about leadership styles and practices. Firstly, Jasmine Huang, a keynote speaker, and entrepreneur from China, explained and spoke about the tea ceremony as a new leadership style in China in a video on the Youku streaming platform (Huang, 2017, 6:22). In her opinion, the finest Chinese tea culture has given her the wisdom to rejuvenate her relationships with both herself and employees, insofar as it helped her discover the Yin-and-Yang leadership style (Huang, 2017, 16:44). More specifically, she has successfully translated the meaning of the Chinese tea ceremony to the context of business relations in China. Another way to target the Chinese audience is through Bilibili, which is what Ying Sheng is doing to promote leadership style and practices in China. Ying Sheng is an Employee Trainer, who runs a training program for different enterprises in China. In this particular video, he stresses that he believes that a manager's job is to focus on the firm as a whole rather than on their personal work (英盛网, 2022). Notwithstanding this, his particular conceptualisation of excellent leadership is focused on mentoring subordinates and selecting the appropriate individuals for the right task (英盛网,

2022, 1:02). In a further video from Bilibili, Huang Jing, Dean of the Reproducible Leadership Institute, shares her thought on five realms of leadership. She started with an explanation of the first realm of leadership, quoting an interesting saying from Mr. Jin Weichun to illustrate this: " *A person only needs to do one job in their life*."(职场指北针, 2022, 2:44). In the third realm of leadership, employees follow the leader to have food and money, so a good leader must provide their basic needs. With respect to the highest realm of leadership, that is, the finest leader, Huang Jing states that they must create a culture of belief for their employees, in order to help them flourish and perform at their best (职场指北针, 2022, 4:26).

In-country leadership bestseller

Chinese Leadership is a book by Barbara Xiaoyu Wang and Harold Chee. Barbara Wang has a PhD, and specialises in cross-cultural leadership and management in China, while Harold Chee has multiple master's degrees and specialises in executive coaching and leadership. Both authors are renowned for publishing multiple books related to leadership, management, and business in China. This 2011 best-seller explores the concepts of *Miànzi* (面子, face), *Guānxì* (关系, social relations), and *Héxié* (和谐, harmony). For instance, the old Chinese proverb that is based on Confucianism states that: *"If you want one year of prosperity, cultivate grains. If you want ten years of prosperity, cultivate trees. If you want one hundred years of prosperity, cultivate PEOPLE."* In other words, to be an effective Chinese leader, one must take care of their employees. In reality, these traditional cultural values have consistently influenced leadership and management practices in China. Furthermore, this book also outlines different leadership styles as well as specifying what kind of leadership style the authors believe works best in contemporary Chinese businesses. Generally speaking, the Confucianism leadership style is still the most widely and accepted leadership style. Overall, this book presents three effective principles for becoming a successful (foreign) manager in China. Firstly, one must learn and come to understand the Chinese ways and mindset. For example, gaining basic knowledge of Chinese history and culture is invaluable, as once one has obtained this basic knowledge, then one will come closer to understanding the Chinese people and its organisational culture. Secondly, striking the balance between Western leadership styles and ancient Chinese leadership practices and cultural wisdom is incredibly important, given that contemporary China is exposed to ever-more leadership styles as a result of being integrated into the global economy. Finally, the best leaders are ordinarily regarded as those who can turn their in-depth knowledge into simple words, and are often referred as *Jūnzǐ* (君子, gentleman). However, making these changes individually is insufficient for making employees listen. Therefore, this is a practical book to help leaders working in China to both understand how to manage a workforce that has a distinct cultural mindset and show them how to do so sensitively and empathetically.

Local leadership book	
Title	*Chinese Leadership*
Subtitle	-
Author	Barbara Xiaoyu Wang and Harold Chee
Publisher	Palgrave Macmillan
Year	2011
ISBN	978-0230248182

Barbara Xiaoyu Wang and Harold Chee
CHINESE
LEADERSHIP

Chinese leadership YouTube/Bilibili review

Lin Bendong, a well-known trainer, and professional team manager in China, discusses why effective leadership is necessary for a company and what constitutes effective leadership (Bendong, 2022). In his words: "*When the three dimensions of craftmanship and science are combined, management style is effective. Craftmanship is based on real experience to achieve mastery while science promotes integration*" (Bendong, 2022, 2:58). Currently, finding the right management style is essential for ensuring that companies can keep up with the rapid changes in Chinese society. In the next video, Jan Ketil Arnulf, Dean Associate Professor at BI Norwegian Business School provides his perspective on Chinese leadership and culture, noting that Chinese leaders place value on relationships, innovative thinking, and having an optimistic view of the future (Youku, 2012). Thirdly, Pascal Coppens, an international keynote speaker and published author about innovation in China, decodes China's leadership model in business through different schools of thought (Pascal Coppens, 2022). From her perspective, Confucianism (family morals, loyalty, respect, altruism education, harmony) has had the largest influence upon the business leadership style (Pascal Coppens, 2022, 8:03). Pascal also put forward an interesting argument that successful Chinese companies often follow one basic management philosophy, whilst also incorporating other schools of thinking into their leadership style (Pascal Coppens, 2022). To illustrate this, Fang Ruan, a management consultant, indicated in her speech that business management in China is changing, especially now that Chinese entrepreneurs, long guided by Confucianism's emphasis on authority, are now looking to Taoist philosophy for a new dynamic leadership style that posits that things spontaneously transform and naturally achieve perfection when they are supported, rather than being controlled (Ruan, 2020). Referring to the chain store Dumpling Xi as an example, Fang Ruan said: *"Most Chinese entrepreneurs are very good at growth strategies, expanding territories (慨激昂口吐), but not so good at what we call converting people's best practices into company policies for the long run (治国安邦)"* (Ruan, 2020, 3:45). She stressed that the frontline manager should have tolerance for making mistakes and be open to receiving new ideas from below (Ruan, 2020). This last point about encouraging employees to learn and make mistakes is shared by Jack Ma, the former CEO of Alibaba Group, who spoke about entrepreneurship in a meeting in Johannesburg in 2018. In the video, Jack Ma said*: "Learning from mistakes is not because you want to avoid mistakes. When you see mistakes, where you have this kind of problem, you know how to face it*" (凤凰网科技, 2018, 16:20).

Understanding hierarchy in China

Since ancient times, hierarchy has been deeply rooted in Chinese culture as well as in *Guānxì* (关系, social relations) between people. The hierarchies are primarily predicated on the principles of Confucianism (Zhang, 2011). In order to understand hierarchy within Chinese organisations, the *Quánlì jùlí* (权力距离, Power distance) should be considered. Power distance reflects the distribution of power between members of society (Wang et al., 2020). For instance, Li and Sun (2018) argued that there is a high-power distance within Chinese society and Chinese organisations. In other words, employees are obligated to be obedient. As a result, employees will carefully consider whether to speak up or out to others, and especially employees from lower down the corporate ladder feel less secure to share their opinions with their superiors. If the consequences are negative, then employees will remain silent in general (Li & Sun, 2018). This has consequences for the information flow inside organisations, insofar as information does not flow freely around a high-power distance culture, but rather follows strict hierarchical lines, which slows down the flow (Cheng & Li, 2001). Moran et al. (2014) found that cultures with a high-power distance are generally less individualistic and prefer collectivism, that is, they prefer to work as a group for the benefit of all rather than for the benefit of the individual. This is evidenced by the fact that China scores low on the individualism scale, which indicates that Chinese society is primarily grounded in the interdependence of its people and the importance of relationships (Hofstede, 2001). This is corroborated in the CCBS Survey (2017), where half of the respondents stated that leaders do not wish to keep a personal distance from their subordinates. This is partly because relationships play an important role in Chinese business activities. However, while Chinese leaders are team-oriented, they are also highly protective of their position and authority. Hence, while they may consult with their employees, the final decision-making authority ultimately lies with them (Wang et al., 2020). This is confirmed by Guangqing Bai (白光清), a General Manager for an import and export business, who explained the Chinese hierarchy as follows: *"In China, leadership means respect and obey with no hesitation all because of one party in power. The main leader has the absolute authority, when a management decision has been made, it will not be changed very easily"* (CCBS Survey, 2017). Due to the high-power distance and collectivism, Chinese employees are more likely to accept authoritarian leadership than their counterparts in other cultures (Li & Sun, 2018). Historically, based on Confucianism principles, Chinese men were placed higher in the hierarchical system than women (Li, 2000). Confucius' infamous quotation "*women and small men are difficult to deal with,*" often referred as *Xiǎorén* (小人, small men/people) served to make Chinese woman inferior for thousands of years. Other quotes such as "*ignorance is the virtue of a woman*" and "*beauty is dangerous*" also served to restrict Chinese women (Wang & Chee, 2011). Given the historical background, in China they do not have feminism by Western definitions or standards. There is no neutral concept for both men and women even in the workplace. Chinese men respect a female colleague as a woman rather than as a person; therefore, they might praise her beauty rather than her intelligence (Wang & Chee, 2011). Through this, men have been able to position themselves in the upper echelons of the corporate hierarchy. As a result, these factors have made it more challenging for women to be recognised as equally competent by others in society or their immediate work environment (Rosenlee, 2012). In conjunction with this, Chinese society is also masculine oriented, which means that there is a strong emphasis on performance and competition (Hofstede Insights, 2017). Generally speaking, these factors bring the male aggression to the surface, thereby further increasing the gender hierarchy.

How Chinese achieve leadership empathy

The Chinese are known for their *Miànzi* (面子, face), not always showing their emotions, and preferring a more indirect form of communication (Fang, 2014). The latter two traits are based on *Wǔcháng* (五常, Five constants). These are *Rén* (仁, benevolence), *Yì* (义, righteousness), *Lǐ* (礼, ritual propriety), *Zhì* (智, wisdom), and *Xìn* (信, trustworthiness) that are considered to be the basic moral codes that have influenced life in China for several millennia (Li, 2015; Liu, 2010). Although the hierarchical functioning of organisations in China involves authoritarian leaders demanding loyalty and absolute obedience from subordinates at all levels of the organisation, the embedding of Confucianism within Chinese culture also means that leaders are obliged to be benevolent towards their employees and promote prosocial behaviour in their organisations (Fu & Guo, 2018). In other words, the importance placed upon social-harmony and human relationships manifests in being polite to others with the aim of generating a positive social effect (Yuan et al., 2022). *Guānxì* -based business practices can reduce uncertainty, lower search, and other transactional costs, along with providing usable resources and a sense of connectedness. *Miànzi* (面子, face) can be seen as a shortcut through which Chinese people build their network and tap into other's social resources (Tan et al., 2010). This concept shows that empathy plays an important role in Chinese society and the philosophy of life. For the Chinese, empathy is about seeing the world on a spiritual level and, essentially, is about how to be kind to others. Relationships are central to business success in China, and, consequently, empathy takes on vital importance in business interactions. As a result, empathic people, including leaders, are better at building positive relationships (Cremer & Tao, 2019). This is important because Chinese employees want their leader to be considerate and benevolent, adhere to the Confucian parental role, along with being self-restrained, honest towards colleagues, trustworthy and impartial (Wang, 2011). Michelle Liu, who works at the University of Hong Kong (HKU) in China, confirms the importance of these values when describing a good leader as follows: *"A Chinese leader has to be loyal and ethical. They should be devoted to society, honest and humble"* (CCBS Survey, 2017). Leadership empathy is thus most likely achieved by leaders who treat their employees with respect and include them with purpose and enthusiasm in the workplace. These characteristics align with the advanced leadership style that is mostly adopted by CEOs in POEs (Wang et al., 2005; Cheng et al., 2004). Although traditions are still adhered to in these organisations, insofar as there remains a discernible devotion to Confucian principles, other cultural values are also coming to be recognised with respect to how Chinese leaders should behave. The economic reforms in the late 1970s have had a major impact upon the expectations of Chinese leaders. The legalisation of POEs resulted in a significant decrease in SOEs, which up until that point had served as the archetypal example of what employees were looking for from Chinese CEOs (Shen, 2008). Aside from the radical systematic and financial changes, the legalisation of POEs also brought greater diversity into workplaces, both in terms of foreign investors and foreign employees (Cheng et al., 2004). Because of this, CEOs had to adapt their leadership style to be more compatible with foreign employees, while, simultaneously, continuing to keep their predominantly Chinese employees satisfied. This resulted in a more "open-door" policy and modern way of thinking, in turn, leading to the newer generation of Chinese leaders' decision making and behaviours becoming ever-more compatible with Western values (Ralston et al., 1995, 1999; King & Wei, 2014). The most important of these emergent behaviours are being attentive to talent and learning, good communication and being considerate towards employees. According to Gao et al. (2011), these Western-influenced behaviours are also deemed to be good leadership by Chinese employees working in China (Gao et al., 2011).

Colombia

Ikram Ammy Driss, Tamara Ruiz del Arbol Ramirez, Teun Kloosterboer, Chacaya Zwaaneveld & Hedda Smith

Due to its colonial past, most Colombians are an eclectic ethnic mixture of Native Americans, descendants of Spanish colonisers, and African immigrants (Chhokar et al., 2007). This Spanish influence can also be discerned in the prominence of Roman Catholicism within the country (Londoño-Vega, 2002). Colombia is as geographically diverse as it is ethnically heterogeneous, insofar as it can be divided into six distinctive natural regions, encompassing everything from the Andes Mountains to the *Llanos Orientales* (plains), and coastal landscapes of the Atlantic and Pacific oceans (Romero et al., 2020). The coffee bean is not only their chief export, but also plays a pivotal role in the culture and relationships of Colombians (Doga, 2019). Indeed, some strains of Colombian coffee have been shown to have homeopathic benefits, while *pasilla tinto* coffee is credited with generating the energy and close connection that characterises the energetic relationships and conversations in Colombia (Sierra Restrepo, 2013). Another aspect of this energy is spontaneity, which is highly valued in Colombian culture. Indeed, Colombians generally are renowned for their *joie de vivre* (enjoyment for life) and live by the mantra: work hard; play hard (Hernández & Bebbington, 2010). Chhokar et al. (2007) reiterate this aspect of Colombian culture, drawing attention to their passion for living in the moment, and not suppressing their thoughts and feelings. This culture of passion is profoundly affiliated with human relations and building trust through relationships. This is strongly reflected in the prevailing leadership style in Colombia, whereby managers must possess the requisite inspirational charisma to connect well with both their employees and business partners (Ogliastri, 2007).

How do Colombians characterise leaders?

The Colombian population is predominantly Catholic, and, indeed, both religion and the country's colonial past have played a pivotal role in terms of how the country's business landscape has developed over time. As Cardoso and Faletto (1979) argue, Latin American countries share predominant features due to their shared common link to Spain. These principles and values have led to the paternalistic leadership style being historically widely practiced in Colombia, an approach which points towards a highly elitist and collectivist culture (Romero, 2004). *El patrón* (the boss) best represents this traditional leader, who is described by Romero (2004) as being autocratic and directive and using formal top-down communication. *El Líder Moderno* (the modern leader), Romero (2004) argues, is more participative and supportive in their approach, which they explain is a result of the increasing number of women occupying senior-level management positions in Colombia. This is evidenced by the fact that Colombia has one of the largest percentages of women in business leadership roles in Latin America, with just under half of business leaders being women (Bosma et al., 2021). With respect to the qualities that are preferred in leaders, Colombian managers are expected to demonstrate emotional and practical trust by connecting with their employees through building rapport with them (Castaño et al., 2015). This is a key factor that distinguishes Colombia from other Latin American countries, such as, for example, Argentina, where mutual loyalty is expected (Altschul et al., 2007, as cited in Castaño et al., 2015). Consequently, managers in Colombia who are unwilling to disclose personal information are viewed suspiciously and are not easily trusted, notes Ogliastri (2007). Ogliastri (2007) proceeds to characterise Colombian leadership as, above all, being grounded in human relations, with personal integrity, negotiation and conflict resolution abilities all seen as being part of inspirational charisma. This was corroborated by one of the survey respondents, a CEO in Bogotá Colombia, who noted: *"Creo que el carisma e incluso la apariencia física son más importantes para determinar el éxito de los líderes en Colombia que en otros países"* (I believe that charisma and even physical appearance are more important in determining the success of leaders in Colombia than in other countries) (CCBS Survey, 2022). This preference for charismatic, relationship-focused leaders is also noted by Torres et al. (2015), who argue that good Colombian managers provide proactive direction to their employees, while, simultaneously, delegating, listening, acknowledging, and encouraging them. In this respect, Torres et al.'s (2015) framing of Colombian leadership goes against commonly held historical views that Colombians prefer authoritarian managers (Luthans and Doh, 2012). and instead indicates that managers should be participatory rather than dictatorial in order to be effective in Colombia.

These more recent findings suggest that there is a discernible shift in the qualities, traits and behaviours that are preferred in Colombian leaders, namely from the colonially informed style of leadership towards Romero's (2004) *el Líder Modeno* (the modern leader), which is more representative of Colombian leaders at this historical juncture.

Survey results and what local respondents say

Over 100 experienced Colombian C-level executives completed the CCBS Survey in 2021 and 2022 to provide detailed information about local leadership styles and practices in the country. In this section we describe the most noteworthy findings emerging from the survey. The first significant result is the importance that leaders place upon subordinates' welfare. This was demonstrated by the fact that 96 per cent of the respondents agreed with the assertion that managers in Colombia should actively spend time guaranteeing the personal well-being of their team members (CCBS Survey, 2021/2022). As one of the respondents, a Risk Manager in Bogotá Colombia, noted, *"En Colombia es muy importante que el líder pueda inspirar al equipo con ejemplo, cercanía en el trato personal y profesional, calidéz y confianza"* (In Colombia it is very important that the leader can inspire the team by example, through closeness in personal and professional treatment, warmth and trust) (CCBS Survey, 2021). In addition, a sense of care and relationships between leaders and employees was evidenced by the fact that 88 per cent of the respondents expressed that employees are able to address their leaders by their first name (CCBS Survey, 2021/2022). Alongside this, there were heterogeneous opinions expressed in relation to whether subordinates needed to address leaders by their titles, with 35 per cent of respondents agreeing it is important to use titles or position, while 51 per cent disagreed (CCBS Survey, 2021/2022). These divergent views were also reflected in relation to whether older generations tend to prefer greater power distance, while younger generations do not share these values (Tarapuez Chamorro, 2016). Another interesting result was that 50 per cent of the respondents agreed that men and women have equal opportunity to attain senior-level leadership positions (CCBS Survey, 2021/2022). This divide with respect to this question is interesting insofar as the stereotype and commonly held belief is that Colombia is an overly patriarchal and masculine country (Garcés, 2008). These contradictory views were also reflected in the interview with Luis Torres, a local scholar, who expressed that foreigners conducting business in Colombia might be surprised by the amount of gender equality in Colombian leadership. In his words: *"Of course, there's still a lot of opportunity to improve gender equality. But for decades too, Colombia has had some great women leaders."* (9 November 2022). Hence, despite a legacy of patriarchal machismo culture, women are now more likely to hold senior-level leadership positions in Colombia.

Local leadership analysis

Luis Torres: a Colombian leadership scholar

Luis Torres is an associate professor at Georgia Gwinnet College, a GDC, and director for the Center for International Business and Exchange. Torres stated in our interview that leadership in Colombia has undergone changes in recent years. The new prevailing leadership style is more welcoming, insofar as experience is shared and management has become more about leading by example (9 November 2022). Leading by example entails managers taking responsibility for their mistakes, exhibiting growth and welcoming feedback from their employees. The introduction of more of an open door policy regarding feedback from employees ultimately leads to happier and more productive employees, albeit Torres stressed that leaders still provide guidance of what they need done (9 November 2022). In response to a question on what caused this shift in leadership behaviour, Torres explained that it is perhaps a response to the changing and unstable political landscape outside of the business sector (9 November 2022). Torres then proceeded to discuss how leadership is not necessarily homogeneous, but rather varies across Colombia, insofar as the size and range of climates leads to differences even across the biggest cities: *"language, formality, the whole exchange of ideas is different"* (Torres, 9 November 2022). He then went on to explain that the warmer and humid *Medellín* is characterised by a more casual approach towards business, which can be espied in everything from clothing to management style. He further elaborated that this is markedly different in Bogotá, where air-conditioning is more readily available and suits are expected (Torres, 9 November 2022). In response to how this impacts upon the business culture, he elucidated that this translates into a much more formal business style, which is mirrored in the management style. Towards the end of the interview, Torres noted how there were also differences in the management styles between the older generation of leaders and the younger generation, particularly in startup companies, where there is far less of a traditional hierarchical structure, which can sometimes presentt challenges for managers who are more used to a stricter hierarchy. Moreover, the younger generation are more focused on personal well-being *"they prefer to be just happy, satisfied"*, so if they are unhappy with aspects of their jobs, then they do not hesitate to move elsewhere. This presents further challenges for managers who historically have not dealt well with high turnover rates due to high unemployment levels in Colombia. Overall, Luis Torres (9 November 2022) shared insights into manifold aspects of Colombian leadership, most notably, how both generational and geographical factors impact upon the prevailing leadership styles and practices.

Hector Godoy Hernandez: a Colombian cross-cultural trainer

Professor Hector Godoy Hernandez is a freelance leadership consultant and teacher with over twenty years of experience in leadership and management in Colombia. He helps integrate international relationships between universities, companies, and organisations. In our interview with him, Professor Hernandez explained that most Colombian organisations follow the structure of "*Pequeñas y medianas empresas*" (small and medium sized enterprises, SMEs) (3 November 2022). He proceeded to discuss how most of these SMEs are family businesses, which means that leaders are generally more concerned with and connected to the emotional well-being of their employees. Furthermore, he explained that Colombian CEOs must ensure that they know or understand how their subordinates are doing if they are to be a good leader. This is best summed up in the following extract from the interview: "*If the people are emotionally at 100 per cent, then they can give 100 per cent in their job, and this is why [leaders] try to connect [with them]*" (Hernandez, 3 November 2022). This is in accordance with the findings from the CCBS Survey (2021/2022), where 60 per cent of the respondents disagreed with the statement that Colombian leaders should retain personal distance from their employees. Moreover, Hernandez agreed with Torres' (9 November 2022) sentiment that Colombian leadership has changed in recent decades, noting towards the end of the interview that Colombian leadership had undergone a profound transformation in the last 15 to 20 years. As a consequence of this change "*leaders are more conscious of the importance of being prepared to be a good leader*" (Hernandez, 3 November 2022). Here, Hernandez drew attention to the fact that leaders are more aware now and are more likely to actively learn how to be a better leader, by, for instance, taking university classes or working with leadership consultants. Overall, our interview with Professor Hector Godoy Hernandez (3 November 2022) corroborated our findings that the business and leadership landscape in Colombia has dramatically changed, whilst, simultaneously, also adding additional context for the lack of personal distance within organisations.

In-country leadership bestseller

One of the best-selling books about leadership in Colombia is *Memoria de un liderazgo conciliador* (Memoirs of a conciliatory leadership), which is an autobiographical work by Jorge Cárdenas Gutiérrez that was released in 2022. Jorge Cárdenas Gutiérrez was born in Colombia in 1930. He was appointed the

President of the National Federation of Coffee Growers of Colombia in 1983. The book explains how important the coffee industry was and remains for the Colombian economy. In this context, the coffee federation had an enormous amount of power and responsibility and therefore leaders of the national coffee federation were more than just industry managers, both in terms of their impact and responsibilities. The importance of leaders displaying humility and charisma in Colombia is emphasised in the book in relation to Gutierez, who is arguably one of Colombia's most influential figures of the century. Despite his power, Gutierez never lost his simplicity and humility over the course of his career. He began as a public servant, transitioned to the coffee industry and later dedicated himself to education, culture, and philanthropy. Cárdenas Gutiérrez (2022) notes that Latin American cooperation and international cooperation is pivital for succsessful leadership in Colombia, citing the example that previous presidents of the coffee federation had been appointed solely for their contribution to trade agreements such as don Manuel Mejía's work and a subsequent trade agreement with Brazil. The great importance placed upon Latin American collaboration can be understood in terms of the fact that there is no progress if there is no stability in the external income of the countries of Latin America. Another interesting point raised by Cárdenas Gutierez is the importance of conciliatory leadership in Colombia, which is a style of management that focuses on building cohesion within the organisation and amongst employees (Kohlhoffer-Mizser, 2020). Cárdenas Gutierez demonstrates that it is important to prioritise relationships above all else when leading organisations, as he believes that this is fundamental for both the current and future success of an organisation. Overall, *Memoria de un liderazgo conciliador* provides both historical and contemporary context for the importance of relationships in successful Colombian leadership.

Local leadership book	
Title	*Memoria de un liderazgo conciliador*
Translation	-
Author	Jorge Cárdenas Gutiérrez
Publisher	Paidós
Year	2022
ISBN	9786280004488

Colombian leadership YouTube review

In the first vdeo to be discussed, Claudia Restrepo, a Colombian businesswoman and academic who specialises in politics and business management, talks about women in leadership positions during her 2020 appearance at San Vicente Fundactión's *Charlas con Propósito* (Talks with purpose). This episode explored female leadership in organisations, with Claudia Restrepo sharing her twenty years of experience in this field. Restrepo studied business Administration and Management at Universidad Pontificia Bolivariana, specialising in financial management, administration and strategy. In the video, she expresses how the patriarchal society in Colombia has impacted upon women's ability historically to access senior-level leadership positions. Restrepo acknowledges that being educated and socialised into masculine values provides someone with the skills needed to be a successful leader in Colombia, such as, for example, being autonomously strong, which she feels connects to the values that stipulate that Colombian leaders must be brave and display strong perseverance. According to Restrepo, the most significant struggles she observes in business meetings stem from breakdowns in relationships due to formality subconsciously being lowered when men are talking with senior-level women in organisations. Overall, Restrepo (2020) believes that women encounter challenges, but are often able to use these to their advantage and express masculinity in ways to make them more successful leaders. Mirroring Restrepo's (2022) sentiment of gender equality, José Luis Suárez Parra, managing partner of Colombia's Gómez-Pinzón, received the 2022 Latin Lawyer's Law Firm Leader of the Year Award. One of the contributing factors to winning this award was his approach towards gender equality. His subsequent interview with Young Partners Retreat Latinoamérica, which formed part of their Young Partner series, discusses leadership from the basis of his experience as an organisational leader. When a new manager joins, Jose Luis Suárez Parra (2022), advises that in order for them to have a genuine impact on the organisation, they must be seen, both internally and externally, as exceptional professionals, leaders, and team players in Colombia. Parra (2022) goes on to characterise an exceptional professional in Colombia as someone who not only has exceptional knowledge in their field of expertise, but also is an expert in the whole market. The expression he uses *"tiene madera para llevar el título de socio"* (they have the material or wood needed to carry the title of partner) reflects the importance placed on leading by example in Colombia (Parra, 2022, 5:08). Parra (2022) then proceeds to characterise the role of a leader as a team coordinator, thus, once again, highlighting the importance of relationships in Colombian organisations. These relationships mean that good managers spend the requisite time to understand their subordinates and cultivate the most cohesive work environments. Overall,

José Luis Suárez Parra (2022) demonstrates the importance of knowledge in successful Colombian leadership as well as how vital it is to build relationships with one's employees.

Understanding hierarchy in Colombia

Colombian society is typically categorised by a level of high power distance, which is to say that the majority of the population believe that business leaders should have a high position in the organisation and surrounding community (Marriaga, 2016). Power distance in Colombia is connected to a leader's decision-making power and level of control, which connects to the elitist culture that has prevailed for a long time in the country (Chhokar et al., 2007). This is in line with the findings of the CCBS Survey (2021/2022), insofar as 60 per cent of the respondents agreed that strong decision-making is required of leaders (CCBS Survey, 2021/2022). Despite this, in our interview with Hernandez, he shared that in Colombia, a linear scheme is used, which although often confused with a hierarchical structure, is actually not the case in practice (3 November 2022). Only in extreme cases when negotiations are not working out does hireachy come into the equation. Laura Esguerra Villegas, a CEO in Bogotá Colombia, gives an alternative perspective on this, *"el liderazgo es transversal, incluyente y colaborativo con los colaboradroes y el líder"* (leadership is transversal, inclusive, and collaborative with collaborators and the leader) (CCBS Survey, 2022). This perspective makes sense in light of the fact that Colombia is the fourth most collectivistic culture in the world (Hofstede Insights, n.d). This means Colombian society has a high degree of interdependence. This is similar to countries such as Venezuela, South Korea, and Indonesia (Hofstede Insights, n.d). In practice, this collectivism can be discerned in the way that employees are expected to report to their superiors. In Colombia, there tends to be many layers of superiors who report to their respective superiors (Botero & Van Dyne, 2009). Consequently, it might take considerable time to get approval for something, as permission has to first be reviewed by multiple authoritative figures. However, as the workforce is currently undergoing a generational switch from Baby Boomers and Gen X to Millenials and Gen Z employees, the power distance in Colombia is in the process of gradually decreasing (Tarapuez Chamorro, 2016). This is illustrated by the fact that a survey conducted amongst Colombian university students in 2016 found that prestige was becoming a less desirable career goal. Furthermore, many young Colombians aspire to be 'free' from corporate hierarchy through achieving the ambition of becoming an entrepreneur. This change is influenced, at least in part, by the large quantity of freely available on information for aspiring entrepreneurs, the presence of lifestyle coaches and social media influencers (Tarapuez Chamorro, 2016). Further evidence for this *"shift in empowerment"* can be seen in the high turnover rates despite relatively high levels of unemployment (Torres, 9 November 2022). In our interview, Torres stated that this means that managers can no longer simply give out orders to employees, as this is now an ineffective leadership style, especially for younger Colombians (Torres, 9 November 2022). Despite the high-level of collectivism, Colombians also value independence, competitiveness, and ambition as well as materialistic wealth and a high income (Soria et al., 2016). In the context of Colombian organisations, this competitiveness can be observed in the fact that the majority of the respondents in the CCBS Survey (2021/2022) stated that leaders encourage competition within their teams to achieve better results. Overall, power distance in Colombia is best connected to a manager's decision-making power and control. However, despite this, power distance is changing amongst the younger generation insofar as less emphasis is placed on an elitst culture.

How the Colombians achieve leadership empathy

In the words of Professor Hernandez:*"To connect with the Colombian people, you need to adapt and act like a Colombian"* (3 November 2022). Empathy for a Colombian leader is achieved by building a strong connection and relation with their employees. From the interview conducted with Professor Hernandez, it became clear that leaders in Colombia differed with respect to how empathic they are towards their employees. In SMEs, most of which are family-owned and family-run businesses, it is more common for leaders to be more connected with the emotions of their subordinates (3 November 2022). In these types of organisations, employees appreciate their leaders' concern by connecting with their emotions. CEOs in these organisations tend to be aware of their employees' private lives and are able to know if the person can work and achieve the right balance between their work and personal life. However, in large companies there is no connection with people's emotions at all. It is strictly about work and not about employees and their personal problems (Hernandez, 3 November 2022). However, the results of the CCBS Survey (2021/2022) paint a wholly different picture, insofar as over 96 per cent of the respondents reported that it is very likely that managers actively spend time ensuring the personal well-being of their team members. Moreover, 58 per cent of the respondents noted that leaders do not prefer to retain a personal distance from their employees, in order to maintain the right level of respect (CCBS Survey, 2021/2022). These findings are important, because other research has shown that in Latin American business cultures, leaders who practice empathy as part of their leadership approach positively influence the bond they have with their employees, which, in turn, enhances employees' productivity, engagement and commitment to the leader and organisation (Bravo, 2017). Furthermore, Professor Torres also stated that today, Colombian leaders tend to be more open and have implemented more of an 'open-door policy' with their employees. The consequence of this is that leaders are both more open to and responsive to receiving feedback from their employees, which makes their employees feel happier insofar as they feel listened to, appreciated and respected by their leaders. Moreover, and most importantly, this positively influences the degree of mutual empathic understanding between leaders and employees in Colombian organisations (Torres, 9 November 2022).

Croatia

Sheher Anwar, Stijn van Beugen, Josipa Cirkveni, Amber Hazebroek, Daantje Meurs

"*Lijepa naša domovino*" (Our Beautiful Homeland). These are the 187-year-old opening lines to the Croatian national anthem, which perfectly encapsulates the tremendous pride that Croatians have in their country. Although territorially small in size, this country is characterised by a rich array of geographical offerings, ranging from the crystal-clear sea where more than a thousand islands are scattered, over the whitewashed mountain peaks, to the sandy desert (Kapusta & Wiluś, 2017). Situated on the eastern border of the European Union, Croatia is a melting point of traditional values and modern ideas upon which the Western world rests (Fuerst Bjeliš & Glamuzina, 2021). However, this post-transition country still lags behind its neighbours to the right in terms of economic prosperity and, indeed, has seen almost a million people migrate since it gained its independence (Census 2021, 2022). Because the regions that now make up Croatia were formerly a part of the former Yugoslavia, several different ethnic groups coexist there. In contemporary Croatia, its citizens identify as either Croats, Serbians, or members of other ethnic groups, such as Bosnians, Hungarians, Slovenes, Czechs, and Roma (Valenta & Gregurović, 2014). This Soviet influence still resonates within the business sector today, insofar as Croatian organisational culture continues to be characterised by a soft authoritarian style that contains sizable amounts of consultative elements, especially at the higher levels of management (Valenta & Gregurović, 2014). Given the contemporary business trend towards greater forms of consultative and participatory leadership styles, it is interesting to observe how this has impacted upon the authoritarian style that formerly prevailed in the country's business sector (Buble et al., 2014). The following chapter will explore the tension between the country's former Soviet past and new more western styles of leadership by examining in detail Croatian leadership skills, practices, and the prevailing organisational culture. We will do so by engaging with academic literature and empirical research from interviews and surveys conducted with Croatian business professionals and experts.

How the Croats characterise leaders

There are several things that must be taken into consideration when examining the qualities, traits, skills, and behaviours that are preferred in Croatian business leaders. Generally speaking, the prevailing leadership style in Croatian reflects the socio-cultural importance placed upon friendships and family ties. This is illustrated by the fact that, according to research conducted by Studentski Poduzetnički Inkubator (2021), integrity, which the authors describe as a synergy of values and behaviour, is the most important trait that is valued in Croatian leaders (Studentski Poduzetnički Inkubator, 2021). This can be observed in the way that Croatians generally care about both their position in society and how they are perceived by both their peers and subordinates (Omazić et al., 2018). This is reflected in the fact that business leaders in Croatia play an important role in wider society, which explains, at least in part, why it is more important for leaders to have powerful and useful acquaintances than it is to have a strong educational background (Bobanović, 2013). This was supported by the results of the CCBS Survey (2022), which showed that Croatians value personal relationships highly. Specifically, when asked about a specific trait or skill that was required of Croatian leaders, one of the respondents answered, "have value put on personal relationships in all areas of business." With respect to the prevailing style of leadership, historically, Croatian leaders have been of the belief that it is critically important for employees to take responsibility over completing their tasks and fulfilling their objectives. This explains why an autocratic leadership style has been the preferred approach within Croatian organisations for some period of time (Miloloza, 2018), and one continues to see it in the way that modern Croatian leaders carry themselves. This aspect of leadership is corroborated by Bobanović (2013), who posits that the most critical trait required of a leader in Croatia is self-confidence. The principal way through which Croatian leaders demonstrate their self-confidence and authority over subordinates is through the way they verbally communicate with their employees, which is invariably direct and abrupt (Bobanović, 2013). This communicative style is one of the main ways through which Croatian leaders maintain a professional distance from their employees and cultivate a work-oriented atmosphere within the workplace. This is also observed in the fact that Croatian leaders are formal, career-oriented and work hard to ensure the organisational goals are achieved and expect the same in return from their subordinates (Bobanović, 2013). This was evidenced by one of our survey respondents, who noted: "It is expected of the leader to be the one who works the hardest" (CCBS Survey, 2022). However, there has been an observable shift in recent years, as noted by one of the leaders in the CCB Survey (2022), who explained: "Croatian companies are mostly separated into two distinct leadership styles. First one is directly or indirectly connected to established power structures that behave similarly as in socialist past, in which connections and authority is the most important thing. The second leadership style is oriented more globally and tries to follow the latest global trends." One reason for this schism in leadership styles and practices is that these more authoritarian-style leaders tend to run state-owned companies, schools, and hospitals, while the latter more modern leaders tend to be found in more innovative industries such as IT (Vrdoljak Raguz, 2017). This latter point is also corroborated by the fact that for most Croatian leaders, creativity is more important than following procedures to achieve results (Mihelčić & Karlovčan, 2008, as cited in Bobanović, 2013).

Survey results and what local respondents say

In order to understand Croatia's leadership styles and practices, C-level executives in Croatia with extensive knowledge and experience were asked to share their insight by completing the CCBS Survey (2022). This insightful information has provided us with considerable knowledge into the relationship between leaders and employees in Croatia as well as what the prevailing organisational culture looks like. The most noteworthy of the findings emerging from the survey are discussed in turn in this section. Firstly, the majority of the respondents were in agreement over the fact that in Croatian business culture, a rather authoritative leadership style continues to predominate. This was illustrated by the following extract from one of the respondents, *"it is expected of a leader to have a firm hand and not be weak...That way they gain the respect of workers. If not, then workers gossip about their leaders and are unmotivated"* (CCBS Survey, 2022). Further evidence for this authoritarian streak amongst Croatian managers can be discerned in the fact that the majority of the respondents stated that leaders are prepared to confront subordinates during staff meetings in order to obtain the desired results (CCBS Survey, 2022). With respect to what traits, qualities and behaviours are preferred in leaders, as aforesaid, the respondents placed considerable value on leaders cultivating personal relationships with their business peers and employees (CCBS Survey, 2022). However, Martinović, a local business academic, claims that employees' expectations of leaders differ considerably depending on both the industry itself and the size of the company, stating that *"a leader in the IT industry and a leader in the food industry are not the same. So, some industries are very propulsive, and people need to be gathered around an idea in some way, in order to achieve something new, to make a breakthrough"* (15 November 2022). Martinović proceeded to add that in smaller and more creative organisations, leaders are both more charismatic and personally involved in implementing changes in their organisations, while, conversely, leaders of larger companies like to retain a certain distance towards being personally involved in the lives of their subordinates (15 November 2022). Furthermore, as aforesaid, a local leader highlighted the existence of two distinct styles of leadership within Croatian organisations, which stemmed from the tension between the country's Soviet past and more modern trends in global leadership that are making their way into the country, particularly within more creative privately-owned industries (CCBS Survey, 2022). In relation to such modern trends, Martinović argued in our interview that *"some branches have to be more creative... [so that they can] allow inclusion and thinking outside the box because that is what is required there [in Croatian organisations]"* Here, Martinović is drawing attention to the fact that Croatia is slowly opening itself up to more modern leadership practices, but that this is still sometimes at odds with established traditional values (15 November 2022).

Local leadership analysis

Maja Martinović: a business academic

Maja Martinović is the Associate Dean at the Zagreb School of Economics and Management, where she teaches in the field of marketing strategy. Alongside this, she has extensive experience of working on the supervisory boards of organisations such as Croatian National Television, an international bank, and an electrical engineering company. In response to a question about what constitutes a typical Croatian leader, Martinović pointed out that the definition of leadership varies from country to country. In contradistinction to the western definition of a leader as generally someone who is consultative, discusses things, and questions, in Croatia the leader is often considered to be the *"big boss"*. For her, however, *"leaders [should] always lead people towards a vision, motivate them through their ideas, and look for those who will follow that spirit and realise those ideas"* (Martinović, 15 November 2022). With respect to this normative ideal of leadership, Martinović believes that Croatia is currently lacking the requisite academic literature, education, and workshops to bring about the development of leadership within the country. To illustrate this point, she proceeded to cite the example of when companies pay for leadership training, invariably the senior-level leaders do not take part. *"Then, there is a discussion there (in the training) about what should be done at the top, and there is no top, and then all those below, some managers, some mid-level, some maybe higher-level, but not the highest, go to these training courses, but what message is ultimately being given to them?"*

(Martinović, 15 November 2022). Their absence from such leadership training courses, Martinović argues, is reflective of the prevailing attitude amongst Croatian leaders, who she characterised as being *"benevolent dictators,"* that is, authoritative leaders who reward and praise when they approve of something and ignore and punish when they disapprove. Martinović proceeded to state that this is a typical example of what happens in many Croatian companies as a result of society, culture, and the fact that Croatians still have a somewhat paternalistic attitude towards leadership, which, in turn, leads leaders position themselves the way people expect them to (15 November 2022). Martinović also drew a parallel between paternalistic Croatian leaders and the role played by the father figure historically in Croatian families. In so doing, she underscored the fact that this leadership style prevails in organisations due to the influence of national culture upon the business climate. Martinović brought the interview to a close by noting that leadership styles also vary across industries in Croatia, or as she put it, *"the lower the level of education of people in a particular industry, the lower the level of inclusiveness"* (Martinović, 15 November 2022).

Velimir Srića: a leadership scholar and consultant

In the following interview, Professor Velimir Srića shared his ideas about leadership in Croatia. He has been working as a Professor of Leadership and Innovation Management for years at the Croatian University, as well as around the world. Alongside this, he has direct experience of political leadership insofar as he held the position of President of the Zagreb City Council, was the head of a political party, and held the position of Minister in the Croatian government. Dr. Srića also acts as a business consultant to a large number of leaders throughout the region, the most famous of which are Rimac Automobili and Infobip, which are currently two of Croatia's most successful companies. He has translated his experiences and knowledge into numerous books, the last two of which are in English and published in the USA. In our interview, Srića cited an anecdote that illustrated the problem of Croatian business leadership. On one occasion, when he was talking to Jack Welch, he noticed that Croatia is extraordinary in terms of success in sports. Jack Welch named it the *"winning spirit"* of the nation, which Croatia can certainly identify with. However, this small nation that can simultaneously hold the first position in a dozen disciplines cannot boast of the same results when it comes to business success. According to Srića, *"It reflects the fact that our people like to compete, but they want to compete in a fair environment, they like to compete where the rules are right. And in business, as I mentioned, politics is also involved, and the rules are not right"* (15 November 2022). This political involvement in the business sector has had a deleterious impact upon Croatian business development, Srića argued. In fact, he proceeded to discuss how politics has an influence over 80 percent of Croatian companies, most of which are government-owned enterprises and agencies. In these large companies, management is highly traditional and is characterised by a strong and rigid hierarchy (Srića, 15 November 2022). The consequence of such rigid bureaucratic organisations is that employees adopt a risk-averse attitude and play it safe, so as to avoid getting in trouble. He also espoused that it is often the case that the heads of such organisations are incompetent people, who attained their positions by dishonest means. As Srića noted, *"that is why we had a brain drain which was very serious. In the last couple of years, we have lost almost a tenth of the population and most of it have really been well-educated young people who chose some other parts of Europe and the world to live there and not in Croatia"* (15 November 2022). However, when it comes to leaders with Croatian origins in other countries, Srića claims that *"when people leave Croatia, they are above average successful, not only in leadership and business but also in science and other areas of work"* (15 November 2022). Foreign managers who come to Croatia, on the other hand, can expect support and multiculturalism, good communication, humour, and a relaxed lifestyle. Croatia is a very safe country, it is a country where people like to drink coffee, talk about anything, and network privately and professionally (Srića, 15 November 2022).

In-country leadership bestseller

Leadership books in Croatia are relatively scarce. One of the first books in Croatia to treat modern leadership in an original way is *Biblija modernog vođe* (The Bible of the Modern Leader), which was written by the above interviewed professor Velimir Srića. Not only is Srića a writer, but he is also a Professor at the University of Zagreb. Alongside to the functions explained above, he is honorary member of the Croatian Helsinki Committee and the Croatian branch of the Club of Rome. Srića has written and published hundreds of scientific and professional books in Croatia and the USA. As a writer he presents his unique and individual perspective on effective leadership in Croatia. He explains that to be a leader one must strive for internal harmony in one's spiritual, cognitive, strategic, and operational endeavours. Together with the team, a leader must develop the skills that are required to play the role of educator, visionary, guide, and encourager. Through so doing, they remove coercion, unnecessary control, conflict, and other instances of bureaucratisation from the system they oversee. This book describes that bad systems are led by bad leaders. Conversely, good systems that have produced the most significant historical, political, scientific, economic, and artistic successes, are achieved with the guidance of winners. Hence, Srića argues, ultimately, organisations win when they are led by true leaders.

Local leadership book	
Title	*Biblija modernog vođe*
Subtitle	- Haramony-modernog vođe
Author	Velimir Srića
Publisher	Znanje, Zagreb
Year	2004
ISBN	953195447X

Croatia leadership YouTube review

Marija Kalinić, business coach and director of a Croatian consulting company, talks about the qualities required to be a leader in Croatia as part of the "Student digital HUB" project, which is implemented by the Split Entrepreneurship Centre in cooperation with the Student Entrepreneurship Incubator. In her lecture, she placed special emphasis on authentic leadership and its importance within Croatian culture. She claimed that the success of the organisation is greater when there is an authentic, that is, ethical leader at the top of the company (Studentski Poduzetnički Inkubator, 2021, 31:55). In the next video to be summarised, president of the Management Board of Wiener Osiguranje VIG, Jasminka Horvat Martinović, shared her recent professional experience at the Entrepreneurial Mindset 2021 conference in Zagreb. This leading insurance company in Croatia managed not only to overcome the pandemic and a series of earthquakes that hit Croatia at the beginning of 2020 but was also able to outperform the competition with enviable excellence at the time of the crisis (Časopis Poduzetnik, 2021, 7:30). Horvat Martinović discussed their approach and pointed out that in their organisation, the ultimate goal of leaders is to engage their employees. More specifically, their task is to stimulate people and encourage them to find new solutions, and ultimately become leaders themselves, rather than followers (Časopis Poduzetnik, 2021, 3:16). In the final video to be summarised, Velimir Srića, a prominent Croatian Professor, elaborated further on this aforementioned topic. In order to describe what human potential looks like, he used the analogy of the seed of a plant whose growth depends on the hands of the gardener (Srića, 2020, 9:53). Of course, in this context the gardener represents a leader who has the potential to directly affect their employees' performance. However, Professor Srića also drew attention to the frequent examples of employee distrust in their leaders due to the questionable motives of candidates for management positions. He then proceeded to state that in Croatia, there are numerous cases of incompetent people in leading positions who use their position merely to satisfy their own ego (Srića, 2020, 12:45). In this respect, Srića posits that Croatian culture is still used to a traditional manager who expects unquestioning obedience to their orders and acts in a transactional manner with those working under them. Nevertheless, he believes that a modern Croatian manager must also be a leader in order to reach out to employees and get the best out of them (Srića, 2020, 16:45). To end the video, he further stated that an effective leader should not treat all employees the same, insofar as not everyone performs the same. Rather, he espouses that everyone needs an individualised approach depending on their respective level of excellence, and, for him, this is a realistic and best-practice approach to leadership in contemporary Croatian organisations.

Understanding hierarchy in Croatia

Since Croatia left the former Yugoslavia and gained its independence in the early 1990s, it has transitioned from a centrally planned to an open market economy (Stojcic, 2012). Therefore, the term "*druže*" (comrade) is no longer heard when addressing a business partner, Professor, or neighbour. Today, it is more appropriate to address someone as Mr. or Mrs, while it remains rare to address leaders on a first-name basis in a professional environment. This degree of formality was discussed earlier as being a predominant trait of Croatian organisational culture (Bobanović, 2013), and is also espied in the fact that duties are delegated from upper to lower levels of the organisational structure (Saiti, 2020), which, according to Globocnik et al.'s (2022) research, reflects the high level of trust Croatian managers have in their employees. This perspective of Croatian organisations as being characterised by guidelines and the prevailing top-down approach is corroborated by the fact that Croatia is a high-power distance culture. This means that Croatians accept hierarchy without further explanation and see their ideal leader as an autocrat (Hofstede Insights, 2021). This was further evidenced by Srića (2022), who explained in our interview that, *"hierarchy in many companies is something that our managers are accustomed to, and they like it. In principle, most people like to be bosses in big hierarchies, and they enjoy autocratic leadership and one way communication from top to bottom."* With respect to the dimension of uncertainty avoidance, Croatia also scores high, thus indicating that they have rigid beliefs and behaviours and do not tolerate unorthodox behaviour (Hofstede Insights, 2017). This was also something that was pointed out by Martinović, who explained that Croatia lags behind the rest of Europe in terms of holding on to outdated values, customs, and beliefs (15 November 2022). For example, in the family sphere, *pater familias* is simply expected, and, moreover, is often reflected in companies where an authoritative figure is expected and whose hierarchical structures are pyramidical (Babarović et al., 2017). However, there is a historical shift going on in the country with respect to how willing employees are to put with such an autocratic leadership style in their organisations. For example, Babarović et al. (2017) analysed Croatian workers from different generations and discovered that younger workers were typically less devoted to their employers and more self-centred, desired promotions more quickly, and did not place the same high value on their employment in comparison to their older counterparts. Similarly, Srića noted in our interview that the *"young[er] generations are very pragmatic, unfortunately also very selfish and focused on their private interests and their goals more than on [the] social good."* (15 November 2022). Furthermore, according to Twenge et al. (2010), social and intrinsic values have declined overtime insofar as the younger generations place greater emphasis upon leisure time and extrinsic values. Nevertheless, Croatia is, as explained in the Hofstede Insights (2021) analysis, a long-term oriented country and tends to be more pragmatic. Moreover, its society is considered to be collectivistic, rather than individualistic, insofar as its members take responsibility for each other and nurture strong interpersonal relationships, which, overall, results in an interesting hierarchical structure in Croatia (Hofstede Insights, 2017).

How the Croats achieve leadership empathy

Tomulić & Grmuša (2017) researched *'suosjecanje'* (empathy) in the working environment in Croatia and noted that there was a strong correlation between effective communication in a company and a positive organisational culture. More specifically, the authors noted that displays of empathic understanding from leaders to employees was critically important for enhancing the quality of internal communication within the workplace, not to mention that it improved the quality of employees' work and their level of satisfaction with their work (Tomulić & Grmuša, 2017). Tomulić & Grmuša (2017) proceed to discuss how the respondents in their study explained that Croatia, like many other post-Soviet countries, is experiencing a disjunction between the practices and beliefs of older leaders who grew up in and worked in the Soviet era and the newer generation of leaders. The reason for this disjunction is that Croatia has undergone a radical economic-political shift over the last thirty years (Finn, 2019), with the resulting increased globalisation having exposed the younger generation of employees and leaders to ever-more international leadership styles, practices, and cultures, which, in turn, has impacted upon the prevailing leadership style in the country (Bobanović, 2013). For example, in large international companies, leaders are fiercely product-oriented and focused on international success. This appears to be corroborated by the results of the CCBS Survey (2022). Interestingly, while employees in large Croatian organisations expect their leaders to possess a charismatic personality, asking them personal questions or interfering with their personal affairs is most certainly not the norm. Rather, as indicated by half of our respondents, leaders generally like to retain distance from their employees in order to preserve a certain sense of formality and retain a level of professionalism during working hours (CCBS Survey, 2022). This might explain, at least in part, why Bobanović (2013) argued that leaders sometimes find it difficult within large Croatian companies to personally supervise and motivate their employees. In smaller companies, however, it is easier to get to know one's employees, motivate them individually and display empathy towards specific challenges that they might be facing (Bobanović, 2013). It is important to stress here that an equal number of our respondents indicated that they disagreed that the leader should retain distance from their employees, which suggests that this approach depends on, amongst other things, generational differences, corporate culture, and the personal traits of leaders themselves. Due to the significant variation in the responses, it can be concluded that the way empathic understanding is achieved and practised differs across organisations. Overall, Croatian managers can be strict towards their employees, in order to maintain distance and obtain the desired company results, while, simultaneously, Croatian leaders can gain respect from their employees if they listen to them carefully (CCBS Survey, 2022).

Fiji

Mariléne Hoekstra, Roos de Boer, Liam Riethorst, Jeroen Godee, Daniëlle Verlaan & Dani Brink

Fiji, which is often referred to as the "*soft coral capital*" of the diving world, is an island country in Melanesia, which forms part of Oceania in the South. Fiji consists of more then three-hundred islands and is home to approximately 900,000 habitants (Dearie et al., 2021). Historically, Fiji was a British colony from 1874 up until the country finally gained its independence in 1970. The inhabitants of Fiji comprise multiple ethnic groups: native Fijian, Indian, Chinese, and European, an amalgamation which, as one might imagine, results in a wide variety of religious denominations in the country (Harrison, 2004). This heterogeneity is also reflected in its language, as, interestingly, Fiji is one of the few countries in the world that has three official national languages (Mangubhai & Mugler, 2003). Specifically, the 1997 constitution established English, Fijian, and Fijian Hindi as the official languages in Fiji, with all of them being of equal status. Consequently, whether you say *namaste* in Fiji-Hindi, *bula* in Fijian or hello in English, you will almost certainly be understood. In terms of the country's economy, the islands have a rich array of natural resources such as sugar, timber, fish, gold and copper at their disposal. It is for this precise reason that a sizable portion of the nation's agricultural industry is devoted to subsistence farming. Besides the extensive natural resources, Fiji also has a burgeoning tourism industry (Harrison, 2004). In fact, the tourism and agricultural sectors are amongst the largest employers in Fiji and constitute an integral part of the national economy; indeed, the sugar industry alone provides employment to over 51,000 Fijians (Mahadevan, 2009), while the gross domestic product (GDP) in Fiji in 2020 was 4.376 billion US dollars (Fiji Bureau of Statistics, 2022). At the societal level, in Fiji, traditional leadership is based on ascription, which is to say it is hereditary. Alongside this, culture, tradition and religion all play a major role in Fijian leadership, which is a powerful force not only amongst Fijian people, but also in terms of the wider political life of the country (Norton, 2015). To gain a better understanding into Fijian Leadership skills and practices the following chapter will analyse the leadership and business culture in Fiji according to data gathered from Fijan managers, scholars and leadership consultants.

How Fijians characterise leaders

Leadership in Fijian cooperatives is diverse and embedded in an ever-evolving cultural and political context. Historically speaking, a tansactional leadership approach has been the dominant style adopted within Fijian organisations, with additional styles having been subsequently integrated in response to cultural changes brought about by local, political, social, economic and cultural factors (Eti-Tofinga et al., 2017). The ever-evolving leadership culture in Fijian society has implications for the way that leaders are expected to behave, which, in turn, informs the attitudes that they hold with respect to leadership in organisations (Elias, 10 November 2022). While a transactional leadership was the dominant style historically, and by today's standards may appear to be somewhat outdated, according to our interviewee, Mr. Elias, a Fijian leadership scholar, it is necessary for leaders in Fiji to follow established regulative, constitutional and administrative rules as well as to conform to cultural roles and standards (10 November 2022). Alongside this transactional style, a delegative leadership approach has also become increasingly prominant in Fiji in recent years according to Eti-Tofinga et al. (2017). The reason for the emergence of this approach stems from the prevailing culture of respect upon which Fijian society is grounded, which normalises the fact that it is wholly acceptable for a respected person in authority to give orders and expect others to do the work. Delegative leaders instruct others to carry out prescribed tasks, ordinarily with a relaxed and less overt approach to supervising work (Eti-Tofinga et al., 2017). This relaxed manneris also evident in Fijian leaders' attitude towards time, which is slighty different from other leaders in Asia, Europe and Australia, in that the decision- process making process takes a considerable amount of time (Elias, 10 November 2022). Notwithstanding the importance of culture in a delegative approach, it is also important to stress that transactional leaders are also expected to be conscious of Fijian culture within their practices, as inidicated by our interviewee, Mr Elias, who stated that: *"Fijian leadership focusses on people which focusses on tradition which focusses on religion. All these things are important parts of the Fijian culture which is quite different from other parts of the world"* (10 November 2022). Moreover, this cultural awareness is critically important irrespective of whether leaders are iTaukei, non-Indigenous Fijians or foreigners. For example, the iTaukei leaders acknowledge their intention to not offend their culture of traditional chieftainship when doing business, and since these leaders show their respect by listening to their chiefs, leaders from other ethnic groups are expected to show their appreciation towards them also (Eti-Tofinga et al., 2017). With respect to the specific kinds of qualities, traits, attributes and behaviours that are expected of

Fijian leaders, Eti-Tofinga et al. (2017) posits that Fijian leaders are expected to display a dual commitment towards empowerment and inspiring others, which indicates that leaders in Fijian cooperatives are respectful and have a desire to work towards a common good. Finally, although Fijian leadership like other countries across the world continues to mostly be concentrated in the hands of men, it is interesting to note that women are slowly attaining leadership positions as public perceptions of women continue to evolve in the islands (Eti-Tofinga et al., 2017). This is evidenced by the fact that in Fiji, women are more easily able to hold chiefly titles, while more women are also beginng to take on senior-level leadership positions within Fijian organisations (Coventry, 2009). In conclusion, then, in order for leaders to be truly successful in Fiji, they need to exhibit an inclusive approach, and display their understanding of Fiji as a nation and how it works (Leadership Fiji, 2021). Moreover, leaders should be cognisant of the fact that the nation is culturally sensitive, grounded in traditional customs, rituals, religious beliefs as well as being relatively hierarchical.

Local leadership analysis

Arun Elias: a Fijian leadership scholar

The interview with Mr. Elias provided several new insights into leadership styles and practices in Fijian organisations. Mr. Elias is a Dean and teacher at the University of Fiji. He specialises in business, leadership and tourism management. Before Mr. Elias came to Fiji, he spent twenty-two years as a Dean at the University of Wellington, New Zealand. In response to our question about what a typical Fijian business leader looks and behaves like, Mr. Elias noted that a Fijian business leader is extremely sensitive to culture, due to the high level of cultural tension in Fiji (10 November 2022). He then proceeded to describe that a Fijian business leader is highly process-oriented, insofar as they find processes very important and expect employees to adhere to them. Moreover, the decision-making process in organisations in Fiji differs markedly from what one sees in other countries. Most notably, in Fiji, decision making takes a considerable amount of time, Mr. Elias noted (10 November 2022). He added that when Fijians conduct business internationally this aspect of their organisational culture can sometimes cause irritation for their partners, because decisions are not made as fast as other countries are used to and would like (Elias, 10 November 2022). Mr Elias then moved onto highlight another difference in Fiji's leadership style compared to other countries, which is that Fijian leadership is focused largely on people, tradition and religion. This is because, Mr. Elias argues, Fijians are highly culturally sensitive, so understanding the cultural language and heritage of the country is critically important if you want to successfully lead organisations there (10 November 2022). When asked about the importance of age in leadership, Mr. Elias made it abundantly clear that there is a difference between familial leadership and business leadership. Specifically, business leaders are, generally speaking, relatively young in that they are aged 30-40 years-old, whereas in the family sphere the leader is almost aways the eldest member. Mr. Elias then turned to the issue of hierarchy within Fijian organisations, explicating that hierarchy is very important on the islands. In his words: "It's not who you are, it is what you are" (10 November 2022) that ultimately describes how hierarchy functions in Fiji. That is to say, people with an important function demand respect, not only in the workplace but also outside of work. With respect to the latter, he contrasted the situation in Fiji to other countries where outside of the workplace everyone is of equal status (Elias, 10 Novermber 2022). Conversely, in Fiji, you carry your function with you in daily life, which means that people will treat you with a lot of respect and reverance if you are a business leader. He proceeded to discuss that managers show their authority by occupying the main seat in meeting rooms, talking the most and eating first when food is provided. Towards the end of our interview, Mr. Elias explained how important it is for Fijian leaders to establish and maintain trust and respect between themselves and their employees (10 November 2022). According to Mr. Elias, such trust is built through religion, because Fiji is a deeply religious country, and, in fact, it is entirely normal for a workday to start with a quick communal prayer. Mr. Elias summarised this scenario as follows: *"So the empathy comes through that relationship (religion), trying to help the Lord."* (10 November 2022).

Fijian leadership social media review

Alongside YouTube and academic literature, social media is also a useful source for gaining insight into Fijian leadership skills and practices. Firstly, Leadership Fiji shares information on leadership skills and development in Fiji using its social media platforms. The Leadership Fiji initiative seeks to assist future leaders in Fiji in dealing with the challenges of an ever-changing world in order for Fiji to realise its full potential in the broadest sense (Leadership Fiji, n.d.). The initiative allows Fijians to explore their own values, philosophies, prejudices, and beliefs via a variety of topics included in the programmes offered by the initiative. Leadership Fiji works very closely with leaders from the commercial sector, non-governmental organisations, government agencies, youth, and faith-based groups in Fiji. Aside from those aspiring to be effective leaders, successful leaders also attend

Leadership Fiji to develop themselves and gain new perspectives (Leadership Fiji, n.d.). Leadership Fiji's Chief Executive Officer, Ms. Sharyne Fong, often shares insights about leadership and equality on her social media platforms. On her own social media, she stated the following: "*Any of us that have platforms, we need to open them to other leaders, global leaders, female leaders, young women coming up behind us. This is not one generation that is going to solve this problem. It is going to take all of us to move forward in the world.*" (Fong, 2022). This shows that Leadership Fiji is also working on eliminating inequality with respect to accessing senior-level positions within Fijian organisations. Ultimately, Leadership Fiji believes that the lessons learned through their programs will build a new generation of leaders capable of leading Fiji forward as an unified vibrant nation. The next online source to be summarised is Fiji Village, which is a Fijian online news website that shares articles with valuable and encouraging lessons related to business, leadership, politics, and cultural issues in Fiji. Graduate Ms. Krishnan of ANZ Fiji says she learned about national concerns and how to connect with cultural issues on the island. She claims that in this respect the program also forced her to step outside of her comfort zone as a Fijian leader (Bhan, 2022) Another graduate, Krishnan, believes that leadership in Fiji is all about taking action and giving back to the country and local population. She says that the most difficult aspect of her job was collaborating with individuals outside of her own organisation to achieve the goal of designing their advocacy activities (Bhan, 2022). According to William Parkinson, the founder and Chairman of Leadership Fiji, this is their way of telling future business leaders in Fiji that it is not simply about sitting in their offices listening to other people talk, but rather leadership involves getting out there, engaging with the local culture and experimenting and trying things to figure out what is best for the organisation. The third website to be summarised is the International Women's Development agency website, which published an online report that sought to provide the Fiji Women's Forum with information concerning public perceptions of female leaders, both in the political and business sectors (IWDA, 2014). There were three main results. Firstly, the majority of people in Fiji feel that women are under-represented in leadership positions in business and the government, and that changing this would be beneficial to the nation as a whole. Second, the conservative perspectives that favour male leadership are a small but significant minority, with women and young people in the country calling for greater equality. Third, people recognise that the qualifications and attributes of Fijian leaders are not unique to men, but rather are common to both men and women. With respect to the latter point, a rural Indo-Fijian man is quoted as follows on the website: "*The leader should be a patriotic person and should be equal to everyone regardless of their economic status whether they are poor or rich, everyone should be treated with equality. The leader should look after their people first then themselves they should not be biased"* (IWDA, 2014).

Survey results and what local respondents say

To gain a deeper understanding of Fijian leadership practices, various local and experienced leadership professionals completed the CCBS Survey (2022). There were several significant findings, which will be discussed in turn below. First of all, the CCBS Survey (2022) revealed that while there are different viewpoints on what competencies a leader should posssess in Fiji, all the respondents noted that mutual respect is extremely important. Moreover, this mutual respect should be the norm regardless of one's status within the organsiation. It is also critically important to respect elders within Fijian culture. This was corroborated by one of the respondents who noted: *"There is a cultural setting where we respect those who are older then us, deep desire of personal connection where we help each other at work or socially"*. The next finding pertains to the fact that when asked if managers should actively spend time ensuring the personal well-being of their team members, almost every respondent answered that this was "very much" like them (CCBS Survey, 2022). The importance of connection and closeness between leaders and employees was also observed in the fact that two-thirds of respondents disagreed that a leader needs to maintain personal distance from their employees in order to be respected (CCBS Survey, 2022). This means that Fijian leaders value relationships with their employees more than maintaining status through hierarchical structures. One respondent who works as a Project Analyst noted in relation to this point that: *"It is more important to be recognised as a role model and mentor than a manager"*. Leaders gain status and respect from employees in Fiji by both exhibiting good empathic leadership and leading by example. In return, respected leaders in Fiji will be addressed in a respectful manner, as evidenced by the fact that the vast majority of the respondents agreed that employees should address leaders by their titles or positions within Fijian organisations (CCBS Survey, 2022). A further noteworthy finding from the survey is that almost all of the respondents reported that they are prepared to confront subordinates during staff meetings in order to get the desired objectives (CCBS Survey, 2022). This does not mean Fijian leaders will burn you to the ground during a staff meeting; rather, in Fiji, confrontation and feedback is given through a '*talanoa*'. A '*talanoa*' is a group session where issues are discussed, and then followed up on in private. A Fijian leader will use this private follow-up meeting to explain their feedback in greater detail, but also to talk about more personal issues that employees may be experiencing. This style of feedback was confirmed by one of the respondents, who said: *"So to really achieve what you want to acheive as a leader, the best way is through a 'talanoa' ... Direct confrontation, raised voices, etc., do not work"*. This, once again, demonstrates the deeply personal and empathic approach Fijian leaders use to create a bond between them and their employees. The final findings from the survey, which support previous literature, concern the required leadership competencies in Fiji. The majority of the respondents noted that Fijian leaders need to be powerful decision makers, good listeners and must have strong organisational experience (CCBS Survey, 2022). Furthermore, some respondents noted that Fijian leaders need to be visionary thinkers who have strong connections with the right public figures. With respect to gender inequality in Fiji, the vast majority of Fijian executives reported that men and women have equal opportunities to advance to senior-level leadership positions in Fijian organisations (CCBS Survey, 2022)

In-country leadership bestseller

Local leadership book	
Title	*Leadership in Fiji*
Translation	-
Author	R. R. Nayacakalou
Publisher	Oxford University Press
Year	1976
ISBN	978-0195504620

The local leadership book *'Leadership in Fiji'* is written by Rusiate Nayacakalou. Who was born in 1927 and passed away in 1972. He was one of Fiji's most distinguished administrators. He studied the roles of traditional and modern forms of leadership in Fiji. After his death, Professor R. G. Crocombe of the University of the South Pacific edited his work for this posthumous publication. The book is about the problems of modern Fijian leadership and how it relates to traditional leadership. For example, because of the interlocking of different types of groups, ideals, and aspirations, there sometimes is friction between Fijians. Some people favour the abandonment of the old leadership styles in favour for the new styles, while others remain more conservative in their approach. Although Fijians may appear to want change, it seems unlikely that this will occur rapidly, because traditional leaders prefer the traditional hierarchy, where they demand and are accorded a certain level of respect, sit on the main seat in meeting rooms, and have the ultimate responsibility for making decisions. For Fijians, the traditional leader is the person who occupies the customary office of chief of the group. The chief has a definite right to make decisions and the chief or leader's jurisdiction encapsulates all matters related to *'ka vakavanua,'* which means matters of the land and involves the relationship between groups or businesses in the village or outside of it. Another topic the book addresses concerns the dilemma between how leadership is rapidly changing and Fijians wanting to hold on to their traditions and religion. The writer argues that modern leadership must be more flexible and functional and less about tradition. According to Nayacakalou (1976), such flexibility and functionality in leadership style is better equipped to the modern context. This book is especially of interest to students, researchers or anyone involved in leadership problems in developing states (Nayacakalou, 1976).

Fijian leadership YouTube review

YouTube is also an interesting source of information on leadership skills and practices in Fiji. The first video to be summarised here concerns the following organisation: Leadership Fiji. Leadership Fiji offers a program to develop and enhance the quality of leaders in Fiji. The video states that Leadership Fiji was established as a means of providing an alternative perspective on what it means to lead (Dave Lavaki First Fighter, 2017, 1:18). Mr. Daryl Tarte is one of the founders of Leadership Fiji. He emphasises in the video that while there are a lot of talented people In Fiji, they are too focused on their vocations. As such, they do not take sufficient time to consider the broader socio-economic issues that the country faces. Mr. Tarte says that to be a well-rounded leader in Fiji you need to adopt a broader perspective upon these issues. In a testimonial, Mr. Atunaisa Siwatibau talks about how the program improved his own leadership skills. Specifically, he talks about how he came back to Fiji after being away for fifteen years and how the program helped him *"put down his roots"* (Dave Lavaki First Fighter, 2017, 4:37). Meeting a lot of different people and leaders from all parts of society gave him a deeper understanding of the country and, consequently, made him a better leader and decision-maker because he was more involved with the culture, habits, and rituals of local Fijian people. Mr. Siwatibau explains this process he went on as follows: *I felt like, I was like a potted plant when I was traveling around. And then I got taken out and then got put back in the soil. I had been planted and could actually put my roots down* (Dave Lavaki First Fighter,

2017, 4:50). Mr. David Aidney, who is a Managing Director and long-time sponsor of the program, talks about why the program is so successful. He explains that the aim of the program is to expose participants to leaders from across Fijian society but also other sectors of society, because these visits deepen their understanding of their country as well as its history and economic and social structures. This deeper understanding is a critical component of being a good leader in Fiji. They hope that their program will result in the development of a new generation of leaders who are suitably equipped to take Fiji forward in the 21st century as a united and dynamic nation (Dave Lavaki First Fighter, 2017, 9:35). The second video to be summarised involves Opetaia Ravai, who is the CEO of the Water authority in Fiji. The video shows what Mr. Ravai does on an average workday. Mr. Ravai is a family-oriented person, not only for his family at home but also with respect to his family at work. Mr. Ravai starts his day in his office doing paperwork. Paperwork includes things like approvals, signing cheques and resignation and termination letters. Mr Ravai explains that because he sees employees as his family, he finds it hard to decide on termination letters. He adds that it is a challenge to separate emotions and being objective (N Studios Fiji Multimedia Company, 2017, 2:20). After the paperwork is completed, Mr. Ravai has a briefing with his employees where they discuss several subjects pertaining to their company. In the video, Mr Ravai is seated at the head of the table. The rest of Mr Ravai's day consists of several meetings and briefings with different people and project teams. The goal of these meetings is to keep up to date on progress and prepare for in this case a press conference. The video does a good job at showing what kind of Person Mr. Ravai is. Above all, you can see that he is a religious man and that he is close to his employees (N Studios Fiji Multimedia Company, 2017, 0:50). This is illustrated by him walking outside with his employees at the workplace (N Studios Fiji Multimedia Company, 2017, 4:40).

Understanding Hierarchy in Fiji

Leadership in Fiji is based on traditional values. In the past, governance was arranged through a hierarchal system of chiefs. The elements that are ranked are social categories or positions defined in terms of age, seniority of descent, and gender, while the whole in relation to which they are ranked is a social system grounded in rituals. Elders are superior to juniors, chiefs are superior to commoners, and males are superior to females (Turner, 1992).). With respect to how hierarchy functions within organisations in Fiji, most meetings are casual and friendly, yet respectful. This connects back to the aforementioned point about the importance of mutual respect between leaders and employees in Fijian organisations (CCBS Survey, 2022). This stems from the fact that Fiji is a highly collectivistic society, which is to say that Fijian people find long lasting relationships to be of vital importance (Hofstede Insights, 2017). However, according to our interviewee, Mr. Elias, who explained that status is very important in Fijian organisations, and, ultimately, people with a higher function get a lot of respect from subordinates. Because what you are is more important than who you are (10 November 2022). Moreover, this respect and status is not only granted in the workplace but also carries forward outside of the workplace (Elias, 10 Novermber 2022). This is corroborated by the fact that the majority of our survey respondents strongly agreed that leaders' academic title should be on their business card or email signature (CCBS Survey, 2022). This status is also reflected in the fact that leaders will sit at the main seat at the table and, ultimately, will make the final decision after every employee has expressed their ideas (10 November 2022). Ideally, this decision will be made after a compromise has been reached (Turner, 1992). This aspect of Fijian leadership was also supported by the results of the CCBS Survey (2022), where the majority of the respondents noted that Fijian leaders need to be powerful decision makers and have strong organisational experience (CCBS Survey, 2022). This portral of Fijian organisational hierarchy is also supported by the fact that Fiji has a high score of 78 on Hofstede's power distance dimension (Hofstede Insights, 2017). Power Distance is defined as the extent to which the less powerful members of institutions and organisations within a country expect and accept that power is distributed unequally. This indicates that Fiji is still a very hierarchical society where subordinates expect to be told what to do (Hofstede Insights, 2017). This can be traced back to Fijian culture, specifically the fact that in Fijian culture it is less common to speak up in groups. Therefore, in order to really achieve what you want to acheive as a leader, the best way to do so is through organising a 'talanoa' a group session where leaders talk through issues, and then follow up on them later in an additional private session (CCBS Survey, 2022).

How Fijians achieve leadership empathy

To properly empathise with Fijian employees, it is particularly important for leaders to realise that Fijians are deeply culturally sensitive people. They take pride in their culture, and they place significance value upon traditions. Besides this, they are also profoundly religious people. This latter point is critically important, because according to our interviewee Mr. Elias: "*Empathy comes through religion*" (10 November 2022). When examining empathy in the context of business leadership this becomes especially particularly important, as according to Mr. Elias employees and leaders that come to Fiji from foreign countries often fail because they do not understand the cultural language well enough (10 November 2022). Another crucial component of Fijian culture that leaders have to exhibit empathic understanding towards by understanding it and sensitively dealing with it, is the conflict between Indigenous natives and people of Indian origin. Indians originally came to Fiji during the British colonisation in the 19th century (Nanda, 1992). The origin of the conflict is that the government and the traditional power structure within Fiji has always favoured the Indigenous Fijians with respect to land ownership and control (Nanda, 1992). Mr. Elias confirmed during our interview that while a lot has changed in Fiji in recent decades, the conflict between these groups still continues today in ways that have implications for organisational leadership (10 November 2022). Specifically, leaders must always make sure to understand and balance the tension between these groups. However, understanding the cultural language and tension between Fijian Indians and Indigenous Fijians is not the only way to establish and maintain empathy with employees. More generally, Fijian employees see their leaders as parental figures, who they treat with a lot of respect and trust (Elias, 10 November 2022). While this respect is due, in part, to the leader's function, in order to earn full respect and, more importantly, trust from employees, Fijian leaders must show that they care for their employees on a more personal level. This is in accordance with Eti-Tofinga et al.'s (2017) research, which showed that Fijian leaders must display a dual commitment towards empowerment and inspiring their employees. One way through which leaders can do this is to ensure that their employees are feeling good and listen to their personal problems if they are struggling with something. This has historically always been the case in Fijian culture, insofar as Meo-Sewabu (2014) argues that Indigenous leaders were always highly devoted to empathy, understanding, and developing relationships with their followers, which are built on respect, trust, and emotion. Further evidence for the importance of leaders displaying empathic understanding comes from the CCBS Survey (2022), where two-thirds of respondents disagreed that a leader needs to keep personal distance from their employees in order to be respected (CCBS Survey, 2022).

The importance of connection and closeness between leaders and employees can also be observed in the cultural practice known as a *'talanoa'* (CCBS Survey, 2022). *Talanoa* is part of the Fijian culture and can be defined as a specific setting that allows for knowledge and emotions to be shared. In the context of modern Fijian organisations, as aforesaid, a *talanoa* is the way in which Fijian leaders provide feedback and confront their employees. To maintain leadership empathy, it is important that managers do this on a daily basis, rather than on isolated occasions (Meo-Sewabu, 2014).

Kazakhstan

Buraççan Cellatoglu, Ramazan Ercelik, Marie-Hélène Geisler, Teun Meijer, Aaron William & Glenn Zonderop

Kazakhstan (Қазақстан), which is located in Central Asia and surrounded by Russia, China, Kyrgyzstan, Turkmenistan, and Uzbekistan, is often referred to as the land of wanderers; indeed, the word *Kazakh* is Persian for wanderer or explorer, while *stan* is translated as nation or land (Kassymova et al., 2012). It is currently the ninth largest country in the world, with a distance from one end to the other that is equivalent to the distance from London to Istanbul. Despite the enormity of its territorial boundaries, the country is sparsely populated with only around twenty million inhabitants, but, interestingly, more than 120 nationalities (Votpusk, 2016). The most prevalent nationalities in Kazakhstan come from its neighbouring countries, which can be discerned in the wide range of languages that are spoken in Kazakhstan, which includes, amongst others, Kazakh, Russian and Ukrainian (Bartholomew, 2017). The other nationalities are a result of the country's colonisation by the former Soviet Union, due to the fact that people from all across the empire were deported to Kazakhstan for the purposes of hard labour (Kassymova et al., 2012). The multi-lingual nature of Kazakhstan presents notable advantages with respect to its economy. Currently, the economy in Kazakhstan revolves around the export of its natural sources, such as, amongst other things, crude petroleum, refined copper, petroleum gas, ferroalloys, and radioactive chemicals (Bartholomew, 2017). As Kazakhstan is an independent country on the edge of becoming the bridge between Europe, Russia, and China, it is interesting to take the country's leadership preferences into account.

How the Kazakh characterise leaders?

There are a diverse range of leadership styles and practices utilised in Kazakhstan, as a result of both generational differences between older and younger leaders and differences between state-owned organisations and private enterprises. This is because the older generation of leaders and state-owned organisations are still steeped in the mentality of the former Soviet Union, while the younger generation and private enterprises have been more exposed to modern and western-influenced leadership styles and practices (Muratbekova-Touron, 2002). According to one of our interviewees (2022), the first style of leadership that is preferred in Kazakhstan is personally -interested leadership, which is a style of leadership in which leaders exercise good listening skills and inquire about the personal lives of their subordinates. Alongside good listening skills, these types of leaders are also characterised by their good communicative abilities, which the interviewee explained derives from the fact that Kazakhs used to be nomads and, as such, have a rich cultural history and tradition of telling stories (2022). It is important to note that this leadership style not only pertains to the workplace, but also extends into after-hours, insofar as personally-interested leaders will become friends with their employees and often meet them outside of working hours. As a result of this relational approach, these leaders thus see and treat their employees as individuals and are willing to stand up for them if they see they are being treated unfairly (Wengler et al., 2021). The advantage of this leadership style is that the respect that leaders earn by virtue treating employees in this relational way translates into an organisational culture in which everyone in the organisation feels they are voluntarily working with each other to achieve the stated interests of their manager and organisation (Wengler at al., 2021). However, it is also important to stress here that Kazakh leaders also exercise some degree of caution with this approach, as if they are deemed to be too open and soft as a leader, then this can actually undermine their authority in the eyes of their subordinates (Wengler et al., 2021). Consequently, this lack of authority can result in an unmotivated workforce that is not willing to go above and beyond to achieve the organisational goals. Alongside this personally-interested approach, Muratbekova-Touron (2002) also argues that in post-communist countries like Kazakhstan, an authoritative leadership style tends to remain popular amongst the older generation of leaders in the country, particularly those running state-owned enterprises. This leadership style involves exercising close supervision over employees as well as centralised forms of control. For example, decisions are typically made by five or six employees, who need to all individually agree and ratify the decision before it can be actioned. This testifies to the level of control that authoritarian leaders have in Kazakhstan. Notwithstanding the prevalence of authoritarian characteristics of Kazakh leaders, one of our interviewees (2022) described a typical Kazakh leader as someone who should be innovative, proactive and responsible during crises. This was corroborated by the results of the CCBS Survey (2022), insofas as being a powerful decision-maker and a visionary thinker were deemed to be important qualities for leaders to possess in Kazakhstan. Despite the preference for leaders who can demonstrate responsibility during difficult situations, Trevino and Brown (2004) argue that Kazakh managers tend to be ethically silent leaders, by which they mean that they tend to be more concerned about financial results than holding people accountable for their (un)ethical behaviour, as evidenced by the low score accorded this aspect of leadership in their survey with Kazakh managers (Trevino & Brown, 2004). Consequently, when viewed in terms of the "global moral compass" for business leaders, although Kazakh leaders tend to be moral persons in the sense that they personally follow their company's moral code of conduct, they need to improve their moral performance when it comes to encouraging others in the organisation to act in an ethical manner more broadly (Thompson, 2010).

Survey results and what local respondents say

Over fifty C-level executives shared their experience and knowledge by completing the CCBS survey (2022), which provided comprehensive insight into the various leadership styles and practices adopted in Kazakhstan. The most noteworthy of the findings emerging from the survey will be discussed in turn below. Firstly, the majority of the respondents reported that employees look up to their leaders on the basis of their organisational experience and market expertise. Alongside this, being a powerful decision-maker and a visionary thinker were also deemed to be important according to the respondents (CCBS Survey, 2022). This point was corroborated by one of our interviewees who described a typical Kazakh business leader as a '*middle-aged male who is pretty authoritarian*' (CCBS Interview, 2022). The second finding to be discussed pertains to the fact that most of the leaders are from the older generation, but that this "*[has] began to change over the last 5-10 years*" (CCBS Interview, 2022) In this respect, there appears to be somewhat of a genarational gap between leaders from the older and newer generation, who have been more exposed to western influences and leadership trens over the last three decades. This, in turn, has led to the emergence of a newer form of leadership in which "*team-based decision-making*" is a key element (CCBS Interview, 2022). The third noteworthy finding is that the respondents were relatively divided with respect to the question of whether women and men have equal access to senior-level leadership positions within Kazakhstan organisations (CCBS Survey, 2022). This divergence of opinions was similarly visible in the respondents' answers to the questions of whether there are differences between the leadership styles of men and women. Alena Geydt, who works for HRD VTB Kazakhstan Banking, described the difference in leadership between the genders as follows: "*Women tend to compromise, while men are more likely to make power-based decisions*" (CCBS Survey, 2019).

Local leadership analysis

An Kazakh leadership scholar: Onajoma Akemu

The first interviewed expert has been an Assistant Professor at the Nazarbayev University Business School in Astana, Kazakhstan, for the last five years. Onajomo "Ona" Akemu has a PhD in Management and has worked and studied in several countries. One of the specific characteristics of a Kazakh leader that he identifies is that they tend to be somewhat more authoritarian in their approach comapred to some other cultures. Akemu proceeded to discuss his own experiences of the high level of power distance between leaders and employees in Kazakh organisations (27 March 2019). Moreover, Akemu explianed that the style of communication in Kazakh businesses tends to be very direct and top-down in nature, as evidenced by the following quote from him *"It is not uncommon for people to say things like: The boss is always right"* (Akemu, 27 March 2019). The second key element in Kazakh business is personal loyalty. In Akemus's own words: *"This personal loyalty is bi-directional, it is a natural system between leader and employee. I give you a job, in exchange I expect you to be loyal"*. The scholar proceeded to explain that this is a form of personal loyalty towards the personhood of the leader themselves, rather than towards the organisation necessarily (27 March 2019). Therefore, when a leader or someone in a senior-level management position leaves the company, it is common in Kazakhstan for leaders to take their entire team with them because the loyalty lays with the leader and not with the company. *"Again, it's loyalty to them, not to the organisation"* (Akemu, 27 March 2019).

A Kazakh cross-cultural trainer

The second interviewee is a Kazakh expert in youth empowerment and leadership. He led several high-profile research projects that were focused on economics, ecology, and human rights. Alongside these specialisms, his own podcast about youth leadership was rated in the top-20 podcasts in Kazakhstan. In our interview, the trainer opined that leadership in Kazakhstan is changing. They proceeded to explain this shift as follows: *"Leadership used to be centralised, there was a top-down system in place where only the executives were able to make the decisions"*. They argued that, today, leaders are more proactive, responsible, innovative and resilient in their approach. However, the interviewee did stress that this shift was not the case across Kazakh organisations as a whole. Rather, they noted, there is a generational gap in Kazakhstan between the older generation of leaders, who were primarily influenced by the former Soviet leadership styles, and the younger generation of leaders, who have a more well-rounded knowledge of international leadership best-practices, and, moreover, are open to incorporating these insights within their own leadership styles. In response to a question about what opportunities Kazakhstan is offering for the future, the interviewee stated that the new emerged leadership styles will afford a different perspective on leadership as whole. This is because: *"Leadership should not be individual, centralised and autocratic; it should be more open to team-based decision-making."* He brought the interview to a close by stating that good leadership in Kazakhstan should not only be business-orientated, but also focused on the well-being and personal development of employees, with *"respect"* and *"trust"* being vitally important to this process.

In-country leadership bestseller

The book entitled *Difference in Leadership Views (2011),* by Sanjar Alin, is a best-selling leadership book in Kazakhstan. The book is based on mainstream western views presented in academic literature and three Kazakh leaders who are executives in three different business sectors; in the book, they explain their perspective on these business sectors and the government of Kazakhstan. Future orientation, gender differentiation, uncertainty avoidance, power distance, institutional emphasis, collectivism versus individualism, in-group collectivism, performance, and humane orientation (Bokus, 2011) are just some of the topics that are addressed in the book. Furthermore, the book also explains how these topics can be implemented and how the Kazakh leaders approach these kinds of situations. Finally, the book incorporates the discussion of the main findings and suggests the direction for future considerations based on the results.

Local leadership book	
Title	*Difference in Leadership Views*
Subtitle	How Do Three Leaders Operating in Different Sectors of Business in Kazakhstan View the Role Played by Their Leadership
Author	Sanjar Alin
Publisher	Lap Lambert Academic Publishing
Year	2011
ISBN	9783844314212

Sanjar Alin
Difference in leadership views
How do three leaders operating in different sectors of business in Kazakhstan view the role played by their leadership
LAMBERT Academic Publishing

Kazakhstan leadership YouTube review
In an interview carried out by CCBS (2016), interviewee Alexander Pakemonov, Chief Research Officer and a Senior Teacher at Kazakh National University, defines *"respect, recognition, authority, and reputation"* (Pakemonov, 2016, 0:47) as the essential elements for successful leadership in Kazakhstan. According to Pakemonov, reputation is of critical importance, because he argues that it is not possible to be an effective leader in Kazakhstan without a good reputation. In order to be an effective manager, you must be recognised, and this recognition must be positive to have a good reputation, he stated. To uphold and maintain a good reputation, Pakemonov encourages leaders to regularly request feedback from their subordinates, even though the Kazakh hierarchical structure in public institutions is based on a top-down structure. In a second interview, Maxim Maximov, Founder of CNL TV-Network, agrees with the arguments stated by Pakemonov. Maximov believes that good Kazakh leaders should encourage their employees. He proceeds to discuss that employees should not be punished for their own wrongdoings. Rather, Maximow argues, adopting a more participative leadership approach would ensure that leaders in Kazakhstan are both more involved with, and provide greater recognition to, their subordinates (Maximov, 2015, 0:11).

Understanding hierarchy in Kazakhstan

The influence of both Islamic culture and the continued influence of the former Soviet Union are crucial for understanding the prevailing organisational hierarchy within Kazakstan. Kazakhstan can be characterised as a high power distance society (Karibayeva & Kunanbayeva, 2017). This high-power distance is visible in a survey conducted by Karibayeva and Kunanbayeva (2017), who asked their respondents to rank Kazakhstan on the power distance scale. Their results indicated that power is distributed unevenly between Kazakh leaders and their employees. This is corroborated by Nezhina and Ibrayeva (2013), who argue that the hierarchical order in Kazakhstan is so important that managers function as role models for their employees and are regarded as flawless and untouchable by them. As a result, employees have little interaction with their leaders and instead merely do what they are told (Nezhina & Ibrayeva, 2013). One reason for this, according to one of our interviewees, is that Kazakh employees can become very stressed in uncertain situations, so they need rules and regulations from a strong leader who can cope with this uncertainty (CCBS Interview, 2022).

This helps explain why the respondents in the CCBS Survey (2022) reported that being a powerful decision-maker and a visionary thinker were important qualities for leaders to possess. Ilimkhanova et al. (2014) confirms this, noting that Kazakhs expect that their eldest, or the person with the highest position, will make decisions in the best interest of the group. A further reason for the rigid hierarchy is that Kazakh leaders are more business-orientated in their approach, which is to say that they are more focused on working than interacting with their employees. This aspect of Kazakh organisational culture was corroborated by one of our interviewees, who stated that "*Kazakh companies do not have long-term visions and therefore the subordinates are only focused on day-to-day life*" (CCBS Interview, 2022). Furthermore, the influence of Soviet culture and values continue to be felt in Kazakh society. According to one of the interviewees, the older generation of Kazakhstan are still profoundly influenced by Russian values and norms in the field of leadership, insoafar as all the decisions are made at the top, because the leaders are strong decision makers (Danish Kazakh Society, 2019). However, a new approach is slowly being adopted by the younger generation of leaders, who place moral integrity and individual equality at the forefront of their leadership style. The organisations led by these leaders tend to be less hierarchical than those run by their older counterparts (CCBS Interview, 2022). Indeed, the younger generation of leaders tend to discuss personal matters with their employees and sometimes even becomes friends with some of their subordinates (Wengler et al., 2021). Furthermore, one of our interviewees stated that hierarchical differences not only exist with respect to the older and younger generation of leaders, but also regarding state-owned businesses and private enterprises, noting that: ''*The government sector is probably not moving in the new leadership direction. They are keeping their older traditions*'' (CCBS Interview, 2022), which is grounded in a more transactional approach. Politicians are a good example of transactional leadership insofar as they "*exchange one thing for another; jobs for votes. As long as this style of leadership and the hierarchical structure still forms the basis, it seems that the arrival of the new leadership approach seems far away for the time being*" (Mukazhanoca, 2012, p. 23).

How the Kazakh achieve leadership empathy

In Kazakhstan, there is an emphasis on autocratic and paternalistic forms of leadership. Clear rules make subordinates feel safe under the umbrella of a good leader that will protect them from a crisis and lead them towards a common goal (CCBS interview, 2022). In high power distance cultures like Kazakhstan, a distant and status-conscious leader is not seen as arrogant, but rather as a leader who has the requisite knowledge and power needed to lead an organisation (Akemu, 27 March 2019; CCBS Survey, 2022). This explains, in part, why leaders are often viewed as parental figures, insofar as they offer support, security and comfort to their subordinates (CCBS Interview, 2022). Indeed, for Kazakhs, family and bonding between a leader and other individuals are essential for establishing a strong sense of connection. As aforementioned, Kazakh leaders who adopt a personally-interested approach will often become friends with their subordinates and meet them outside of work. In so doing, these types of Kazakh leaders thus view and treat their employees as individuals, and are even willing to go to bat for them if they perceive them as being treated unfairly (Wengler et al., 2021). The realtional approach between leaders and their subordinates not only comprises a caring and concerning attitude towards fairness ar work, but rather also extends to include an interest in the welfare of employees. In this respect, as Ardichvili and Kuchinke (2002), empathic understanding comes more naturally if the leader is seen as being a quasi-parental figure. This empathic aspect of Kazakh leadership was also observed in the CCBS Survey (2018), where the majority of the respondents indicated that leaders should spend time actively on the well-being of their team members.. An additional way in which it is important for Kazakh leaders to be empathic pertains to the multicultural nature of Kazakhstan society and, as such, Kazakh organisations. As aforesaid, Kazakhstan is a rich multicultural country with a lot of citizens from different ethnic backgrounds (Votpusk, 2016). Therefore, it is is vitally important that Kazakh leaders display empathic understanding towards these different cultures working within their teams. This is why tolerance is one of the most deeply held and practiced values within Kazakh culture, as evidenced by the fact that there are manifold versions of the word 'tolerance' in Kazakhstan to reflect the many cultures in the country (CCBS lesson Kazakhstan 2022). Given this, Kazakh leaders must be both cognisant of and tolerant towards all of these different nationalities and strive to display sufficient empathic udnerstanding as to be able to bring them together to work effectively in the organisation (Busi, 2014).

Panamá

Jairo Diaz, Darryl Oppong-Kyeremeh, Romée Caprino, Nam Doan, Dimas Sarkam, Mustafa Bakhsh & Nora Ruijpers

Puente del Mundo, Corazón del Universo (bridge of the world, heart of the universe) is a famous Panamánian phrase through which people express their national pride (López, 2007). Panamá is in Central America and is renowned above all for the *Canal de Panamá*, which is close to the city and around 80 kilometres in length (James, 2006). Given that it was the first Spanish colony (Benítez, 2014), historically, it served as a trans-shipment point for gold and silver bound for Spain. Panamá continues to serve as a land bridge between the Caribbean Sea and the Pacific Ocean connecting North and South America, which makes Panamá one of the most strategic transportation hubs in the world (Gollasch et al., 2006). As one would expect, Spanish is the primary language spoken, which also explains why it is home to several indigenous groups from primarily Latin countries (Andrade et al., 2016). The country has a population of over four million people (Sullivan, 2020), most of whom are mestizos or of mixed European and indigenous American ancestry. Most Panamánians are also Roman Catholics, and the country is deeply religious (Hassig et al., 1996). Panamá City, the capital, is a contradictory combination of beautiful natural reserves and a bustling business environment with skyscrapers, colonial monuments, and buildings. It is the largest and fastest-growing economy in Central America, with transportation, banking, commerce, and tourism being the key sectors driving economic growth (Cordoba, 2022). Panamá is well-known for business, but also for *fiestas* (parties) and festivals, which are a huge part of Panamánian culture. These festivals reinforce a strong sense of community and togetherness, insofar as everyone is involved and all shops and companies are closed during the festivities (Cheville & Cheville, 1981). This democratic country places considerable value upon respect, which helps explain why Panamánians adopt a formal approach to communication in their leadership styles. Indeed, such formality is regarded as the utmost form of respect and, as this chapter will demonstrate, is vital to the organisational culture in Panamá (Becker, 2004).

How the Panamánians characterise leaders?

El liderazgo es una relacion (leadership is a relationship) is a well-known saying in Panamá, thus indicating the importance of leaders building a bond with their followers to achieve effective leadership (Bieberach Vanegas, 2004). Another important trait of a leader in Latin America that is in accordance with the aforesaid statement is *personalismo* (personalism), which means that leaders must personally value and validate each of their followers to gain respect (Bordas, 2013). Abdiel Ledesma, a Panamánian cross-cultural trainer, states that Panamánian leaders gain respect by building trust, empathising, and connecting with their employees (Ledesma, 15 November 2022). Further support for this comes from the CCBS Survey (2022), where the majority of the respondents stated that the well-being of staff should be a leader's top priority. To better understand the preferred leadership style in Panamá, it is instructive to examine in more detail how business is conducted. According to an article on American investment and business practices in Panamá, the attitude towards business practices is similar to that seen in America, due, at least in part, to the profound influence of American television and radio stations in Panamánian culture (Panamá, 1996). Consequently, Panamá 's multifaceted leadership styles and practices are a combination of North and Latin American influences. For example, a typical Latin American mindset that conflicts with the North American approach is the *"Do not take things so seriously"* mentality. In other words, if there is a conflict or challenge, then Panamánian leaders are expected to be gracious and exhibit humour towards the situation. In a similar vein, it is also of paramount importance for Panamánian leaders to be kind, according to Karen Garcia Saucedo, a Panamánian cross-cultural trainer, who explained that publicly yelling at employees or confronting them about their mistakes is simply unacceptable (14 November 2022). Instead, Saucedo argues, showing kindness and empathy is the right way to handle such situations, because, ultimately, how things are said in Panamánian organisations profoundly impacts upon how employees understand what has been said (Saucedo, 14 November 2022). The display of good humour and kindness serves to foster a pleasant working atmosphere, but also boosts productivity once prolonged, strenuous work is required of people (Bordas, 2013). Alongside this more relational approach, prior studies on the preferred leadership styles in Panamánian Higher Educational institutions have also indicated that leaders adopt a transactional leadership style (Smith, 2020). Within this approach, leaders value order and structure. They often do not deviate from the norms for anyone or anything. Luz Nelly Garcia Rivera, a leadership coach and motivator, argues that Panamánian followers see someone that uses power to achieve their objectives as a leader (Rivera, 2017). While some leaders also occasionally employ the laissez-fair leadership style, which primarily comprises delegating tasks to subordinates, ultimately, the final decision and power are always concentrated in the hands of the leader (Bieberach Vanegas, 2004). Alongside this, it is important for leaders in Panamá to actively listen to the opinions and voices of their subordinates (Smith, 2020). This was confirmed by the results of the CCBS Survey (2022), which showed that leaders in Panamá need to be decision-makers and good listeners. In Smith's (2020) findings, the leaders also viewed themselves as inspirational motivators, which makes sense given that motivation and leading by example are characteristics viewed highly in Panamánian society (Smith, 2020). Like Bieberach Vanegas (2004) Garcia Saucedo noted that it is important for Panamánian leaders to be driven and result-oriented, while, simultaneously, defining each team member's role and assigning tasks, however, she argues that Panamánian leaders must redirect their focus on creating a humanistic connection to communicate with and inspire employees, rather than applying a directive leadership style (Saucedo, 14 November 2022). Finally, Saucedo noted that Panamánian leaders must be visionaries who know the ins and outs of the market they are operating in (14 November 2022).

Survey results and what local respondents say

The CCBS Survey (2022) was conducted in order to gain additional empirical insight into leadership styles, skills, and practices in Panamá. The findings below are based on the knowledge and expertise of 88 local C-level managers from two different periods: 2019 and 2022. This is because the survey was completed by 38 respondents in 2022, but this data is complemented by primary survey data on leadership skills and practices in Panamá from 2019, which had a sample size of 50 respondents. The most important findings that emerged from the survey are summarised in turn below. The first noteworthy finding is that the respondents reported that it is necessary for leaders to actively spend time ensuring the personal well-being of their team (CCBS Survey, 2022). This finding is in accordance with that of Rivera, a coach and motivator, who describes a Panamánian leader as someone who must have the ability to feel the emotions of others as well as understanding their view and taking an active interest in their concerns (2017, 6:49). The next main finding from the CCBS Survey (2022) was that just over half of the respondents stated that it is essential to address leaders by their titles or positions within Panamánian organisations. In response to what qualities, traits and behaviours are preferred in Panamánian leaders, the respondents agreed that Panamánian leaders should have a strong charismatic personality, in conjunction with having access to the right networks and a high intellect. Furthermore, successful leaders in Panamá must be "*powerful decision-makers*" and "*good listeners*" according to the respondents (CCBS Survey, 2022). With respect to the treatment of women in Panamánian businesses, there were contradictory responses from the participants. Some leaders agreed that men and women have equal opportunities to attain senior-level leadership positions, while others disagreed that this was the case, which is in accordance with the research of Cardenas et al. (2014), who argued that *Machismo* makes it difficult for women to gain access to higher-level positions. Furthermore, in response to the question of whether men and women utilise different leadership styles, one respondent stated: "*Women are more reactive*" in their approach in comparison to men (CCBS Survey, 2019). Finally, sixty-five per cent of the respondents agreed that managers should encourage some degree of competition within a team to achieve better results, while sixty-two per cent disagreed with the notion that leaders should retain an emotional distance from their employees to maintain respect. These final two findings are in line with Rivera's perspective that Panamánian leaders should motivate and influence subordinates to reach specific objectives (Rivera, 2017, 1:52).

Local leadership analysis

Karen Garcia Saucedo: A Panamánian cross-cultural trainer
Karen Garcia Saucedo holds a master's degree in Business Administration with a particular interest in Management and Operations. She graduated from Universidad Latina de Panamá and Universidad de Panamá, two of the most respected universities in the country. Garcia Saucedo has twenty years of experience in the corporate world, and most of her career was spent in the area of talent management. In 2015, she decided to dedicate herself to being a consultant. Today, she is a consulting director partner at Gente Smart Corp, an organisational development agency in Panamá. Garcia Saucedo leads a team that focuses on developing leadership skills for multinationals and medium-sized companies. During the interview, Garcia Saucedo stated that a Panamánian leader should have a clear vision and be result-oriented (14 November 2022). For her, this means finding a way to progress in the market. A leader must know the ins and outs of the market to be able to navigate and strategically lead an organisation effectively. Conversely, a leader must be driven and eager to attain results. As Garcia Saucedo states, the drive to push through obstacles and get results is crucial for Panamánian leaders (14 November 2022). She went on to argue that more leaders should focus on connecting with their subordinates to

communicate and inspire them, rather than implementing a directive approach (14 November 2022). Her experience is that Panamánian leaders lack people skills, which, in turn, results in a lack of connection between leaders and their employees. It is, therefore, crucial for leaders to connect with their employees on a human level and see them as people rather than mere subordinates. One way to achieve this humanistic connection, Garcia Saucedo argued, is to periodically question employees on how they feel and what can be done, from a leader's standpoint, to facilitate their performance at work (14 November 2022). Panamánian leaders can build trust by developing communication skills and connecting with their employees. Saucedo believes that yelling at employees and making their mistakes publicly known is not the way to improve such situations. Rather, leaders must be kind, and sometimes it is more important how things are said rather than what is said (Garcia Saucedo, 14 November 2022). Furthermore, Garcia Saucedo stated that Panamánian leaders are not accustomed to change, and, as such, are slow to adopt new processes and stuck in their old ways and procedures. As Garcia Saucedo said, *"We do not rush or drive to get things done immediately and stress all the time"* (14 November 2022). This is because the Panamánian culture is laid-back and reacting to stress is simply not in their DNA (Garcia Saucedo, 14 November 2022). However, Saucedo did note that Panamánian leaders are keen to learn from other cultures: *"we have a culture where we are open to other ways of doing things"* (14 November 2022). In the same way that the American business culture was partially adopted (Panamá, 1996), Panamánians have no difficulty in learning from other cultures and adopting their methods. In her experience, leaders embrace multinationals and quickly adopt them as part of their team (Garcia Saucedo, 14 November 2022).

Abdiel Ledesma: a Panamánian cross-cultural trainer

Abdiel Ledesma began his career by getting a bachelor's degree in Computer Systems Engineering. After holding several management positions in Panamá, Ledesma decided to do a master's in Leadership at the Project Management Institute. Today, he works as a leadership consultant and facilitator in Panamá, where he helps to improve leadership skills and practices in Panamánian organisations. Over the course of the interview, Ledesma stressed on multiple occasions that it is essential to treat people as human beings, not as things when leading an organisation in Panamá (15 November 2022). This approach is also reflected in the leadership system he developed that focuses on servant leadership. He believes that servant leadership consists of five main aspects: generating trust, being able to develop your team, creating an emotional connection, sharing a vision and being able to build high-performance teams (15

November 2022). Before doing business in Panamá, it is important to empathise and create a social bond with people. This can be achieved by asking simple questions such as: *"How was your son's activity last weekend*?" (Ledesma, 15 November 2022). There are still leaders in Panamá that like to display their authority because it is regarded as an element of power. According to Ledesma, these leaders do not allow teams any autonomy to operate without constantly giving them orders (15 November 2022). This autocratic style of leadership is changing; however, insofar as ever-more leaders are beginning to implement the open and servant leadership style in Panamánian organisations. Within this leadership style, it is acceptable for employees to directly approach their leaders without going through an intermediary, even if it is to give feedback (Ledesma, 15 November 2022). Panamánian leaders can earn respect by showing they have the requisite experience, building trust, empathising, and connecting with their employees. Besides this, older people, irrespective of their educational title or hierarchical position in an organisation, are always treated with more respect due to the prevailing social norms (Ledesma, 15 November 2022). Ledesma states that the critical factor in being a successful leader is as follows: *"Haz las cosas con amor…"* (do things with love), because as he mentions, love is an ingredient that always adds something extra (15 November 2022).

In-country leadership bestseller

Trasciende: Principios de vida y liderazgo que impactan (Transcend: Principles of life and leadership that impacts) is written by Panamánian writer and motivational speaker Daniel Castell. Castell has over seventeen years of leadership experience in the banking world. He is also a leadership coach and founder of a leadership academy. In this academy, he helps organisational leaders enhance their leadership through self-knowledge to connect with their employees and get the best out of their teams. This 2022 leadership best-seller describes the importance of living and operating in life with a specific purpose, both on a personal and professional level. The book teaches how anyone can strengthen their leadership skills and discover their purpose in life. The author helps the reader to improve their leadership style and communication with their team members and cultivate a better and more productive work environment. Castell provides stories, examples from his life, anecdotes, and strategies. For example, he states, "*Leadership does not start with a position. It is the result of our growth and personal development*" (Castell et al., 2022, p. 25). He also states that leadership is personal first and corporate second. That is to say, everyone's leadership journey should begin by asking themselves about the purpose of their life. After that, the purpose of leaders and the importance of time management are discussed.

Castell brings the book to a close by stressing the virtues of change and how a purpose will never retire (Castell et al., 2022). Overall, this Panamánian book is ideal for anyone who is seeking to develop their leadership skills, both within and outside the workplace.

Local leadership book	
Title	*TRASCIENDE*
Subtitle	*Principios de vida y liderazgo que impactan*
Author	Daniel Castell
Publisher	Editorial Litterae
Year	2022
ISBN	9798446320349

Panamánian leadership YouTube review

Alongside academic research and interviews and surveys, YouTube, an online video-sharing platform, also represents a valuable source of information for gaining insight into Panamánian leadership styles and practices. Raùl Varela Barros (2022), a business lawyer and the General Director of the World Happiness Foundation, talks about who a leader should be and the characteristics that make a good leader in Panamá in an online seminar. He states that the desired leader should be humanistic, and place their employees at the forefront, in order to build a team and achieve their goals. Raùl sees a company as a community of individuals, which explains, in part, why he thinks Panamánian leaders do not need to be extraordinary or have a high IQ to lead an organisation; rather, any qualified person with the required virtues can become a leader (Barros, 2022, 9:40). One of these important virtues is humility, which derives from the Latin word *humus*, and refers to the fact that a leader must display a down-to-earth attitude towards subordinates or business associates in Panamá (Barros, 2022, 12:31). Furthermore, Raùl states that it is important for Panamánian leaders to have a sense of humour because they are managing human beings rather than automated machines. Ultimately, Raùl notes, it is emotions that drive humans, and these emotions trigger qualities such as a sense of belonging, productivity, and hard work, which are essential in team building. He then proceeds to state that Panamánian leaders should be able to motivate and excite their followers, function as a navigator when there is no direction, and improvise and revise the vision when needed (Barros, 2022). To display such flexibility and growth without losing face in front of their subordinates, an open mindset is necessary. Next, he argues that leadership is about exhibiting exemplary behaviour and setting an example to one's employees, as this enhances credibility and trust. Finally, *"a true leader is someone who knows how to surround themselves with the right people"* (Barros, 2022, 11:11). Another video that talks about local leadership is *"Liderazgo Social Efectivo"* (Effective Social Leadership). In this video, Luz Nelly Garcia Rivera (2017), a coach and motivator, explains that leadership is predicated on both love and passion (Rivera, 2017, 1:05). Next, she states that Panamánians see leaders as someone who uses power to achieve their objectives (Rivera, 2017, 1:52). Power, in this instance, is defined as the power to motivate, influence and work with enthusiasm to achieve specific objectives. This kind of leadership is referred to in the video as leadership from the soul. Further, it is argued that Panamánians see a leader as someone who must have the ability to feel the emotions of others, understand their point of view, and take an active interest in their concerns (Rivera, 2017, 6:49). In the conclusion of the video, she explained that Panamánian leaders should be firm and display strong resistance to getting frustrated, so that they can withstand complex and critical situations and practically achieve their set goals.

Understanding hierarchy in Panamá

In Latin America's hierarchical societies, including Panamá, children are raised to obey their parents. This view of parents as authority figures flows over into Latin American workplaces, where hierarchical and unequal power relationships are the norm, subordinates are generally told what to do, and people respect authority (Becker, 2004). In Latin America, titles are important, and it is best to address people using their titles. However, if you do not know the person, then you should address them either as Mr. or Ms., followed by their last name (Poveda, 2016). This is also confirmed by the CCBS Survey (2022), where most of the respondents stated that in Panamá it is vital for subordinates to address leaders by their titles. One reason for this, as Garcia Saucedo explains, is that managers like to show their authority: *"Many leaders like to be noticed as leaders, they like to have authority"* (14 November 2022). The main reason for the use of titles is that Latin Americans view hierarchy as a tool that lets each organisational member know precisely who has authority over whom (Becker, 2004). In Panamá, decisions are primarily made by the managers and rarely by subordinates because they are either not encouraged to contribute to the decision-making process or simply not made aware of them directly (Becker, 2004).

This results in a centralised decision-making structure in which senior-level managers want to hold onto power as much as possible and, to this end, try as much as possible to avoid delegating decision-making (Elvira and Davila, 2005, as cited in Martinez, 2005). According to Ledesma, this autocratic leadership style which has prevailed historically is slowly changing, but it nevertheless continues to dominate in Panamá (15 November 2022). This hierarchy is also characterised by a pronounced gender inequality, insofar as most of the executive positions in Latin American organisations are occupied by men. One reason for this is the persistence of the *machismo* influence in Latin American Countries (Cardenas et al., 2014). *Machismo* is a set of behaviours comprising the content of male gender roles in a Latin society (De La Cancela, 1986). According to Cardenas et al. (2014), *machismo* makes it difficult for women to gain access to senior-level positions in Latin American organisations. Unfortunately, authority in Panamá is still often misused because it is regarded as an instrument of power. "*We still have leaders not only in Panamá but in other Latin American countries as well, who feel that they have the power to control everything that must happen, it is called command and control*" (Ledesma, 14 November 2022). Ledesma proceeded to state that this is unfortunate because authority should not be used as an instrument of power (14 November 2022).

How Panamánians achieve leadership empathy

From the results of the CCBS Survey (2022), it is evident that empathy is of paramount importance to Panamánians. Specifically, the survey shows that more than three-quarters of the respondents stated that leaders should take an active interest in their employees' well-being. This is corroborated by one of our interviewees, Saucedo, who argued that Panamánian leaders have great empathy for others, and, generally speaking, leaders try to understand the different needs and circumstances of their employees (14 November 2022). However, she also acknowledged that Panamánian leaders sometimes experience difficulties reacting to certain situations and circumstances because they do not know what to do or say (Saucedo, 14 November 2022). One of the principal ways through which Panamánian leaders can build trust and rapport with their employees is by developing their communication skills and striving to connect more with them. Despite this, Saucedo believes that there remains a lack of connection between people in the work environment; she explains that this stems from a lack of people skills, and that medium-sized businesses in particular in Panamá need to continue to work on this (14 November 2022). Ledesma shares this sentiment, arguing that empathy is one of the essential qualities that a Panamánian leader should possess in order to maintain a healthy relationship with their employees (15 November 2022). According to Ledesma, leaders can achieve this by asking a simple question: "*how was your son's activity last weekend?*" Above all, Ledesma believes that working is a social activity, and, as such, leaders must first empathise with their employees before engaging in conversation about work (15 November 2022). This is in accordance with Saucedo, who explicated that leaders could empathise with their colleagues or subordinates by asking them simple personal questions in a friendly way (14 November 2022). Similarly, Bordas (2013) describes that Latin American leaders establish personal, genuine, and caring relationships, because Latin American leaders, unlike Americans, do not segregate work from their private life. As aforesaid, Panamánian leaders are expected to be gracious and humorous, insofar as this helps to foster a pleasant working atmosphere for employees (Universidad de Panamá, 2004). One way to maintain this atmosphere is to be cognisant of being empathic and respectful when communicating bad or unpleasant news to employees (Robles et al., 2014), because, as Saucedo states, how a leader communicates a message in Panamá is just as important as the message itself (14 November 2022). The final important way to exhibit empathic leadership in Latin America is to be observant and a good listener, so as to be able to pick up on nonverbal cues, silence, and indirect verbal communication from one's employees, which, in turn, makes them feel listened to and appreciated.

Perú

Andrea Nicole Chumpitazi Vidal, Giorgio Sancipriani, Iwan de la Fosse, Jasmijn Roeper, Mehdi El Farhouni Boudour & Turan Semen

Incan values and beliefs, most notably, collectivism and a shared sense of solidarity are a deeply embedded aspect of Peruvian culture (Hofstede, 2017). The Incan Empire relied on a vast network of roads to keep connected and used *'Chasquis'* (Inca runners) to transport information and supplies (Brown, 2016). Even today, the importance of rapid communication from leaders through exchanges of information with all stakeholders is critical for successfully managing the decision-making process in the country (McIntosh, 2012). Leaders often communicate in Spanish, which is the official language of Peru, albeit Indigenous languages like Quechua and Aymara are still used throughout the country (Garcìa, 2005). In fact, there are 44 native languages in Peru and part of the Andes Mountains, with Quechua speakers being predominantly located in Peru's Andean regions, while Spanish is the main Romance language used (Zúñiga, 2008). This is reflected in the common Peruvian saying, *'El que no tiene de Inga tiene de Mandinga,'* which means that every Peruvian has either some Indigenous or African ancestry (Albiez-Wieck et al., 2020). Peru is located on the west coast of South America, with most of its 33 million inhabitants being Roman Catholic. Alongside this, Peru is renowned for its beautiful nature and world-famous landmarks like the Amazon Rainforest. Economically speaking, Peru's GDP was 235 billion USD in 2021 (National Institute of Statistics and Informatics, 2021). The service sector accounts for 60% of this, with telecommunications and financial services accounting for 40%, with its modernised industrial sector accounting for 35% (INEI, 2021). The business relationships in these sectors are invariably built on trust and mutual respect, which, in turn, necessitates a democratic form of leadership. Peruvian leaders maintain these democratic-style relationships by engaging with subordinates in private, during meetings and staff outings (Elvira & Davila, 2005). Other values such as organisational expertise, status and employee-engagement also differentiate Peruvian leaders from other counterparts in the region (McIntosh, 2012). The following chapter seeks to provide additional insight into the Peruvian business leadership culture by drawing upon empirical data and academic research.

How the Peruvians characterise leaders

According to Lenartowicz and Johnson (2002), who compared management principles across twelve Latin American nations, Peruvians placed the greatest emphasis upon virtues such as civility, self-direction, and integrity. These values are embedded in terms such as "*el patron*" (owner or boss), whereby the leader of a company treats their employees as if they were part of their extended family (Romero, 2004). Integrity comprises two other qualities that are of paramount importance to leadership in Latin American societies, namely honour and paternalism. In Peruvian culture, a paternalistic approach to leadership is of fundamental importance. The Peruvian manifestation of "*el patron*" encompasses two distinct management philosophies: on the one hand, a Peruvian "*el patron*" is expected to express interest in helping to develop the potential of their staff, while, on the other hand, leaders are also expected to practice "*mano dura*" (authoritarian leadership) (Sully de Luque & Arbaiza, 2005). Indeed, being a competent communicator and exhibiting a paternalistic disposition towards one's employees has also been found to be closely related with power and authority in Peru, insofar as these qualities are expected of Peruvian leaders (Romero, 200). In addition, one of our interviewees underscored that Peruvian leaders are characterised by being open and flexible (Cicilia Parra, 24 October 2022). One of the ways in which this flexibility expresses itself is with respect to the Peruvian work ethic, namely a willingness to work longer than the typical working day (Parra, 24 October 2022). In fact, according to both Parra (24 October 2022) and '*Naciones Unidas*' (United Nations) (2019), Peruvian leaders work the longest hours each week in Latin America. In this regard, a 12-hour working day for a Peruvian manager is more the norm than the exception (Parra, 24 October 2022). Notwithstanding the Peruvian work ethic, Brown et al. (2019) argue that the candidness of Peruvian leaders results in less authoritarianism and greater democracy in the workplace. This stems from the fact that the more cordial approach to fulfilling the wishes of employees and seeking their input serves to reduce the level of power distance within Peruvian organisations . This is evidenced by the fact that the employees who took part in Brown et al.'s (2019) research made it clear that a more participative work environment is both wanted and necessary for Peruvian businesses to thrive. This is in contrast to both Hamill (1992) and Wolfsohn's (2021) framing of Peruvian leaders as displaying *'caudillo'* (political leader) characteristics. *'Caudillismo,'* which means *autocracy,* is a type of governance in which a strongman archetype rules a faction, city, or state. 'Caudillo' leaders are respected, and people feel comfortable working under them because they feel heard (Wolfsohn, 2021). This was corroborated by one of the respondents from the CCBS Survey (2018), who when asked: *"Do you feel that there is something specific about leadership in your own* country that makes it different from what we see in the leadership literature from abroad?", answered: *"The closeness and confidence of the leader with the team without losing respect and authority"* (CCBS Survey, 2018). This Peruvian style of *caudillo'* leadership is a little different than the typical authoritarian style of leadership, where a leader is only capable of outlining the goals, issuing directives, monitoring, and overseeing, and rewarding or punishing subordinates based on the outcomes they achieve (D'Alessio, 2006). In conclusion, the Peruvian work ethic is highly influenced by its culture. Being emotionally invested and having close relationships with employees are key characteristics of being an effective Peruvian leader.

Survey results and what local respondents say

Overall, 51 respondents shared their experience and knowledge of Peruvian leadership skills and practices by completing the CCBS Survey (2022). The most significant findings from the survey administered to C-level professionals will be discussed in turn below. Firstly, the leaders' responses indicate that the relationship between employers and employees is *"Lado humanitario,"* (on the humanitarian side) in Peruvian organisations (CCBS Survey, 2022). For example, when asked about specific leadership practices in Peru, one of the respondents noted that: *"Round trip transportation is included, as well as lunch every day. When there is an event, they are paid in cash for overtime and snacks"* (CCBS Survey, 2022). The General Manager of PepsiCo Foods Peru conformed this perspective of Peruvian leadership, opining that: *"Peruvian leadership is democratic; leaders are always in contact with their subordinates to see about their concerns."* (CCBS Survey, 2022). Secondly, more than 10% of our respondents reported that teamwork is what distinguishes a Peruvian leader from other leaders in the region (CCBS Survey, 2022). According to one of our respondents, a General Manager of a commercial company, this teamwork manifests in having regular meetings to evaluate results which may pose new challenges for the company's growth (CCBS Survey, 2022). On the contrary, however, Carlos Escala Cisneros, who is a consultant in leadership and team management systems, argued that leadership in Peru is still closely related to the concept of authoritarianism (CCBS Survey, 2022). This framing of Peruvian leadership as autocratic and underpinned by the masculine notion of *el patron* was also reflected in other results from the survey; for example, 13% of the respondents strongly disagreed with the statement that men and women have equal opportunity to attain senior leadership positions, while another 11% somewhat disagreed with this (CCBS Survey, 2022). However, the culture of leadership appears to be changing in Peru, insofar as more than 70% of the respondents reported that there are equal or somewhat equal opportunities today for both men and women (CCBS Survey, 2022). With respect to changes in the hierarchical structures within Peruvian organisations, a Head of Finance in a Peruvian organisation stated: *"Before the structure was very vertical, and it still is in traditional of family companies, but in companies such as start-ups or multinationals the desired structure is more horizontal, considering everyone equally despite their hierarchical position"* (CCBS Survey, 2022).

Local leadership analysis

Ofelia Brown: a Peruvian Leadership Scholar

Ofelia Brown has been a Professor in Business Administration at the University of Lima for over twenty years and trains Peruvian professionals in leadership. She has also written multiple publications on leadership in Peru. During the interview, Ofelia Brown argued that there are multiple characteristics that define leadership in Peru. Brown emphasised that a typical Peruvian leader has a strong sense of how the collective is feeling, stating that the well-being of the group matters a lot to them (25 November 2022). She proceeded to discuss how, from her experience, she finds Peruvian leaders to generally have an inward vision, by which she meant that they tend to focus on the company rather than the market (25 November 2022). Moreover, Brown stated that Peruvian organisations maintain hierarchy via *"a culture of high-power distance. Peruvians assume there are people higher-up than themselves."* (25 November 2022). In response to a question about what the decision-making process looked like within Peruvian organisations, Ofelia Brown noted that: *"Foreigners have a hard time understanding why decision-making takes so long in Peru, because it is necessary for everyone to agree."*(25 November 2022). She then proceeded to shed light on what the communicative process looks like in the context of Peruvian organisations and such delays, noting that *"Peruvians do not tell you upfront what they think. Peruvians give you detours to tell you things are delayed. They're not direct."* In addition to this, Brown suggested that Peruvian leaders are expected to be transparent, citing the following reason for this fact: "We *[Peru] are a country that has suffered from corruption .... So, for a leader to be respected, they must show that they are not corrupt."* (Brown, 25 November 2022). Delving deeper into what qualities, traits and behaviours are preferred in Peruvian leaders, Ofelia Brown described that a

Peruvian leader *"has integrity, honesty, transparency, respects values and has their own values."* Nearing the end of the interview, Ofelia Brown pointed out that a Peruvian leader loses respect if they are seen to be a little manipulative or to have a double agenda. To combat this, a Peruvian leader should always be *"professional and always look for ways to lift up their employees."* (Brown, 25 November 2022).

Miryam Parra: a Manager and Trainer in Leadership and Development
Miryam Parra is a Pedagogical Advisor at the Los Robles school and an Executive Director of San Agustín school in Peru. After 35 years of working, she will soon retire. Alongside being an Executive Director, she is also a leadership consultant in Peru. Miryam began the interview by stating that there are two types of leaders in Peru: first, there is the authoritarian figure; and secondly, an emergent leaderships tyle that is associated with the younger generation of professionals. *"[who] have a different type of education which is more leaning towards equality and showing power and authority in a different way... Peru is developing by the day and so is their education system."* (Parra, 24 October 2022). Miryam followed up on this by noting that the new generation of leaders have a greater capacity to observe and understand other cultures as a result of globalisation, which, in turn, exposes them to different leadership approaches that inspire and influence them (24 October 2022). They have also improved their language skills and leadership capacities by virtue of having studied or worked abroad, or just due to greater exposure to international best-practices as a result of the internet. Moreover, she stressed that flexibility and openness are key characteristics of Peruvian leaders. Alongside this. Peruvians are also highly ambitious and driven when it comes to achieving both their own and the organisation's goals. This is why they are used to working between 10 and 12 hours instead of 8 hours each day. *"It is not because anyone expects it from them, but because the Peruvian leaders want to achieve the goals as quickly as possible."* (Parra, 24 October 2022). When discussing how hierarchical the country is, Parra opined that leaders are treated with great respect, as a result of their positioning in the upper echelons of the organisational hierarchy. Towards the end of the interview Miryam pointed out that *"The respect one has is not [borne] out of fear, but out of respect."* This respect stems from an appreciation of the complex competencies needed by leaders to be able to steer the company. Finally, Parra concluded the interview by stating that she believes that an individual performs better when they feel heard, and that is also

important that leaders give employees the responsibility and space they require in order to be able to branch out on their own and develop (Parra, 24 October 2022).

In-country leadership bestseller

Liderazgo y comportamiento organizacional (Leadership and Organisational behaviour) was written in 2017 by Lydia Arbaiza Fermini. This book provides up-to-date information and tools from the study of organisational behaviour that make it easier to comprehend how individuals and groups behave inside Peruvian organisations and, consequently, how system dynamics operate. In addition to enhancing the success of organisations and increasing process quality, the analysis of organisational behaviour also attempts to assure employee welfare by foreseeing events that may impact upon both the quality of life and job performance, such as, amongst other things, interpersonal difficulties, lack of motivation, and stress. Active listening, teamwork, conflict management, and effective communication with employees are just some of the aspects of Peruvian leadership that are promoted through exercises and situations, so that the reader can put the lessons they are learning in the book into practice. If leadership training programs cover these aspects of Peruvian leadership and are well-planned and consistently administered, then this will have a positive impact upon Peruvian organisations, namely in terms of talent retention, knowledge transfer, and increased productivity. Therefore, studying organisational behaviour entails paying attention to the intangible factors that impact upon daily life at work, such as personality characteristics, attitudes, learning preferences, and, most importantly, the methods via which Peruvian leadership is exercised.

Local leadership book	
Title	*Liderazgo y comportamiento organizacional*
Subtitle	-
Author	Lydia Arbaiza Fermini
Publisher	Alfaomega Esan
Year	2017
ISBN	9789587784527

Peruvian leadership YouTube review

Baltazar Caravedo Molinari, a Peruvian author, and Director of the Centre of Leadership at the Pacific University in Lima, discusses recent developments related to what constitutes good organisational leadership in Peru, arguing that *"the business paradigms of the past are under discussion"* (Molinari, 2013, 0:03). According to Molinari, the leadership style in Peru is changing from a pyramidical structure in which the boss or leader adopts an autocratic role, to a more democratic circular structure. In this circle, knowledge and decisions are shared, rather than the authority being concentrated in the hands of a single person. This creates loyalty towards the leaders, which, in turn, benefits employee retention within companies. For this to be realised, Molinari stresses that there is a need for adequate internal communication in that it is a projection of one's image to the outside world. "*Because the messages that we all give [combined] with the way we act is a message that reaches everyone*" (Molinari, 2013, 4:42). Peru has experienced significant economic growth over the course of the last decade, which, in turn, has created opportunities for businesses across many industries; however, as Ofelia Brown notes, the role of the leader remains critical if organisations are to capitalize on this growth (ESAN, 2022). Organisational changes are also brought about by globalisation, and therefore a more "transformational" style of leadership is required in Peru (2019, 1:27). In this video, she gives her perspective on this transformation of the Peruvian business culture. For her, transformational leadership means that a leader possesses an adaptive form of leadership in which communication and action take place interactively. In her words: *"All of us who have risen to leadership have learned to lead by imitation: seeing how they lead and trying to pick up their habits. Today, a different leadership is required, and Peru has quite a challenge in this regard"* (Brown, 2012, 02:23). This so-called challenge steams from the fact that, according to her, Peru is in a *"tremendous leadership crisis"* (Brown, 2020, 08:01). This crisis is fuelled by scandals and transgressions that happen daily in companies and institutions all over the country, which, in turn, creates a social problem. These issues stem from an incorrect communication style that can lead to misunderstandings. Ofelia Brown wrote a book entitled *"Sin Comunicación no hay Liderazgo"* (Without Communication there is no Leadership) in which she emphasises the importance of communication. She states that a good leader must be a good communicator, one that primarily listens and respects the opinion of others. Those who control both these leadership attributes can bring out the best in people, thus making everyone feel desirable and making subordinates want to succeed. Consequently, in her opinion, this is what makes a good modern Peruvian leader.

Understanding hierarchy in Peru

A recent study shows that most organisations in Peru have an informal vertical organisational structure, as a result of Peru's vertical-collectivistic cultural practices (Brown et al., 2019). Undoubtedly, Peru's rich history and culture profoundly influence how Peruvian subordinates operate, in turn, earning them status according to their age or the position they hold within a company (Mcintosh, 2012). In addition to this, House et al. (2004) observed that Peruvian self-protective leaders expect to receive, and are dutifully granted, many privileges in society. This explains, at least in part, why Peruvian leaders tend to retain a certain distance between themselves and their employees, due to the high-power distance in the country. According to Hofstede (2017), power distance is defined as the extent to which the less powerful members of institutions and organisations within a country expect and accept that power is distributed unequally. Peru scores 64 on the power distance scale of Hofstede, thus indicating a notable gap between those at the top and bottom of the hierarchy (Mcintosh, 2012). Societies with high-power distance like Peru are often characterised by polarized and emotional supervisor-subordinate relationships (Hofstede, 2001). One reason for this is that leaders higher up the corporate ladder have access to more information and resources than their subordinates, which, in turn, establishes and perpetuates this sense of power distance between employer and employee (Stephens, 1981). Peru's history and culture very much influence how Peruvian subordinates operate (Mcintosh, 2012). This is illustrated by the fact that, culturally speaking, Peruvians prefer to their leaders to be powerful decision-makers and visionary thinkers (CCBS, Survey 2022). Given that Peruvian culture id heavily gendered, these preferred traits of leaders serve to create more senior-level opportunities for men, insofar as they are seen as embodying these aforesaid traits along with being more self-reliant than women, who in Peru are generally seen as caretakers (USAID, 2020). However, the gender roles in Peru have been gradually changing. Specifically, women are becoming more influential and gaining more attention, both in the business and political sectors (USAID, 2020). This is occurring in parallel with other changes that are taking place, both in Peruvian society generally and within Peruvian organisations specifically. For example, Mcintosh (2012) proposes that Peruvians desire a change in leadership practices, namely a shift away from the autocratic 'traditional' leadership style to a more democratic participative one, that serves to reduce the level of power distance within organisations. In conclusion, then, the hierarchy in Peru is currently undergoing a transformation away from the hereditary autocratic leadership style towards a more transformative participatory leadership style.

The longstanding power distance has also been getting smaller in recent years, as a result of Peruvian organisations further adapting their leadership styles to establish equal gender opportunities and introduce greater democracy across organisations.

How the Peruvians achieve leadership empathy

Evidence for Peruvian leaders displaying empathic understanding towards employees can be found in the CCBS Survey (2022), insofar as 22% of the respondents reported that leaders in Peru are good listeners. Further evidence comes from the fact that the majority of the respondents reported that Peruvian leaders tend to spend time on the personal well-being of their staff (CCBS Survey, 2022). Moreover, Peruvian leaders are also expected to show compassion and stand alongside their employees in times of trouble (CCBS Survey, 2022). An example of a Peruvian leader displaying their empathic skills is a leader who claims to know over 90 percent of their employees personally, who gives their workers an open line of communication, allowing them to e-mail or call them with any work-related concerns they may have (Sully de Luqu e & Arbaiza, 2005). Our interviewee, Mariella Delgado, lends support to this description of empathic leadership, noting in response to the question 'How do you practice empathy and make employees' voices heard?' that Peruvian leaders must *"allow spaces for dialogue, including not only on work issues but also, in some cases, on personal issues."* ((15 November 2022)). Furthermore, she elaborated on this statement by saying *"I show compassion in the personal life of my employees by asking about their family and if any difficulties are present, I call them to inquire about their situation*" (Delgado, 15 November 2022). Alongside this, as aforesaid, Peruvian leaders strive to create strong informal and interpersonal relationships, with business contacts and those working under them, which is par for the course in the business sector there (Romero, 2004). Given that, as aforesaid, business relationships in Peru are predicated on trust and mutual respect, Peruvian leaders seek to treat their employees as if they were part of their extended family, by engaging with them during meetings and also on staff outings (Elvira & Davila, 2005). Research on leadership and Latin American culture provides a clearer picture of the expectations of leaders in this region (House et al., 2004). Specifically, both House et al. (2004) and Sully de Luque and Arbaiza's (2005) research found that Latin American cultures generally prefer leaders who are charismatic and team-oriented, which they display through being friendly, participative and compassionate towards employees. When asked to elaborate further on what Peruvian leaders do to establish and maintain respect and empathy with their employees in the workplace, Mariella Delgado stated *"Leaders themselves want to set an example via the following actions; follow the institutional rules, arrive early, hand in work on time."* (15 November 2022). In a similar vein, the General Manager of PepsiCo Foods Peru, opined: "*Peruvian leadership is democratic; leaders are always in contact with their subordinates to see about their concerns."* In conclusion, then, Peruvian leaders achieve empathy by creating strong emotional bonds with their employees, by showing commitment, working hard, building trust and respect, being charismatic, friendly, and compassionate towards them.

Poland

Klaudia Rubacha, Ali Atilgan, Bastiaan Rethmeier, Ryan Timmers, Bart Koper & Bob Groot

Rzeczpospolita Polska (Republic of Poland) is located in the heart of Europe. The country is twice as large as Greece and half the size of Ukraine, and is inhabited by almost forty million residents (CSO of Poland, 2021). The official language is Polish, which has a variety of dialects spread across the country, including, amongst others, Silesian, and Kashubian (Gębal, & Nawracka, 2021). Despite the heterogeneous dialects, there is one main religion: Catholicism. According to Knecht (2021), Catholicism has a profound impact upon Polish values and norms, which is reflected in the common saying *Gość w domu, Bóg w domu* (Guest at home, God at home). This saying specifically captures the strong interdependence between Polish culture and Catholicism and is uttered to show excitement at having a visitor to one's home. Alongside religious-based values, Poland also has a long history of conflicts with other countries. For instance, it was part of the Soviet Union until its dissolution in the final decade of the twentieth century (Stachura, 2008). Many Poles strongly resisted the loss of economic and political independence (Goldberg & Kremen, 1990), and, indeed, Sielski (2020) argues that resistance is one of the defining features of Poles. Poland would not be what it is today without leaders like Lech Wałęsa, whose charisma and influence positively impacted on society and helped it develop (Sielski, 2020). Poland's economy has tripled in size since the early 2000s (IMF, 2022). Brown (2016) notes that this is because Poland became a democracy and made their European Union (EU) membership a success. Currently, the country has the eighth largest economy in the EU, with the most profitable sectors being agriculture, manufacturing, energy, and tourism (Klug, 2006). The economic growth in the country has also made it increasingly attractive for international companies to do business there.
The consequence of this is that Poland has had to respond to the needs of international businesses to further grow its economy, which, in turn, has led to the internationalisation of the country and a greater demand for developing leadership skills and practices within Polish organisations.

How the Polish characterise leaders?

Polish leadership has undergone a profound shift over the course of the last four decades. According to Ardichvili and Dirani (2017), Polish managers in the 1980s and 1990s were more autocratic than American or French organisations, for example. Moreover, they tended to restrict employee participation in the decision-making process when attempting to address organisational problems. As aforementioned, Poland has undergone many changes since gaining its independence from the Soviet Union in 1990 and becoming an EU Member State in 2004. According to *Polski Instytut Ekonomiczny* (2020), Poland's diverse history has contributed to the economic growth of the country and made it one of Europe's fastest growing economies. These profound economic-political changes have undoubtedly transformed what qualities, traits and behaviours are preferred in Polish leaders (Sielski, 2020). At this juncture, to be acknowledged as an effective manager in Poland, it is important to possess and display a specific skillset, which includes, amongst other things, being an honest and trustworthy person who has both a strong sense of values and ethics and is continuously striving to maintain these morals in the organisation (Kretek & Karczewski, 2018). Polish leaders exhibit their ethical prowess by promoting open communication in their organisations and dedicating themselves to ensuring the dignity and rights of others are respected (Shollenberger, 2014). This point was corroborated by one of our interviewees, Andrzej Kuras, who stated that the younger generation of Polish leaders is characterised by both a compassionate leadership style and paying attention to the distinct personalities within their teams (2 November 2022). Similarly, Maciej Madziński notes that the servant leadership style is more prevalent amongst the younger generation of leaders, who prefer a less charismatic and delegating leadership style (Escola Mobile, 2022). Furthermore, Mrówka (2010) emphasises that it is important that Polish leaders do not accept the current situation and instead strive to continuously improve, preferably by outlining a strong vision for their organisation to follow. Alongside these qualities, Mrówka (2010) also observes that both monitoring the performance of one's employees and leading them to the visualised goals are key attributes expected in Polish leaders. However, what defines an excellent Polish manager above all is their ability to lead their employees in such a way that they are capable of leading themselves. To do so, Polish leaders must be able to teach their employees and truly care about their individual progress, rather than merely giving them simple commands to follow (Mrówka, 2010). Mnich & Walaszczyk (2022), in their research with senior-level managers of small and medium-sized Polish commercial and production enterprises, found that righteousness and the ability to clearly express thoughts, were the most valued traits for leaders to possess. This is in line with the results of the CCBS Survey (2022), which showed that organisational experience, market expertise and a high intellect were important traits for leaders to possess. Finally, the Polish still tend to equate leadership with males, due to the prevailing mentality that *kobieta powinna zostać w domu, a mężczyzna pracować* (a woman should stay at home and a man works). Such gender stereotypes and norms continue to impact upon both women's ability to attain senior-level positions in Polish organisations and the perceptions of female leaders (Warszewska-Makuch, 2019). Andrzej Kuras argued in our interview that there is no inequality between the genders when it comes to attaining senior-level positions within Polish organisations, noting that the only difference pertained to the level of commitment that men and women show, which is in fact an individual factor (2 November 2022).

Survey results and what local respondents say

By participating in the CCBS Survey (2022), C-level executives from Poland allowed us to gain a better insight and understanding of the local leadership styles and practices in the country. There were several key findings that will be discussed in turn below. First, the majority of the respondents reported that there is a strong possibility that when a decision has been made, leaders will not change their mind. However, the second most selected answer was that Polish leaders are likely to change their decision, which is the total opposite (CCBS Survey, 2022). One explanation for this apparent contradiction in the results comes from Andrzej Kuras, who explained in his interview that *"we [Polish people] are a little bit on the edges"* (2 November 2022). By *"edges,"* Kuras here was referring to the fact that the country remains a mixture of old Soviet remnants and new less authoritarian and more compassionate Western influences that both infuse the prevailing leadership approaches in the country (2 November 2022). However, when it comes to confronting subordinates, 53 percent of the respondents reported that they would confront their employees during staff meetings, in order to obtain the desired results (CCBS Survey, 2022). Indeed, one of the respondents claimed that it is common for Polish leaders to have *"a very strong emphasis on their subordinates achieving the desired results"* (CCBS Survey, 2022). Surprisingly, only one-third of the respondents noted that they do not mind hearing criticism during a team meeting, while the rest expressed that they preferred not to hear it directly (CCBS Survey, 2022). One potential explanation for this result is that Polish leaders do not like to be humiliated or seen as incompetent (Kuras, 2 November 2022). The next interesting result emerging from the CCBS Survey (2022) pertains to how Polish leaders value empathy in their leadership styles and that they actively implement it, which is reflected in the fact that three three-quarters of the respondents answered "very much like me" and "like me", when asked whether managers should actively spend time ensuring the well-being of their team members. Similarly, just over half of the respondents stated that they do not retain personal distance from their employees, which means that the Polish leaders find human connections important and do not insist on retaining a high-power distance from their subordinates (CCBS Survey, 2022). This was supported by one of our respondents, who in response to what differentiates the Polish leadership style from others, stated *"the relationship between [leaders and their] employees"* (CCBS Survey, 2022). Indeed, the vast majority of the respondents reported that employees are allowed to address their managers by their first name, which again shows that the power distance is relatively lower amongst Polish leaders (CCBS Survey, 2022). Next, in response to a question asking on what basis employees look up to their managers, the most selected answers were organisational experience and market expertise. Interestingly, attributes that can only be acquired through hard work were selected much more by the respondents than attributes that cannot be actively changed such as age or one's family background (CCBS Survey, 2022). The lack of importance placed upon family background was also underscored by the fact that the least important attribute for a Polish leader to have according to the respondents was family connections (CCBS Survey, 2022). The importance placed upon expertise was supported by Kuras, who stated that the main criteria for choosing an employee are the hard skills that people specialise in (2 November 2022). Finally, half of the Polish C-level executives opined that men and women have equal opportunity to attain leadership positions (CCBS Survey, 2022), which is in contrast to Andrzej Kuras' argument that he has *"never saw (...) a man or woman treated worse because of their gender"* (2 November 2022).

Local leadership analysis

Anna Czarczyńska: a Leadership Scholar

Anna Czarczyńska is a professor and the head of the department of Economics at the Kozminski University. The interviewee shared her knowledge and expertise on leadership styles and practices in Poland. Firstly, Czarczyńska began by providing an explanation of the historical factors that have influenced Polish leadership styles, specifically drawing reference to over a century of partition, post-World War II changes in Poland's borders and finally a long period of Soviet rule (15

November 2019). Czarczyńska claimed that while the prevailing leadership style in Poland now looks profoundly different than it did during the Soviet juncture, there is still a remnant of the communist era in the current Polish leadership style. Specifically, Czarczyńska refers to the persistence of these old-fashioned leadership models in terms of *"homo Sovieticus"* (15 November 2019). One way in which the old Soviet style lingers today is *"people who do not commit to making decisions because it could backfire on them, should the decision prove to be wrong"* (15 November 2019). However, Polish people's fundamental scepticism towards hierarchies and regulations serves to accelerate the disappearance of this leadership model. Indeed, Czarczyńska stressed above all that *"regulations are commonly seen as oppressive"* in Poland (15 November 2019). She then proceeded to discuss how although trust is by no means commonly the foundation of Polish organisations, this is sure to change in the future. However, Czarczyńska then immediately noted that such changes are indeed time-consuming, which, in turn, culminates in a form of duality with respect to leaders in Poland. She described this duality as follows: *"on the one hand, employees have respect towards hierarchy, while, on the other hand, they utterly mistrust it"* (15 November 2019). To illustrate her point, she described the situation of Polish managers who were employed in Finland. Finnish supervisors criticised Polish employees for being too innovative, whereas Polish managers believed that not being able to solve a problem was itself considered to be a sign of incompetence. This example illustrates Czarczyńska's point about the persistence of these old Soviet beliefs and values about showing strength no matter what. However, as illustrated in the example, in other cultures, such as Finland, it is not deemed to be shameful or a sign of weakness or incompetence to ask for help, which is something that some Polish managers still have to learn (15 November 2019).

Andrzej Kuras: a Polish Leadership Trainer

Andrzej Kuras has worked as a leadership trainer for twelve years. Kuras is also the owner of a small consulting and leadership training company. While the firm primarily focuses on leadership training, coaching and mentoring managers, they also offer consulting services related to various business projects. In response to our first question, Andrzej Kuras stated that *"there is not a typical Polish leader,"* and *"we are a little bit on the edges"* (Kuras, 2 November 2022). This is because, Kuras argued, in Poland there are either managers who adopt an old autocratic approach or a newer younger generation who exhibit a more compassionate management style (2 November 2022. Consequently, it is difficult to place all managers into a singular category with respect to leadership styles. On the other hand, Kuras did go onto say that age is an important indicator of someone's leadership style. More specifically, Kuras opined, leaders who were born during the Soviet regime tend to be more autocratic in their approach and continue to prefer this management style as it worked for them in the past (2 November 2022). It is worthwhile to stress here that although age might influence someone's leadership style, older leaders are not treated any better simply as a result of their age, but rather are accorded greater respect due to personal traits such as work commitment (2 November 2022). Kuras also discussed the issue of gender inequality in the interview, stating that *"I never saw in my career a man or woman treated worse because of their gender."* (2 November 2022). Today, Poland has undergone profound transformations, in part, because of the increased prevalence of international corporations in the country, which, in turn, has led to a change in both the prevailing leadership style and cultural attitudes towards gender equality within business leadership. One of these changes is that Polish leaders have are now cognisant of the fact that they must establish proper connections with their employees if they are to be equipped to deal with every case. This is why Kuras stresses that *"The number one leadership skill is empathy (...) but the main skill is humility."* (2 November 2020). To help leaders achieve empathy and build trust with employees, Andrzej Kuras has established his own formula which combines credibility, reliability, and intimacy. However, these three aspects can easily be forgotten when a Polish leader displays too much ego (2 November 2022). Respect is critical for Polish leaders to build a meaningful human dialogue and establish empathy with their employees. Kuras noted that *"many people feel disrespected, and the main reason for this disrespect is a lack of respect and recognition, so they are being seen like they don't exist"* (2 November 2022). One simple method Kuras recommends for Polish leaders to maintain respect with one's employees is to arrange weekly one-to-one catchups with subordinates (2 November 2022).

In-country leadership bestseller

"Lider wystarczająco dobry" (Good enough leader) is one of the best-selling modern books about Polish leadership and was written by Sebastian Drzewiecki and Piotr Prokopowicz in 2022. Sebastian Drzewiecki is the Vice President of SoftServe, and Piotr Prokopowicz is an organizational psychologist and leadership consultant. Their professional background and experience in Polish business made them write and publish *"Lider wystarczająco dobry"* which is a manual for creating genuine connections with employees. The book comprises a set of informative guidelines through which to improve organisational structures and teaches readers how to apply them in their own businesses. In the book, key paradoxes of Polish leadership and personality traits are discussed and examined, in order

to help readers break away from these to become a more successful leader in Poland. For example, the authors emphasise that being effective is far less important and appreciated by employees than being inspiring in Polish workplaces. Despite this fact, the authors argue that almost every Polish leader continues to be more task-focused rather than people-focused in their approach, which is a critical mistake. To address this, the authors propose the solution of creating a more community-based approach and bringing employees together by displaying kindness and amiability towards them. For instance, in order to build a community, Polish leaders could introduce post-work meetings or weekly check-ins with employees in order to receive their feedback. Moreover, according to Drzewiecki and Prokopowicz (2022), the great five personality traits for Polish leaders to possess are extravagance, emotional stability, conciliation, diligence, and openness to experience. Ultimately, it is the combination between these personality traits and effectiveness, kindness and amiability that result in the perfect Polish leader. Throughout the book, a reader is also able to read about companies that were compelled to act during crises and learn from how they were able to navigate their way through them. Overall, the manual connects practice and learning, which makes it suitable for leaders running both SMEs and large multinational firms in Poland.

Local leadership book	
Title	*Lider wystarczająco dobry*
Translation	*12 lekcji autentycznego przywództwa na czasy niepewności*
Author	Sebastian Drzewiecki, Piotr Prokopowicz
Publisher	Onepress
Year	2022
ISBN	9788328373617

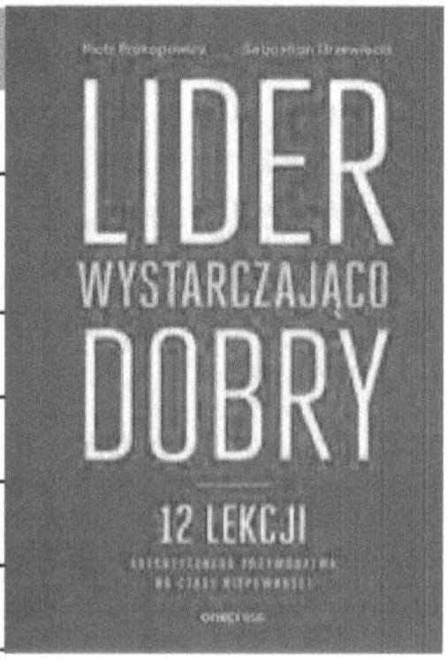

Polish leadership YouTube review

Managing director and future leaders' mentor, Maciej Madziński, was invited on Escola Mobile, a business podcast and videocast channel, to share his story regarding the future development of leadership styles in Poland. Decades ago, a Polish leader would have been described as charismatic and would delegate tasks to subordinates by saying *"go, do"* (Escola Mobile, 2022, 5:44).

In accordance with this, it would have been entirely normal for Polish citizens to have workdays lasting 12 to 14 hours, as this was considered to be the proper way to ensure success. This has changed as a result of the concept of 'turquoise management', which is an approach in which employees are self-organised and believe that they are capable of performing tasks by themselves (Escola Mobile, 2022). This management style tends to focus more on team effort, carrying out tasks together, letting employees feel that they are part of the community, rather than simply following orders in order to pick up a paycheck. Alongside this shift, some Polish leaders are also becoming more focused on the visionary perspective (Escola Mobile, 2022). As aforementioned, in the past, subordinates had the mentality *"im dłużej pracujesz, tym lepiej"* (the longer you work, the better). Today, this has changed, and it is all about the quality of the number of hours worked. Finally, Maciej Madziński promotes the manifold benefits of adopting a servant leadership style within Polish organisations. This leadership style is characterized by helping employees and solving tasks together, which means that leaders must display their willingness to help their subordinates with fulfilling various tasks. The servant leadership style has become more popular in Poland, in part, because the younger generation of employees in the country prefer a less charismatic and more delegatory leadership style (Escola Mobile, 2022).

Understanding hierarchy in Poland

Poles believe in the phrase *bez pracy nie ma kołaczy* (no pain, no gain), which is strongly reflected in their way of working. In the CCBS Survey (2022), one of the respondents argued that *"there is a very strong emphasis on subordinates achieving results"*. Within this approach, all employees focus on performing the specific tasks for which they are held accountable by people in higher positions in the organisational hierarchy. This is one of the reasons why Poland is known for its hierarchical structure, insofar as everyone has a designated position within the hierarchy and people accept this framework without the need for any further justification (Nasierowski & Mikula, 1998). According to Sielski (2020), the older generation of leaders frequently exhibit authoritarian behaviours, namely because of their experiences of working in organisations during the Soviet era. This aspect of Polish leadership was confirmed by Andrzej Kuras, who emphasises that older Polish leaders learned their leadership skills in their "garages" and the authoritarian approach prevailed during the period of Soviet rule (2 November 2022). Because this approach was successful in the past, the older generation is often reluctant to change it and embrace more modern and egalitarian styles of leadership. Within this authoritarian approach, leaders grant their subordinates almost no power whatsoever over the decision-making process, to the point that if they are not there, then decisions are postponed until they are. The persistence of this approach is evidenced in the fact that just under half of the survey respondents reported that once leaders have made a decision, they are not likely to change it (CCBS Survey, 2022). In this instance, leaders thus have sole responsibility over decision-making within organisations and retain ultimate accountability, which, in turn, means that employee participation in decision-making is either impossible or undesirable (Sielski, 2020). This image of Polish leadership was corroborated by our interviewee, who stated that even in instances where Polish leaders delegate tasks, at the end of the day they always make the final decision (Kuras, 2 November 2022). Similarly, one of the survey respondents also argued that *"(unfortunately) the 'boss is always right' rule is still present and hardly anyone dares to express their opinion or ideas."* (CCBS Survey, 2022). Conversely, the newer generation of leaders are distinguished by both establishing a structure, while, simultaneously, being kind to their employees by, amongst other things, showing concern over and checking on their employees' well-being (Rongińska, 2018). This shift was also reflected amongst our survey respondents, insofar as three-quarters of them stated that leaders actively spend time ensuring the personal well-being of their team members (CCBS Survey, 2022). Maciej Madziński referred to this more compassionate and humane style of leadership as the servant leadership style (Escola Mobile, 2022). According to Gorbaniuk et al. (2013), contemporary Polish managers appreciate the active involvement of their employees, and the servant leadership style helps to facilitate the direct transfer of information from leaders to employees, due to the fact that the focus is on cooperation and there is no barrier caused by one's position within the organisational hierarchy.

How the Polish achieve leadership empathy

According to Gierczak and Grodecka (2014), displaying empathy towards one's employees used to be viewed as a sign of weakness from male Polish leaders and as a source of a strength by female Polish leaders. Fortunately, the labour market is constantly changing and being an empathetic leader today in Poland is more of a necessity than a disadvantage. Rongińska (2018) argues that today Polish leaders are responsible for monitoring and leading their employees towards the visualised goal, while, simultaneously, bearing in mind and showing concern over the physical and mental well-being of their employees. Berendt et al. (2018) argue that displaying empathy towards employees not only strengthens the team spirit within an organisation, but also helps to provide solutions in a wide range of situations. Therefore, Winkler (2013) emphasises that in order for Polish leaders to build trust with their employees, managers must engage in open and direct communication as well as cooperation. However, it is crucial to stress here that this is not to say that Polish leaders should strive to become friends with those working under them; rather, the argument being put forward here is that leaders should cultivate relationships with their employees only insofar as they this helps to motivate employees and make them feel comfortable in their workplace (Gierczak, & Grodecka, 2014). In our interview with him, Andrzej Kuras shared how Polish leaders can do precisely this by explaining his formula to build trust (2 November 2022). First of all, Kuras argues, trust comprises credibility, reliability, and intimacy. Only if these three factors are applied together can Polish leaders build connections with their employees. Kuras specifically emphasised that Polish leaders fail to establish intimacy when they, for example, give feedback in front of other employees rather than doing so privately (2 November 2022). In order to build trust with their employees, then, Polish leaders must be credible, reliable, cultivate closer connections with people, and show them that they are not resources, but rather are resources which can be converted into highly valued skills (Kuras, 2 November 2022). Berend et al. (2018) also emphasise the importance of empathic leadership and suggest that one way in which a leader can establish this with their employees is by admitting when they do not know how to solve a problem. In this way, Polish leaders show their employees that they too are willing to learn, while, simultaneously, building trust with them as they now see their leader as being more on their level and are less resistant to put forward their ideas to them (Berendt et al., 2018). Andrzej Kuras also noted in our interview that Polish subordinates often have the impression that they are not being heard and that "*many people feel disrespected, with the main reason for disrespect being a lack of respect and recognition*" (2 November 2022). This relates back to why Berend et al. (2018) advise Polish leaders to be honest with their employees about their own limitations, insofar as it helps create a bond between them. Finally, Kowalik (2021) emphasises that there are specific moral values required of Polish leaders that in turn result in a more empathetic leadership style. These morals are often referred to by Polish managers as *kulturowy klej* (cultural glue) because they serve to bring workers together even more. The most important of these values is getting your employees to cooperate with a storyline. In other words, employees' development experience ought to give them the impression that they are embarking on a genuine journey together, one that has a start, middle, and an end.

Romania

Justin Imansoeradi, Saruta Wantum. Enrique Beukers, Isa van Delft, Floor van Empelen & Sophie Noorman

Romania received its name from the people that used to and still live there, the Romanians, who were known as the *Român. Deșteaptă-te, române!* (Awaken Thee, Romanian!) Is Romania's national anthem and was first sung in the city of Brașov prior to quickly becoming the revolutionary anthem. In fact, Romania has a long history of occupations that have left its mark on the country. Prior to unification, various regions were at one stage ruled or occupied by the Austro-Hungarian, Ottoman, and Russian Empires (Boia, 2001). This has resulted in the country being divided into three parts, each of which has its own distinct cultural and ethnic history: East (centred on Moldova), West (Transylvania and adjoining regions), and South (centred on Muntenia). Alongside these foreign influences, Romanians also have their own distinct cultural practices, such as wooden carvings, beautifully woven carpets, pottery, and glass paintings. Bucharest, the country's capital, is a cultural epicentre and home to the national theatre, the opera house, and the Romanian National Orchestra. Dance also plays a prominent role in traditional Romanian culture and is wholly distinct from the dances one sees in the rest of the Balkans. Traditional Romanian dances are like a Brechtian play, insofar as there are no actors and spectators, no passive onlookers, but only active participants (Giurchescu, 2019). Romanian culture and spirituality are perhaps best captured in the ballad of *"Moirita"*, which is an allegorical tale about a faithful sheep who tries to protect her shepherd and provides insight into how Romanians think about death. The continued popularity of this folk tale testifies to the pastoral nature of Romanian society and shows their attachment to traditions and values (Cordoneanu, 2012). Contemporary Romania is a developing country with a predominantly service-based economy, which has undergone major economic growth from the early 200s onwards. The traditions, importance placed on family, and distinct form of communication employed by Romanians also profoundly influences the prevailing organisational culture in the country as well (Vlaicu, 2019). By drawing on empirical data from surveys and interviews with local professionals, this and other aspects of Romanian leadership will be examined in this chapter.

How the Romanians characterise leaders

It is important for leaders in Romania to always try and adopt the middle ground in their leadership approach. The consequence of this is that they seek to avoid extreme positions, invariably gravitate towards the sensible centre- ground, and do not typically think or act in terms of binary solutions (white/black; yes/no; good/bad) to problems they encounter in the workplace (Benea, 2015). One reason for this is that, historically speaking, given the multi-ethinic nature of Romania, both its leaders and Romania as a country has always sought to find the middle-ground in order to establish and maintain a sense of harmony between its citizens from hetergeneous cultures (Guluţă & Rusu, 2019) . Hence, as Benea (2015) observes, Romanians can compromise with seemingly incongruous ideas and positions. Therefore, it is important that leaders are able to embody this spirit in their day-to-day leadership practices. According to Guluţă and Rusu (2019). the predominant leadership style in Romania can be understood as "*the implication leadership style*". Within an implication leadership style, managers set limits upon their decision-making by either asking employees to make the final decision or allowing the group of employees to decide freely (Guluţă & Rusu, 2019). Furthermore, Catalana et al. (2004) conducted research on leadership authority and CEO motivations in Romania, which consisted of comparing and contrasting Romanian leadership styles and practices to that of Austrians and Germans. The authors concluded that Romanian leaders appear to be more arbitrary, direct and more reluctant to accredit their power (Catalana et al., 2004). Alongside this, Romanian leaders were also found to be more bureaucratic and status conscious than their Austrian and German counterparts, not to mention that they had low levels of trust in those working in the lower echelons of the organisational hierarchy (Catalana et al., 2004). The importance placed on status and directness was also supported by the results of the Cross-Cultural Business Skills (CCBS Survey (2022), insofar as the respondents reported that Romanian employees prefers leaders that are visionary thinkers and powerful decision makers. Notwithstanding the cultural preference for strong decision-makers in Romania, Catalana et al. (2004) also found that Romanian leaders are more focused on cultivating a peaceful and friendly environment within their organisations and treating their employees in a humane way, which contrasts sharply to German speaking countries that are ordinarily very strict towards their teams and distance themselves from such a relational leadership approach. This was corroborated by our interview, Professor Lupu, who stated that Romanian leaders will only earn the respect of their employees, if they ensure that they are happy in the

workplace and provide them with help if needed, even if the problems pertain to issues outside of the workplace (2 November 2022).
Furthermore, the findings of the CCBS Survey (2022) show that 88% of the respondents stated that it is important for Romanian leaders to have a strong charismatic personality. Alongside this, the respondents reported that having access to the right work network (80% of the respondents), a high intellect (90%), organisational experience (94%) and technical competence (78%) were also fundamental qualities for Romanian leaders to possess. Finally, Huţu (2010) posits that within Romanian organizations it is important for leaders to establish and maintain a strong balance between collectivism and individualism. While most of the respondents in Huţu's (2010) research stated a preference for working in groups, senior management tended to prioritise mostly individualistic attitudes (mainly related to power distribution and retention) despite the fact that most of them declared that teamwork was very important. Overall, this section demonstrates that Romanian leaders must strive to establish a good balance between individualistic and collective goals, find the middle-ground in their approach and be visionary thinkers and powerful decision-makers.

Survey results and what local respondents say

Over 70 experienced C-level Romanian executives completed the CCBS Survey between 2015 and 2022 to provide their knowledge and expertise on Romanian leadership styles and practices. This section provides an overview of the most noteworthy findings with respect to leadership in Romania that have emerged in the survey over the period under consideration. First and foremost, based on the respondents' answers, one can discern that the Romanian leadership style is relatively hierarchical. This was evidenced by the fact that 83% of the leaders agreed with, the statement that 'when a management decision has been made, it will not be changed very easily'. This particular finding is in accordance with Guluţă and Rusu's (2019) research, which showed that Romanian managers make decisions on their own without consulting their employees beforehand. The hierarchical nature of Romanian organisations can also be discerned from the fact that 59% of the respondents stated 'employees would not bend the rules without asking in order to improve their performance or achieve better results' (CCBS Survey, 2022). Secondly, according to the respondents, it is important for Romanian leaders to have a strong charismatic personality (88%), access to the right work network (80%) and intellect (90%). Moreover, leaders should also have organisational experience (94%) and technical competence (78%), in addition to being visionary thinkers (86%) and powerful decision makers (84%).

Despite the aforementioned hierarchical nature of Romanian organisations, it is leaders in their day-to-day interactions with employees appear to adopt a relatively informal management style. This was evidenced by the fact that 68% of the respondents reported that employees are able to address their leaders by their first names in Romanian organisations. Further evidence for a relational approach can also be observed in the fact that 85% of the respondents expressed that leaders should actively spend time on ensuring their team members personal well-being (CCBS Survey, 2022). Although they find well-being to be of particular importance, the results also indicate that leaders like to encourage some degree of competition between their employees in the workplace culture, insofar as 77% of the respondents stated that they did this in order to achieve a better result (CCBS Survey, 2022). In response to the question 'What sets Romanian leadership apart from other countries?' one of the respondents answered, *"Romanians tend to micromanage, also most of them have no clue about setting SMART objectives or taking data-driven decisions."* The issue of micromanagement was a recurring theme amongst the respondents as well as the fact that *"people often do not trust the leadership"* in the country. Interestingly, one of the respondents opined that the reason for the lack of trust in leadership stems from the communist background of the country (CCBS Survey, 2022).

Local leadership analysis

Professor Constantin Lupu: a Romanian leadership scholar

Professor Constantin Lupu currently works at the *Universitatea de Studii Europene* in Moldova. Professor Lupu has almost 30 years of experience in several roles in the business industry. He also has extensive experience in leadership as he was President of S.C. Wolf Investment S.R.L. for four years. In our interview with him, Professor Lupu stated that the work culture in Romania has almost little to no difference from the work cultures of other countries in Europe (2 November 2022). He proceeded to note that the people in Romania are well-educated, and work hard because they have certain goals that they want to achieve in their lives, just like their counterparts in France or Germany, for example. However, Professor Lupa then said that what does differentiate Romania from other European countries is their culture and food, however this does not translate back into the business sector necessarily. In response to a question about what constitutes a typical Romanian leader, Professor Lupu posited that a typical Romanian leader is well-educated, not only with respect to their line of business such as management, marketing, or economy, but also on a whole host of other topics. He cited as an example that Romanian leaders would also be highly knowledgeable about the history of language, not only the Romanian language but also with respect to English and/or French, for example (2 November 2022). He moved onto discuss that if a Romanian leader wants to be respected by their employees, then it is vitally important that they focus on and develop strategies that will help to keep their employees happy. For example, Professor Lupu stated that leaders should not only ensure that their employees are sufficiently financially compensated, but rather also provide them with help if needed, even if the problems occur outside of work (2 November 2022). In a similar vein, Professor Lupu opined that a good Romanian leader is someone who has empathy for their employees; this is because employees need a leader that is willing to listen to their problems in order to be able to help them with their issues or simply give advice if needed. In this respect, Professor Lupu noted, it is important for a Romanian leader to keep close contact with their employees to earn their respect. When asked if there is a notable difference between the respect that employees have for older or younger leaders, he stated *"that it all depends on the era of business."* He then noted that if there is a young leader that has managed more companies, then they will definitely be looked at as being smarter than an old leader who has only run one company (Lupu, 2 November 2022). However, if the old leader was working in the agriculture industry and was sufficiently educated, then they will be respected more, both due to the value accorded to what they have learned in school and over their years working in the industry (Lupu, 2 November 2022).

In-country leadership bestseller

One of Romania's best-selling books about leadership is *Ghid practic pentru antreprenoi* (Practical guide for entrepreneurs) and is a compilation of the knowledge of eight Romanian businesspeople, Daniela Cretu, Felix Daniliuc, Radu Manolescu, Mihai Marcu, Robert Maxim, Felix Patrascanu, Luminita Roman, Nicoleta Stoian. However, the book itself is written by Claudiu Vrinceanu. Claudiu describes himself as an ambassador and someone who connects entrepreneurs, investors, multinationals, and the media with the public environment, such as foreign governments and institutions. Daniela Cretu is a Romanian businesswoman with experience in leadership and management. Felix Daniliuc is the head of SMEs at BRD Groupe Société Générale a Romanian bank. Felix has extensive experience working with banks, having worked with BRD, Raiffeisen Bank Romania and ING Romania. Radu Manolescu is the founder and managing partner of K.M Trust & Partners. Radu has experience with Strategy, Executive Coaching, and Management. Mihai Marcu is a country sales manager at Synology and on the board of directors at Medlife.

Robert Maxim is an advisory partner at KPMG Romania. Robert offers consultancy services to the Romanian market and has worked in multiple fields such as finance, retail energy and healthcare. Felix Patrascanu is a board member of TAROM and the Owner of FAN courier. Luminița Roman is a Founder & Managing Director at Hatwit, and specialises in HR, performance and recruiting. Nicoleta Stoian is a General Manager at Vitafoam Romania. All these authors possess extensive knowledge and experience, which is why they are all part of the Romanian Business Leaders (RBL), which is a non-profit organisation that is dedicated to building a future where future generations want to live. They want to make sure Romania becomes a country their children will want to live in. The RBL is one of the founding members of the Coalition for the Development of Romania, along with other representative business organisations in Romania. This book contains nine chapters that educate the reader on a variety of subjects from marketing to human resources. It acts as a guide for starting entrepreneurs who can learn from the experiences of these eight entrepreneurs to make sure not to make the same wrong decisions. It covers all the points of interest when just starting up and is an excellent way to learn from the best Romania has to offer.

Local leadership book	
Title	*Ghid practic pentru antreprenori*
Translation	Practical guide for entrepreneurs
Authors	Claudiu Vrinceanu, Daniela Cretu, Felix Daniliuc, Felix Patrascanu, Luminita Roman, Robert Maxim
Publisher	Evrika Publishing
Year	2021
ISBN	978-606-94903-8-9

Romanian leadership YouTube review

Alongside academic research, YouTube is also an effective resource for learning about leadership skills and practices in Romania. The first video to be summarised here is a video about the audiobook *"Catre leadership prin Management"* (Towards leadership through management) in which Radu Nechita talks about what Romanian managers can do to motivate both themselves and those working for them. According to Radu Nechita (2021), the only real motivation for people must come from inside themselves. Everyone has their own set of responsibilities, for which everyone can come up with their own motivation. What leaders in Romania need to do to encourage and sustain the motivation of their employees is to sufficiently stimulate them through introducing systems of recognition (Nechita, 2021). This could take the form of incentivising them through a system of rewards, offering promotions, or other types of advancements that employees can go through in the professional field. In the next video to be analysed, Daniel Metz, the CEO of NTT DATA Romania, talks about the development of his own company. In this interview, Daniel Metz talks about how important it is that his company in Romania grows without there being a correlation between the increase in income and the increase in the number of people. Results have shown that Romanian employees produce much more in terms of added value than they would have produced if the company involved them. In short, Daniel Metz's company allows its employees to appreciate their value and, in turn, have witnessed that the added value of their employees increases. The third video to be discussed pertains to transformational leadership in Central Eastern Europe. In the video, the guest speaker, Mr. Frank Hajdinjak, who is the former CEO of E.ON Romania, says that the transformational leadership style over the last 15 years has also become strongly visible in Romania (Stein & Partner, 2020, 49:27). Romania is a deeply hierarchical country and because of this it requires a lot of self-confidence from middle-level managers to let go more and involve employees more often in the decision-making process. In this respect, Hajdinjak notes that it is not only leaders but also employees themselves who have to get used to the evolving leadership style, because it is so ingrained that they should simply do what they are told to do, rather than coming up with ideas themselves. According to Hajdinjak, this style no longer works in modern organisations (Stein & Partner, 2020, 50:14). Many organisations in Romania have therefore been changing their leadership style in recent years to a style that is characterised by having a more open relationship with employees and involving them in the decision-making process.

Romanian leadership social media review

Mirela Mihaela Balaban has worked at Maxwell leadership Romania since 2017, and is now their Senior Program Advisor (Balaban, n.d.). She is active in Facebook, Instagram, and LinkedIn, where she posts updates about her work. A few years prior to starting at Maxwell, she graduated from the Maxwell leadership Romania program (Balaban, n.d.). The Maxwell program is designed to help individuals or companies to improve their leadership skills. Their stated goals are as follows: "*Whether your goal is to better yourself or make waves that change the world, there are many ways to feel the call to lead. We are here to help you answer it, and we know without a doubt you can get there. All it takes is a clear plan, daily practice, and a community of fellow change-makers with you at every step as you lead powerful, positive change through values-based leadership*" (Maxwell, 2022). Sorin Popa also works for Maxwell leadership Romania and runs a lot of live training sessions for future leaders dedicated to enhancing their leadership skills (Popa, n.d,). Sorin Popa states on the website one of his favourite quotes that she tells future leaders: "*Nu m-am născut pentru viața asta, m-am crescut pentru ea*." (even if I was not born for this life [being a leader], I grew up to do it). Both Sorin Popa and Mirela Mihaela Balaban believe that even if people are not born with all the leadership skills, they will need to run organisations in Romania, they can be taught those leadership skills. Sorin Popa is active on Facebook (Popa, n.d.), Instagram, LinkedIn as well as on the Maxwell leadership Romania Youtube channel (Maxwell leadership Romania- Youtube, 2011). Andreea Rosca is a Romanian woman who describes herself as an 'explorer.' She co-founded the Romanian Business Leaders Foundation in 2011 with three other entrepreneurs, which serves as the voice and tool for business leaders to build a Romania where future generations want to live (Romanian Business Leaders' Summit, n.d.). This foundation is active on their own website, Facebook, LinkedIn, and YouTube. Furthermore, Andreea has interviewed many people about leadership throughout her career. She writes about Romanian leadership on her website and LinkedIn, noting that: "*The people who irritate us the most, who disappoint us the most, those who do things differently than we would like are the best teachers. It shows us our own limits, the inability to listen and understand, our own fixed ideas*" (Rosca, 2022). Liliana Urziceanu is a leadership & Executive Coach, Business Consultant, Mentor and Coaching Supervisor at Theoxis consulting. Liliana also used to work as a HR Director at Brico Depot Romania, Banca Romaneasca, GRAMPET Group of Companies, which are all located in Bucharest. The services she offers right now at Theoxis consulting are coaching of executives, leadership development, strategic planning, and management consultancy. Liliana is active on LinkedIn as well as Facebook. For instance, she reacted to a post from a business scholar, Professor David Clutterbuck, where she described how beautiful and clearly, he articulated the sense of purpose and the difference between purpose and goals for a Romanian leader (Urziceanu, 2022).

Understanding hierarchy in Romania

As aforementioned, the organisational culture in Romania is in general very formal and hierarchical (Stein & Partner, 2020). This is evidenced by the fact that decisions require multiple layers of approval from those with decision-making power in the organisation. These multiple layers of approval can serve to put people in an awkward position when there are last minute changes, as they need approval from senior-level figures (Pop, 2016). Within such a hierarchical organisational culture, Romanian leaders make decisions on their own without consulting their employees beforehand (Guluţă & Rusu, 2019). Moreover, 83% of our survey respondents agreed with the statement that 'when a management decision has been made, it will not be changed very easily'. The hierarchical nature of Romanian organisations can also be discerned from the fact that 59% of the respondents stated 'employees would not bend the rules without asking in order to improve their performance or achieve better results' (CCBS Survey, 2022). This makes sense when one examines Romanian organisations through the lens of Hofstede's concept of power distance. Romania scores high (90) on the power distance scale (Alt, 2018). This means that there is a large power distance within organisations in Romania, and that people are accepting of inequality within society and organisations. In this respect, it is understandable that Romanian employees assume that leaders simply tell them what to do and therefore merely stick to carrying out their tasks. This view of Romanian organisations is supported by Mr. Frank Hajdinjak, who argues that due to the fact that Romania is a deeply hierarchical country, it requires a lot of self-confidence from middle-level managers to delegate and involve employees more in the decision-making process (Stein & Partner, 2020). Indeed, Catalana et al. (2004) show that Romanian leaders generally have low levels of trust in those working in the lower echelons of the organisational hierarchy. Hajdinjak also discusses how this is because it is so ingrained in both leaders and employees as a result of their Soviet past that employees should simply do what they are told to do, rather than coming up with ideas themselves. This is supported by the results of the Cross-Cultural Business Skills (CCBS Survey (2022), insofar as the respondents reported that Romanian employees prefers leaders that are visionary thinkers and powerful decision makers. This is in line with Laurenţiu Hauser (2014), who stated with respect to Romanian leadership and hierarchy that: "*Formal leaders coordinate, organize, monitor and influence people and processes by strict rules and procedures, which makes it difficult to introduce new ideas and concepts*" (Hauser, 2014, p. 3). Romanian leaders' focus on monitoring and observing was also a recurring theme in our survey data, with one of the respondents noting in response to the question

'What sets Romanian leadership apart from other countries?' *"Romanians [leaders] tend to micromanage."* (CCBS Survey, 2022).

How the Romanians achieve leadership empathy

Due to Romania's history, power and decision-making authority has historically been concentrated in the hands of leaders who predominantly employed an autocratic management style; however, with the collapse of the Soviet Union and greater exposure to western practices and international trends, there has been some changes in recent years (Budrina, 2011). According to Hajdinjak, this style no longer works in modern organisations (Stein & Partner, 2020, 50:14). In Romanian companies today, although leaders ordinarily give out direct instructions to employees regarding tasks that have to be done, before then following up on the progress on a one- to- one basis to see that the task has been completed, it is important to stress accept this micromanagement in return for the protection that leaders bestow upon them. This protective relationship is illustrated nicely by Irinia Budrina, who stated that, *"Managers in Romania often tried to preserve jobs and provide a measure of social protection"* (2011, p. 6). However, with respect to the younger generation of employees, leaders must go beyond more than merely offering protection to achieve empathic understanding with those working under them. This is because the younger generation of Romanian employees are characterised by increased conscientiousness, individualism, flexibility, perseverance in tasks compared to their older counterparts, or at least they are if they are sufficiently motivated by their leaders, which makes leadership more difficult ((Racolța-Paina & Irini, 2021). Therefore, a more diverse management style is needed in order to analyse the individual differences of employees and work out how to best motivate them and capitalise on these unique skillsets, in order to obtain not only a positive result for individuals' personal development but for the organisation as a whole (Racolța-Paina & Irini, 2021). This shift towards more relational and individually tailored forms of leadership in Romania is supported by the results of the CCBS Survey (2022), where 70% of the respondents reported that it is (very) likely that managers actively spend time ensuring the personal well-being of their team members. Moreover, 68% of the respondents stressed that it was important for Romanian leaders to be good listeners (CCBS Survey, 2022). This is also in line with Catalana et al.'s (2004) research, which found that Romanian leaders strive to foster a peaceful and friendly environment and speak to their employees in a humane way. This aspect of Romanian leadership was corroborated by our interviewee, Professor Lupu, who explained that the main way through which Romanian leaders gain their employees' respect and to ensure that they work hard for you is to make sure that they are happy in the workplace and provide them with help if needed, regardless of whether the problem is work-related to otherwise (2 November 2022). He proceeded to note that Romanian leaders achieve empathic understanding by not simply paying people well, but also by listening and responding to the problems their employees experience and helping them to address this (Lupu, 2 November 2022). In this respect, Professor Lupu noted, it is important for a Romanian leader to maintain close contact with their employees to earn their respect.

Thailand

Annelot van Dommele, Berber Kok, Ciovanni van de Groep, Guido Struijvé, Jason Achthoven, Marisa Alberda & Tom Bernard

สวัสดี (*Sawasdee*) is the greeting one hears when meeting local Thai people (Scroope, 2016). This is typically followed with ค่ะ *'kha'* for females and ครับ *'khrap'* for males. This greeting is accompanied with the *wai*, that is, a dip of the head while clasping the palms of your hands together in front of your chest (Cooper, 2019). The *wai* shows the level of respect you have for the other person and is an important custom in Thailand, in part, because of how important it is to both give and save face in Thai culture. This refers to the way in which people acknowledge other people's accomplishments and social position within the social hierarchy (Ukosakal, 2005). Indeed, this concept is deeply rooted in many aspects of Thai culture, and it is very prominent in leadership in Thailand. Alongside this, Thai society is also heavily grounded in superstition, so much so in fact that even some governmental decisions have been known to be made after consulting a medium or fortune teller (Satrusayang, 2015). Buddhism is the main religion practiced in the country, with Selvarajah (2013) arguing that the spiritual authority of the Buddhist religion has a profound influence upon both the thinking and behaviour of Thai people, both on a national and personal level. Given that it is the eighth largest global economy (IMF, 2022), and has over 70 million inhabitants, Thailand is an attractive country for international businesses (Prasartruek, 2003). Thailand is officially classified as a newly industrialised economy with its main sectors being tourism, agriculture, and manufacturing. The currency, *Baht*, is one of the oldest currencies still in use, dating back to the 13th century (Jansen, 2007). During its history, Thailand has never been colonised by the west. Although it has changed names several times, it has always remained politically independent. This fact is also reflected in the name Thailand itself, which directly translates into two meanings: 'land of the free' and 'land of the Thais' (Radu, 2019). Thai culture has been influenced by other countries, however; most notably, China and India (Selvarajah, 2013). This means when one attempts to understand leadership skills and practices in Thailand, it is also critically important to consider the influence of these two countries.

How the Thai's characterise leaders?

Based on research on ความเป็นผู้นำ (*Khwām pĕn p̄hū̂nả* - leadership) styles, it can be said that Thai workers prefer a leader who shows initiative in their leadership approach (Mekhum, 2020). Mekhum (2020) also found that the concept of 'hierarchical learning' is valued within Thai organisations. This consists of building a strong foundation of duty and presenting a mutually agreed vision of the future direction of the company that both leaders and employees can aspire towards (Mekhum, 2020). This testifies to the fact that if Thai workers see that there is a shared goal and that leaders are taking the initiative in achieving this goal, then they are prepared to work hard and play their part in its fulfilment. In a similar vein, Vora and Kainzbauer (2020) posit that a humanistic leadership style is of critical importance for being a successful leader in Thailand. A humanistic leadership style generally is characterised by caring and engaging, which is in accordance with the broader societal values of Thailand and Thai business culture. More specifically, a humanistic leadership approach is in strong alignment with Buddhist traditions, which underpin the prominence of compassion, friendliness, and humility within Thai culture (Vora & Kainzbauer, 2020). Vaughn (2018) also stresses that understanding Buddhism is key to being a successful Thai leader, noting: "*There are ten principles that were highlighted from Buddha, and these are called the Rajadhamma 10 in Thailand*" (Roongrerngsuke & Liefooghe, 2012, as cited in Vaughn, 2018, p.3). These principles encompass certain values like generosity, altruism, patience, and honesty. Given that 94% of people in Thailand are Buddhist, it is important that leaders pay tribute to this and incorporate this within their leadership style. Doing so shows their employees that they care for them and that their work is valued, rather than them merely being a cog in the machine (Vaughn, 2018). This also helps explain why Thai people prefer that their leaders possess both a certain strength and have a caring nature, because, ultimately, they want to feel an emotional connection with their leaders. This is illustrated by one of the leaders interviewed in Vora and Kainzbauer's research, who stated: "*I think that you have to be able to be emotionally involved and attached to people*" and "*If you want to win the hearts of Thai people, you need to lead from the heart*" (2020, p. 9). Another noteworthy attribute that Thai employees prefer in their leaders is that they are sociable, as this helps to get the best out of their teams. As aforementioned, Thais prefer caring leaders, and one way through which leaders can display that they care is by asking their employees how their day was or how their family is doing and connecting to them in this way. One leader in Vora and Kainzbauer's research described this as follows: "*[leaders must] make them [employees] feel that you are approachable*" (2020, p. 9).

Interestingly, this sociability on the behalf of Thai leaders also extends beyond the workplace to include engaging in social activities, such as, for example, team building activities or other types of fun activities. This aspect of Thai leadership was corroborated by one of our interviewees, Vissanu Zumitzavan, who stated: *"The leader needs to understand what their subordinates need and then fill in the gaps"* and *"You need to tell or show them that you care for them and do this by helping them"* (Zumitzavan, 4 November 2022). Zumitzavan elaborated on this further, explaining that Thai employees can tell if you are sincere or not, and that this ultimately impacts upon their work ethic, insofar as if they feel that you do not genuinely care for them, then they will not work to the best of their abilities. Consequently, he stressed how important it is for Thai leaders to show their employees that they are prepared to help them: *"If they have family issues, like not having enough money for clothes or schooling, you can show care by helping them"* (Zumitzavan, 4 November 2022).

Survey results and what local respondents say

To gain more knowledge and insight into leadership in Thailand, research has been conducted through the means of administering an online survey to C-level executives and managers with substantial leadership experience and knowledge in Thailnd. The results presented in this section are based upon two separate CCBS Surveys, one from 2017 and the other from 2022. The survey focuses on, amongst other things, the prevailing leadership styles and practices in Thai organisations, preferred qualities, traits and behaviours of Thai leaders, and gender differences in leadership. This section discusses the most noteworthy findings emerging from the survey. With respect to the importance placed upon failing to adhere to deadlines, the majority of the respondents reported that they did not see this as being synonymous with failure necessarily (CCBS Survey, 2022). In combination with the majority of the respondents reporting that leaders are not prepared to confront subordinates during staff meetings in order to obtain the desired results, this also suggests that failure to adhere to deadlines would be handled in private during one-to-one meetings, rather than employees being confronted in group meetings if deadlines were not met (CCBS Survey, 2017/2022). Another noteworthy finding was that in a majority of the respondents stated that leaders encourage some degree of competition within their teams in order to achieve better results (CCBS Survey, 2017/2022). However, it was evident from the results that this competition should not adversely affect the personal well-being of employees or be conducted in an overly aggressive manner (CCBS Survey, 2017). The next notable finding from the survey pertains to the fact that there is some autonomy with respect to work decisions, insofar as the respondents stated that employees have some leeway over bending the rules as long as they achieve better results or improve performance from doing so (CCBS Survey, 2017). Indeed, Thai employees experience much greater freedom in many respects than other countries, according to some of the respondents in the survey (CCBS Survey, 2017). Finally, in relation to the most recent CCBS Survey (2022), an interesting result is that someone who holds a certain position according to their title or status should be addressed in this way by employees further own the organisational hierarchy. This indicates that Thai employees should tread carefully when it comes to respecting the organisational hierarchy and superiors' respective position within it.

Local leadership analysis

Vissanu Zumitzavan: a Thai leadership scholar

Vissanu Zumitzavan is a scholar in the field of Thai business alongside teaching at Khon Kaen University in Thailand. Besides lecturing, he is also the designated researcher in the department. During our interview, Zumitzavan stated that seniority is strongly respected within Thai culture. This becomes particularly noticeable within the older generation of leaders, who tend to listen less to their teams and give more direct orders (4 November 2022). The orders of a superior are generally not questioned, as Thailand prides itself on exhibiting a high-level of general respect for elders and hierarchically superior members of society (Zumitzavan, 4 November 2022). In response to being asked if older employees have more influence than younger employees in Thai organisations, Zumitzavan noted: *"Yes, because we believe in seniority. If you are older, most of the time the younger generation is going to respect you"* (4 November 2022). He then proceeded to discuss the issue of hierarchy within Thai organisations, explaining that it is more likely that there is a top-down approach adopted in organisations and that employees listen to their boss and follow their orders without questioning them. Zumitzavan noted in this regard that Thai workers are very loyal, a fact which might also underpin the respect and reverence they have for leaders 4 November 2022). However, this loyalty is not the exclusive province of employees, but is also a key component of leaders' makeup also. To illustrate this, he cited the following example from his own experience: *"If leaders have a good idea of your experience, and think that you can do something, they will allow you to participate"* (Zumitzavan, 4 November 2022). When asked about work relationships, Zumitzavan elucidated that the aforementioned strong sense of hierarchy and respect also extends beyond the workplace, with the result being that having more of friendship bond with employees is something that is not yet accepted within Thai culture (4 November 2022). He then moved on to give his opinion about gender differences in leadership, gender (in)equality and how female leaders are treated generally in Thailand, explaining that: *"Everyone is treated equally. Today, I believe that it is equal not only for woman but for any gender. We [Thailand] are quite open in that sense"* (Zumitzavan, 4 November 2022). Zumitzavan also shared his thoughts regarding how a Thai leader can seek to build trust and respect with their subordinates. To achieve this, he explained that first and foremost a leader must understand the needs and wants of their subordinates in order to bridge this gap. In his words: *"You need to have good communication skills, know how to convince them to work with you, show your empathy and show that you understand them"* (Zumitzavan, 4 November 2022). He concluded the interview by stating that if leaders' subordinates feel that they are not being cared for, then they are not going to give their best for them.

Larry S. Persons: a Thai cross-cultural trainer

Larry S. Persons is a leadership development expert who has worked with Thai leaders for many years. He is born in Bangkok and grew up in the northeast of Thailand. He stayed in southeast Asia until the age of 15 while attending Boarding school, which contributed to him being bilingual (Thai and English) and having strong Asian values. He earned a PhD at the Fuller School of Intercultural Studies, teaches anthropology and urban cultures as well as being the cofounder and CEO of CQ Leadership Consulting, LLC. He is also an author of the book, *The Way Thais Lead: Face as Social Capital* (2016). In the book, Persons shares his insights about the importance of gaining, losing and maintaining face in the Thai social hierarchy. During our interview with him, Persons talked about two different ways in which Thai leaders have and continue to lead: through fear and kindness (22 November 2022). According to Persons, the biggest form of exchange between employee and employer is the instrumental exchange. In Persons' own words: *"The whole idea in the instrumental exchange model is the way you gain traction is through indebting other people by using your power in such a way that they then owe you something"* (Persons, 22 November 2022). In response to a question about how the nature of hierarchy in Thai businesses has changed in recent years, Persons answered as follows: *"In business, if it's changing, it's changing very slowly, very slowly. These are deeply entrenched values. Hierarchy in Thai society, I think, comes originally. It's based on Confucian teaching, you know, that the father is always right. The boss is always right'* (22 November 2022).

He proceeded to explain that he has witnessed a change with generation X and the younger generations, which is as a result of the fact that *"Many of them have gone and studied in other countries ... and they even begin to acculturate, you know, they take on other aspects of the UK culture or Australian or Dutch or American culture, so I see them wanting to try new models of leadership"* (Persons, 22 November 2022). In his book, he writes about the importance of maintaining face in Thai culture, and when the question arose as to what is truly unacceptable in Thai leadership he returned to this theme, noting that the worst thing a Thai leader can do *"is to cause another person to lose face, it is sacred. It's a sacred value that and it shapes and forms so many of the dynamics in Thai leadership"* (Persons, 22 November 2022).

In-country leadership bestseller

One of the best-selling books about leadership was written by Professor Suthep Pongsriwa and is entitled *ภาวะความเป็นผู้นำ (Leadership).* Suthep Pongsriwa is currently a lecturer at Chiangrai Rajabhat University. He is highly renowned for his leadership skills within the academic world in Thailand, and, indeed, the book is the main textbook for leadership courses in Thailand. The book was released in the year 2020 and describes the basics concepts of leadership in Thailand. The significance of leadership is explained by acknowledging how much power and influence it bestows upon someone, and that they therefore have a responsibility to display empathy and engage in warm conversations with those below them. The book then proceeds to delineate what constitutes the ideal leader in Thailand, describing, amongst other things, that they should be strong, empathetic, and knowledgeable. Above all, after reading this book, one will understand how important efficient administration is to Thai leaders.

Local leadership book	
Title	*ภาวะความเป็นผู้นำ* (Leadership)
Subtitle	-
Author	รศ.สุเทพ พงศ์ศรีวัฒน์ Prof. Suthep Pongsriwa
Publisher	Expernetbooks
Year	2020
ISBN	9789744143235

ภาวะ
ความเป็นผู้นำ

Thailand's effective administration consists of four key aspects: budgets are decided based on the needs of provincial administration; administration has a clear and concise structure; decision-making power is allocated to provincial administrators; and the authority of the central administration is limited, hence why there is a greater emphasis placed upon area-based administration. The other noteworthy information that readers will take away from the book is the importance accorded to merit and prestige within Thai culture. To ascend to the top of the hierarchy in Thai organisations, leaders are required to work hard and familiarise themselves with the specific skills of decision-making, conflict management and employee motivation that are necessary for becoming an effective leader in Thailand.

Thailand leadership YouTube review

Larry Persons, Founder and CEO of CQ Leadership Consulting and author of *The Way Thais Lead*, talks about the critical importance of saving face in Thai culture in an interview with Thai PBS World (Persons, 2020). Thai PBS World is an online English news service of the Thai public broadcasting service. Persons shares that through his research he found that you cannot lead at any significant level in Thai society without having any form of face. He notes that this is the case because hierarchy is still particularly important in Thai society and that because of this *'slipping up'* is simply not an option. He also shares that new leaders need a sense of inner goodness and outward generosity. Larry also provides advice to the younger generation of leaders in Thai society, noting that they should *"First of all, be patient, be a learner and absolutely learn to speak up"* (Persons, 2020, 24:45). He proceeds to note that the latter will become increasingly important for future leaders because the work dynamic is shifting in the contemporary labour market. He elaborates on this as follows: *"It will be impossible to guide organisations in this day and age with only one person having all the answers"* (Persons, 2020, 25:30). In another video by Thai PBS World, Kattiya Indaravijya, CEO of Kasikorn Bank, talks about female leadership in Thailand (Indaravijya, 2022). She states that although the number of female leaders has been increasing steadily in recent years, greater focus still needs to be dedicated to the persistence of gender equality within Thai society generally and organisations specifically. However, rather than merely focusing on male and females, Thai leaders should think in a broader sense and focus on *"All kinds of genders. We should give them the same opportunities for them to show whether they are able to perform"* (Indaravijya, 2022, 1:11). In the third video to be summarised, Bloomberg Quicktake (2021) spoke to Jittirat Tantasirin, CEO of two Mercedes-Benz dealerships, about breaking barriers in Thai leadership. She explains that creating a safe space is becoming even more important in contemporary society. As a CEO she spends a lot of time and effort on this issue, stating: *"I want to create a space where all staff feel safe and empowered"* and *"When staff do not feel comfortable with a test ride, we equip the car with cameras"* (Tantasirin, 2021, 02:50). In the next video to be summarised, CNBC International TV talks to two CEOs and a company founder about the balance between sustainability and commercial gain in Thai leadership (CNBC International TV, 2022). All three leaders reference the fact that they find sustainability more important than commercial gain, and that this heavily influences their leadership styles within their respective companies, but that there is always a way to make it work. Kotchakorn Vorakhon, founder of Landprocess says: *"if it is not sustained, then it is your job to make it sustained"* (Vorakhon, 2022, 2:14).

Understanding hierarchy in Thailand

The Thai word for hierarchy is ลำดับชั้น (*ladab chan)*. Thailand is a deeply hierarchical country in which tremendous respect and reverence is displayed towards elders and individuals considered to be higher up the societal hierarchy. With respect to interpersonal relationships, both inside and outside of the workplace, people in Thai society are continually striving to determine people's place within the societal hierarchy in order to ensure that they show the required respect (Donelly, 2022). In this respect, hierarchy in Thailand plays a much greater overt role in everyday life compared to the west, for instance (Holmes & Tangtongtavy, 1996). This originates from the fifteenth century when King Borommatrailokanat undertook a ranking of all citizens within the kingdom. The ranking was based on the amount of land owned by a person and the name for this criterion was *sakdi na* (field power). Even though this ranking has subsequently been removed, the country is still deeply hierarchical, starting wit the king on the top and working its way down though the aristocracy, government officials, Buddhist leaders, all the way down to the remainder of the general population. Hence, the majority of Thais still think there should be a clear social hierarchy in society and organisations (Holmes & Tangtongtavy, 1996). Consequently, hierarchy therefore plays a significant role in terms of how people address each other in the Thai language in organisations, which is based on certain characteristics such as sex, age or social position (Kalule, 2013). In Thai organisations, it is thus readily assumed that all orders or directives coming from someone in a higher position within the organisational hierarchy must be completed without questioning the necessity or practicality for carrying them out.

It is for this reason that Thailand has been described as a compliance culture (Gallagher et al. 1997). This is supported by the fact that Thailand scores 64 on Hofstede's power distance index, which although slightly lower than the average Asian country (71), is still higher than some western countries (Hofstede Insights, 2021). Power distance in Thailand is frequently justified by the social position of the leader (Gronn, 1995). This power distance pervades not only the business sector but all social relationships in Thailand. Furthermore, Hofstede (2021) posits that this power distance makes for strong hierarchies within organisations, which, in turn, may lead to the adoption of a paternalistic management approach. Persons states that Thai business culture is: "a *little bit more like a military model. If the general tells you to do something, doesn't matter what your rank is, if you're under him, you go out and you follow orders"* (personal communication, November 22, 2022). Going against these orders is not common for Thai employees, due to the simple fact that Selvarajah (2013) notes that confrontation for a Thai person is taken personally and therefore it is hard for them to separate work conflicts from personal relations.

How the Thai achieve leadership empathy

Thai society is characterised by values and principles that help to facilitate leadership empathy within organisations. Specifically, the high level of respect and reverence in which elders and other people are held in society (Kalule, 2013), certain aspects of Buddhist values, such as, for example, seeking harmony (Vaughn, 2018), not to mention the importance in Thai culture on maintaining face (Persons, 2016), all provide fertile ground for leaders to display empathy towards their employees. In conjunction with this, it has also been shown that the humanistic and paternalistic leadership styles are especially prevalent within Thai organisations, and that both of these leadership approaches are predicated on empathic understanding between leaders and their employees (Vora & Kainzbauer, 2020). One of the main ways through which Thai leaders show empathy, according to Chaiprasit and Rinthaisong (2022). is by placing themselves in the shoes of their employees and showing sincere interest in their life and career development. Moreover, they can also strengthen their leadership position by showing respect for the different points of view expressed by their employees (Chaiprasit & Rinthaisong, 2022). The importance of empathy was corroborated by one of our interviewees, Zumitzavan, who stated that leaders need to be honest in their endeavours, build trust and rapport with their employees and seek to understand them, so that they feel highly valued within the workplace (personal communication, November 21, 2022). The sentiment here is nicely captured in a Thai saying น้ำจากใจ (*nam jai*), which can be literally translated as water from the heart. น้ำจากใจ is kindness and Thais will love people, leaders, friends or politicians or anybody else who exhibits that they possess this water in their heart or น้ำจากใจ, as this shows that you are kind hearted, thoughtful and generous. According to Persons, the most admirable characteristic a leader can possess in Thailand is generosity. This generosity can manifest in different ways, such as, for example, being financially generous, or generous with sharing information, their encouragement and their words (Persons, personal communication, November 22, 2022). Moreover, as noted by Zumizavan (4 November 2022), it is both appreciated and seen as a strong indication of empathic leadership if leaders help subordinates who are experiencing family issues, by, for example, helping to pay for their children's education or paying their medical bills. Such help would simply not be possible if Thai leaders were not already adopting an empathic leadership approach, insofar as they would not be able to pay bills if they did not first get to know their employees, know what is going on in their lives (Persons, personal communication, November 22, 2022).

Uzbekistan

Astrid Bons, Ivo Botterweck, Laura Marell, Sheryl Sodijana, Shiella Valmeo & Thijn van Well

O'zbekiston (Uzbekistan) is one of only two double landlocked countries in the world, which is to say that neither Uzbekistan nor its neighbouring countries are bordered by the sea. Uzbekistan is located at the geographical crossroads between Europe, the Middle East and Asia. The Silk Road, which runs through the heart of the country, formed one of the world's most well-known trade routes from classical antiquity up until the late Middle Ages. The trade in silk and porcelain has brought Uzbekistan tremendous prosperity, especially in Tashkent, Samarkand and Buchara (Cole, 2014), with the latter referred to as "*Madinat Al Tujjar*" (The city of Merchants). Having been ruled by various empires, including being part of the USSR, Uzbekistan gained its independence in 1991 after the dissolution of the Soviet Union. Although Russian continues to be spoken as a governmental language, the official language is Uzbek, which is spoken by the vast majority of citizens (Zhao, 2020). Independence also granted the large population of Muslims, most of whom are Sunni Muslims, the right to practice their religious faith (Office of International Religious Freedom, 2021). The election of President Shavkat Mirziyoyev in 2016 has resulted in various investor-friendly reforms designed to improve Uzbekistan's overall business environment. The setting up of high-profile projects, free economic zones and investment incentives should serve to attract foreign direct investment in the medium-to-long term (Uzbekistan trade & investment risk report, 2022). Today, agriculture accounts for a quarter of the country's GDP, with the main agricultural products produced being cotton, fruits, vegetables, livestock, grain, wool, and silk (Kiprop, 2019). Another important industry is the services industry, key amongst which is transportation and tourism (Tursunbaevich et al., 2020). The importance of the latter likely derives from Uzbekistan's reputation for generosity, hospitality and admirable values, such as tolerance, kindness, and respect for others (Muminov et al., 2020). Indeed, these skills and values are a key driver in terms of attracting foreign business into the country, and profoundly influence how leaders interact with their employees. This chapter will explore these values and other important aspects by providing a detailed analysis of Uzbek leadership styles and practices.

How the Uzbek characterise leaders

A distinct change of leadership has been discernable in Uzbekistan since the country gained its independece from Soviet rule in 1991. Whereas the country used to rate low in charasmatic and transformational leadership and higher in transactional and laissez-faire leadership dimensions during the Soviet era, today a different way of managing and leading has come to the fore and proven to be a determining factor in the success of organisations (Ardichvili, 2001). In Uzbekistan, in order to manage an organisation effectively, it is crucial that leaders are able to give direction to their subordinates in order to achieve organisational goals and objectives. Generally speaking, there are five leadership styles that can be outlined by an associated set of qualities, attributes and traits, which are predominantly applied and successful in the country (Sharipova et al., 2021). A good Uzbek leader is characterised by their tendency to prioritise the needs of their neighbourhood, alongside motivating others and adopting a positive outlook towards the future, believing that any problem can be overcome (Sharipova et al., 2021). In this respect, leaders must be leader-creators, which is to say that they must continually innovate and take risks to solve problems. Further evidence for this comes from the fact that the respondents from the CCBS Survey (2022) stated that Uzbek's definitely like their leader to be a visionary thinker. Such leaders do not simply command their employees what they want them to do, but rather are open to having discussions with their subordinates. However, Shaykhov Alisher, advisor for the Chamber of Commerce and Industry and former ambassador for Uzbekistan in the UK and Northern Ireland, expressed in our interview with him that transparancy about a long term vision, if there even is one, can be a challenge for leaders in Uzbekistan, noting: *"A long term vision is not always incorporated in business."* (18 November, 2022). Furthermore, Sharipova (2021) argues that it is important for Uzbek leaders to be wrestlers, that is, confident, diplomatic, first in line to face uncertainties and strong-willed. The importance of the latter was also corroborated by our survey respondents, who when presented with five desirable qualities a leader should definitely possess, overwhelmingly selected being a powerful decision maker (CCBS Survey, 2022). In fact, this dominant type of leader is the most common leadership style in the country, insofar as authoritarian leaders are very common in Uzbekistan (CCBS Survey, 2022). Next, is a diplomat-leader who knows how to positively influence those they work with. This was supported by Alisher, who noted that empowering employees is essential within Uzbek organisations (18 November, 2022). This necessitates leaders recognising that they do not have to do everything by themselves; rather, leaders should "*see the potential of their staff, make more use of their capabilities, let them train other staff. Look what is inside their pockets.*" (Alisher 18 November, 2022). Finally, sympathetic leaders are valued by employees, who take inspiration from the fact that they can guide them and the organisation through hard times, and from knowing that the leader will respect and support them. Bayzakov (2011) claims that to achieve effective business outcomes, managers and leaders must also understand Uzbek culture, including how it impacts upon management methods. In this respect, the modern Uzbek culture, which integrates both secular Western values and traditional Uzbek values, can most effectively be described as a dualism of values. The secular values are a result of the previous Soviet system's introduction and the society's commitment to develop in the free-market economy sector. Conversely, the conservatism and collectivism that underpin traditional Uzbek values are primarily influenced by both the Islamic culture and the country's rich historical heritage (Bayzakov, 2011). This dualism underpins the the leadership styles and practices outlined above.

Survey results and what local respondents say

To gain additional insight into Uzbekistan's leadership practices, numerous C-level executives and senior managers with notable managerial experience shared their knowledge and experience by completing the CCBS Survey (2022). This provided us with broad knowledge about how the Uzbeks commonly lead their companies and employees. The most noteworthy findings are delineated in this section. Firstly, when asked if they could say something specific about leadership in Uzbekistan, a recurrent response from the participants was that leaders tend to be rather authoritarian in their leadership style (CCBS Survey, 2022). This was evidenced by the fact that managers are extremely unlikely to change their decision once it has been made, alongside the fact that leaders are somewhat prepared to openly confront staff during staff meetings, in order to obtain the desired results (CCBS Survey, 2022). This aspect of Uzbek leadership was corroborated by Alisher Khasanov, a deputy rector and adjunct professor, who stated that "*Uzbekistan is a no mistakes culture in state organisations, where being kind is considered a weakness, but being rude is considered ill-mannered*" (CCBS Survey, 2022). Moreover, "*Most of the leaders prefer subordination* [from their employees]," according to the head of a local think tank department in Tashkent (CCBS Survey, 2022). According to this respondent, leaders in Uzbek society are people that the public, look up to and that hold authority: "*Most leaders demonstrate their status in the society. In turn, some in society tend to show strong respect to leadership, which makes even a modest leader more aspiring.*"(CCBS Survey, 2022). Interestingly, in spite of this authoritarian approach, the survey showed that it was somewhat unlikely for employees to address leaders by their function or title, while around two-thirds of the respondents stated that employees can address their leaders by their first name (CCBS Survey, 2022). In order to attain a senior-level position in a company, having an academic title on your business card or in your email signature is very important, although having access to the right network was deemed to be the most crucial factor (CCBS Survey, 2022). The next noteworthy finding is that Uzbekistan is also a very result-oriented society, at least in the business sector, insofar as failing to meet a deadline is more or less considered the same as failure (CCBS Survey, 2022). To achieve better results, Uzbek leaders strive to encourage a sense of competition within a team. Despite being a highly authoritarian and result-oriented society, one respondent noted that, "*most of them [authoritarian leaders] are learning to be increasingly more empathetic*" (CCBS Survey, 2022). This change in leadership behaviour was supported by the fact that the majority of the respondents noted that managers should definitely spend time ensuring the personal well-being of their staff (CCBS Survey, 2022). In fact, according to Maftuna Akhadova, CEO of IMPACT.T., it is this newfound "*open-mindedness* [that] *distinguishes leaders in our country from leaders from other countries*" (CCBS Survey, 2022). Our interviewee, Oksana Novojenina, explained that this change in leadership can primarily be attributed to the emergence of openminded younger, or middle-aged entrepreneurs, who studied abroad and "*are coming back to the country with the will to improve the situation and to make the country stronger. They bring back important traits, like self-awareness, [...] integrity, endurance, and fairness [...] they try to bring this [new] style of leadership here [...] this transformational leadership style, versus the authoritative leadership style like we had mostly in Uzbekistan.*" (11 November, 2022).

Local leadership analysis

Zebo Sharipova: an Uzbek leadership scholar

Zebo Sharipova, head of Management and Marketing at Kimyo International University (KIU) in Tashkent, Uzbekistan, has been working as a senior lecturer at KIU for three years. Prior to working at the University, she studied and worked in China, where she earned her master's degree in Project Management. She is currently doing her PhD in International Economics in Beijing Technology and Business University. At the moment, she also teaches at the Chinese academy of science in Beijing. She co-authored an article about leadership in Uzbekistan, in which she distinguished between leadership in the public and private sphere within Uzbekistan (22 November 2022). More specifically, she posited that in the public sphere, the system continues to be characterised by autocratic features, which is a remnant from the Soviet era of leadership styles and practices. The last five years have saw changes take place in the private sector, namely a slightly greater degree of liberalisation and democracy. This is a result of both the president's new innovative strategies which have led to changes in the way the business sector is managed and rapid changes in international business companies. According to Sharipova, Uzbek organisations and society are characterised by a high-power distance. Leaders ordinarily do not communicate directly with their subordinates. Rather, a third person will be used to talk to the subordinates. *"Leaders do not like critics, they do not like discussions. Uzbek leaders only search for validation, and are poor in time management"* (Sharipova, 22 November 2022). Furthermore, Uzbek leadership is underpinned by a sense of connection. This explains why hiring trusted family members or relatives is the prevailing culture within organisations in Uzbekistan. Additionally, Sharipova explained, men are often preferred over their female counterparts for the simple fact that men do not have to think about taking care of children. In her words, this occurs *"because the males and females, they have different tasks in a family, and in society as well. And if we are mostly with our family, the females with family like with kids and a husband. So, they have to pay attention too much to the family instead of their career."* Sharipova proceeded to add in relation to this point that men mostly are stricter, more straightforward, and capable of providing convincing arguments for their decisions in comparison to their female counterparts, and that female leaders sometimes have trouble with their emotions and therefore cannot be objective in their leadership style (22 November 2022). This was supported by the fact that the majority of our respondents noted that men and women do not have equal opportunity to attain senior leadership positions in Uzbekistan (CCBS Survey, 2022). Towards the end of the interview, she stated that as a leader herself, she is a little bit strict by nature and straightforward like a male leader. One reason for this is that she grew up with three brothers; however, she noted that she tries to act like a lady by smiling more, communicating more, and asking her employees more questions. According to her, *"management should not be a position; it should just be a duty."* She unpacked this point by saying that she wants to ask her employees, like how they are doing, or how she can help them solve problems. As a leader, this is what she tries to do, but this is not how other managers and leaders approach situations in Uzbekistan necessarily. With respect to this latter point, Sharipova brought the interview to a close by expressing that, *"I would love to see more changes to leadership and especially for the payment process, the payment, you know, and the inequality between male and females in relation to leadership positions. Because we do the same job, we say we perform the same duties, we complete the same tasks and thus it is unfair I guess for anyone not to get paid according to their duty, but rather according to their gender."* (22 November 2022).

Oksana Novojenina: a cross cultural business trainer and consultant
Oksana Novojenina is a business trainer and consultant from Uzbekistan, who manages, designs, coordinates, and conducts training and organisational development design. She supports leadership teams and runs strategic communication programmes within companies. She has been working in management positions for more than 15 years. In our interview, she began by talking about the fact that, historically speaking, leadership in Uzbekistan was about rules, regulations and setting boundaries according to the generation of leaders aged over 50 years old (22 November, 2022). There was also a high-power distance, high uncertainty avoidance, masculinity, hierarchy, and short-term orientation. However, the country has undergone profound changes in recent years, namely as a result of President Shavkat Mirziyoyev coming to power in 2016, which, in turn, opened the door for Western leadership styles and practices to become more widely implemented within the country. Today, Novojenina stated that the younger generation of Uzbek leaders are more democratic and transformational in their approach, rather than following the autocratic style of the previous generation. These younger leaders are open to creativity, have more freedom in terms of their own thinking, in addition to placing value not only on outcomes but also on the process. In her words: *"They are welcoming new ideas and innovations. [They have] an open mindset. It's about transparency, it's about fairness, it's about empathy."* (22 November, 2022). Next, Novojenina moved on to discuss the legacy of the past in which people were used to being managed in a top-down manner by a manager who was more interested in the system than in relationships. This approach is now over according to her (22 November, 2022). In response to a question about which difficulties she has seen foreigners encounter when they come to work in Uzbekistan for the first time, she referred to broken promises, which she explained as follows: *"There is an Uzbek saying 'hop,' it's like an English 'yes'. You will always hear 'hop' and never hear 'no' from your business partners. But that doesn't mean that the required result would be necessarily forthcoming."* (22 November, 2022). Rather, saying 'hop' is merely a form of politeness and a way of trying to maintain face, rather than a concrete confirmation. Therefore, to avoid any ambiguity, it is important to be strict on agreements and to discuss even the smallest details in the business process, according to Novojenina. It is also very important for foreign managers in

Uzbekistan to show respect for local employees, their professional experience and qualifications. In a previous interview (11 November, 2022), she emphasized: *"Expatriates often think that Uzbek people are not educated enough or qualified enough and that there are not many professionals here, which is not true."* Towards the end of the interview, she noted that Uzbekistan has a lot of family businesses and family values are highly appreciated in both the private and business spheres, which is reflected in the way that people address each other (22 November, 2022). She described that many employees view their boss like a father and consider this person to be high ranked, and that this is widely accepted in Uzbekistan business. This is evidenced by the fact that even in a business meeting, subordinates often refer to their Uzbek boss as *"aka"* (uncle), to show them the required respect, while women are sometimes referred to as *"opa"* (aunt).

In-country leadership bestseller

Leadership books in Uzbekistan are rare. According to the CCBS Survey respondents, the majority of them are plagiarised, and thus they prefer to read English language management books (CCBS Survey, 2022). One of the few books written by a local author is the recent publication *Bu kitob siz uchun emas, balki bo'lajak liderlar uchun* (*This book is not for you, bur for future leaders only)* by Hasan Mamasaidov (Asaxiy, 2022), who is an entrepreneur and co-founder of several businesses as well as being a media celebrity.

Local leadership book	
Title	*Bu kitob siz uchun emas*
Subtitle	*Balki bo'lajak liderlar uchun*
Author	Hasan Mamasaidov
Publisher	MFaktor
Year	2022
ISBN	978-9943-6562-4-6

The insights in this book are based on the author's own knowledge and experiences of setting up projects and companies in Uzbekistan. Mamasaidov's focus is on how to succeed, as in his opinion, every person feels the need for success, to live well, achieve their goals and find their place in life. He endorses this perspective through recourse to quotes like, *"Life is a great teacher but his lessons are very expensive"* and *"There are many critics and advisors in the world, but those who really work are few and far between unfortunately"* (MFaktor, 2022). By sharing his thoughts and considerations the author hopes to inspire future business leaders in Uzbekistan to be succesful.

Uzbekistan leadership YouTube review

In a YouTube video of a forum, co-organised by the Central Asia-Caucasus Institute, about the rising private sector in Uzbekistan, young entrepreneurs speak about the challenges and changes Uzbekistan is currently undergoing (Central Asia-Caucasus Institute, 2021). They place considerable emphasis upon the heavy domination of the state and how that has changed since 2016 when president Shavkat Mirziyoyev came to power following the death of the former leader, Islam Karimov. Whereas in previous times nepotism and bribery were more commonplace, the government is now more supportive which means that there is both a more attractive business investment climate and it is easier to set up a private business. Competitiveness, agility, and flexibility are cited in the video as important values in the business sector as well as living up to one's promises. Under these young entrepreneurs, corruption is thus heavily rejected. Zuhursho Rahmatulloev, CEO of Alif Tech, states: *"I do not deal with anyone when there is an element of corruption, bribery or anything else [...] I'm running a very transparent business model in this country and it's working out well alright"* (Central Asia-Caucasus Institute, 2021, 1:15:50). The fact that company data is now becoming increasingly digitalised also contributes to a reduction in corruption within the Uzbekistan system. In a dialogue between European Bank for Reconstruction and Development, President Sir Suma Chakrabarti, and Europe-Uzbekistan Association Secretary-General, Oybek Shaykhov , Chakrabarti underscores the fact that there must be greater support for female entrepreneurs *"because they are often locked out of access to finance"* (Europe-Uzbekistan Association, 2020, 22:15). On top of that, the importance of greater diversification, with respect to people with disabilities, is noted: companies should *"bring in more workers [with disabilities] into the labour force"* (Europe-Uzbekistan Association, 2020, 23:11). This indicates that leaders should open themselves up to diversity and inclusion within their organisations. Finally, in a video session organised by the British Council for young entrepreneurs, Dinara Dultaeva, founder of publishing company Dinara & Co, shares her thoughts about how leadership in Uzbekistan is ultimately about taking responsibility for establishing a healthy and productive environment and providing the conditions necessary for inspiring people, because then *"they will follow you and do it, not because they are your employee, but because they really believe and they really want to be part of the history which you are creating together"* (British Council, 2020, 44.37). In the conclusion of the video, the speaker expresses that a shared vision, integrity, and passion are important values for Uzbek leaders to possess if they are to get everybody in the organisation onboard with their goals and objectives.

Understanding hierarchy in Uzbekistan

One can discern a certain dualism of values within Uzbekistan's hierarchical structures. On the one hand, the influence of Islamic culture and its traditions are of great importance, insofar as they underpin the conservatism and collectivism observed within the country. On the other hand, influences from the former Soviet regime can still be espied in various respects. Most notably, this influence is felt in the predominance of secular values (Bayzakov, 2011). This dualism of values is also reflected in how hierarchy functions within organisations in Uzbekistan. High power distance is both common and accepted by leaders as well as their subordinates (Aminova & Jegers, 2014). An Uzbek CEO will generally not socialise with their subordinates, while those in the upper echelons of the corporate hierarchy will mostly group together with people who are on the same level as themselves. One consequence of this rigid hierarchical system is that subordinates in Uzbek organisations simply do not have the option to say no to someone with a higher status than themselves within the organisation (Aminova & Jegers, 2014). In accordance with this hierarchical system, an assertive and authoritarian management style appears to be the prevailing method through which managers exercise influence over their staff. This is endorsed by one of our CCBS Survey respondents (2022), who noted that authoritarian executive level managers *"aren't leaders, but bosses"* and *"[that] leaders are often result oriented, and feared and respected for their function, instead of their expertise"*. Notwithstanding this, there has been somewhat of a shift in the prevailing management style in recent years, as a new generation of leaders have come to the fore. The majority of the population in the country is aged between 30 and 45. They are ambitious, well-qualified and schooled in Western thought and leadership styles and practices, as a result of having often studied abroad. This younger generation of leaders are less business and profit-oriented and more focused on adopting people-centred leadership: What do subordinates need to perform at their best in a company? (Novojenina, 22 November 2022). Hierarchy is less of an issue for these 'new leaders,' a fact which was reflected in the outcomes of the CCBS Survey (2022), insofar as around half of the respondents reported that a manager should actively spend time on maintaining the personal well-being of their team members. Moreover, almost one-third of the professionals agreed that they do not prefer to retain personal distance from their employees in order to maintain the right level of respect (CCBS Survey, 2022). This illustrates that while traditions still carry notable weight within Uzbek organisations, as new generations come to the fore and take up ever-more leadership positions within companies, the weight accorded to these traditions is being continually re-evaluated.

How Uzbekistan achieves leadership empathy

In modern day Uzbekistan, "*Hurmat*" (Respect) and "*Empatiya*" (Empathy) are two very important factors in the workplace (CCBS Survey, 2022). Interestingly, these two values happen to be closely linked to one another, insofar as an employee that feels respected and appreciated by their manager will, on average, perform better than a colleague that does not feel this (Finney, 2008), and, in turn, display greater empathy to their superior. As aforementioned, historically Uzbek leaders have adopted an authoritarian approach. With regards to developing an empathic understanding with their employees, then, these leaders must be careful that they do not only hold authority because of their job title and function, but rather because of their experience and expertise. As one of our survey respondents noted: "*The leader is often feared and respected because of their leadership, not because of their expertise*" (CCBS Survey, 2022). A leader that relies solely on formal authority to get things done will not be able to influence their subordinates by displaying the positive leadership qualities that are required in Uzbekistan, such as organisational experience, market expertise and being a respectable age (CCBS Survey, 2022), but rather ordering them, which in turn will lead them to lose the respect of their staff. The consequence of this is that employees will feel alienated, which, in turn, will them to feel less happy and involved and therefore less empathetic towards their manager (Brent & Dent, 2010). In order to achieve empathic understanding with one's employees and create a positive working environment and manage productive employees, managers in Uzbekistan must be "*encouraging*" towards their employees, according to one of our survey respondents, Asif Darr, a CEO of an organisation in Uzbekistan (CCBS Survey, 2022). One of the main ways to do this is by taking into account that every employee is different, and thus should be managed differently. This was corroborated by Bakhshillo Khodjaev, Vice Rector at Tashkent State University of Law, who stated: "*Leaders should identify the proper ability and skills of each of their employees, in order to use their capacities in the right and efficient way.*

Choosing the right motivation for each individual is also vital," (CCBS Survey, 2022). In Uzbekistan, Bayzakov (2011) emphasises that leaders will be more effective if they delegate responsibility and provide more independence to their capable subordinates. In this respect, it is important to take into account that Uzbekistan is a high context culture, which is to say that it prioritises in-person contact and strong verbal communication. Consequently, in many instances the way in which leaders deliver the message to employees is even more significant than the words themselves (Bayzakov, 2011). One way in which this high context culture manifests in organisations is that it is important for leaders to properly extend greetings to employees. The idea behind this is that everybody deserves to be welcomed. When greeting someone, it is also considered polite for leaders to inquire about their employees' family and health. Indeed, failure to do so could be interpreted as being rude or insulting to the subordinate (Bayzakov, 2011). Similarly, according to our interviewee, Oksana Novojenina the most effective way for leaders to build trust and respect with their employees is to be open, empathetic towards them and have mutual communication and feedback on a regular basis within teams. More specifically, *"Setting clear goals and explain expectations and providing a safe environment is important."* (Novojenina, 22 November 2022). The final example of how one can discern empathic understanding amongst Uzbek leaders is that, in comparison to other cultures, Uzbek leaders tend to use the word "we" much more often than "I" (Bayzakov, 2011). This is emblematic of the aforementioned shift in leadership style, whereby younger leaders are becoming more people-centred and increasingly empathetic towards their employees (CCBS Survey, 2022). Consequently, leaders in Uzbekistan can achieve greater empathic understanding with their employees by knowing and comprehending these values and practices.

Bibliography

Bibliography

Acerca de. (2022, June 7). BBVA Aprendemos Juntos 2030. https://aprendemosjuntos.bbva.com/acerca-de/

Albiez-Wieck, S., Lira, C. L. M., & Barragán, F. A. (2020). *El que no tiene de inga, tiene de mandinga: honor y mestizaje en los mundos americanos* (1st ed.). Iberoamericana Editorial Vervuert, S.L.

Alt, M. A. (2018). Hofstede's cultural dimensions for Romania and Hungary. https://www.researchgate.net/publication/326004980_Are_bank_advertisement_appeals_adapted_to_local_culture_-_Lessons_from_multinational_banks_present_in_Romania_and_Hungary

Aminova, M., & Jegers, M. (2014). Are Hofstede's national cultures homogeneous?: the case of Uzbekistan. In J. Ahrends & H.W. Hoen (ed.), *Economic development in Central Asia: institutional underpinnings of factor markets* (pp. 85-98). PL Academic Research.

Andrade, C., Rebolledo, N., Tavares, F., Pérez, R., & Baz, M. (2016). Concrete durability of the new Panamá Canal: Background and aspects of testing. In M. G. Alexander (Ed.), *Marine Concrete Structures* (pp. 429–458). Woodhead Publishing.

Aprendemos Juntos 2030. (2020, October 6). Aprendizajes de vida: valores, éxito y liderazgo. Carlos Torres Vila, presidente de BBVA [Video]. YouTube. https://www.youtube.com/watch?v=GidR3MEYIKA

Ardichvili, A. (2001). *Leadership styles and work-related values of managers and employees of manufacturing enterprises in post-communist countries.* https://doi.org/10.1002/hrdq.1003.

Ardichvili, A., & Dirani, M. K. (2017, July). *Leadership Development in Emerging Market Economies.* Palgrave Macmillan.

Ardichvili, A., & Kuchinke, K. P. (2002). Leadership styles and cultural values among managers and subordinates: A comparative study of four countries in the former Soviet Union, Germany, and the US. *Human Resource Development International, 5*(1), 99–118.

Arnulf, J. K. (2012, September 4). *Leadership in China - Professor Jan Ketil Arnulf.* Youku. https://v.youku.com/v_show/id_XNTg2MDUyMTA0.html

Asaxiy (2022). *Hasan Mamasaidov: Bu kitob siz uchun emas**. https://asaxiy.uz/product/hasan-mamasaidov-bu-kitob-siz-uchun-emas?language=uz

Back, M. (2012). Developing a Guide for Internship in Spain. Case: Spain Internship SC (Master's Dissertation). Retrieved December 1st, https://www.theseus.fi/ Thesis_Mia_Back.pdf?sequence=1&isAllowed=y

Balaban, M. (n.d.). Facebook. Www.facebook.com. Retrieved 2022, from https://www.facebook.com/mmirelamihaela

Balderas, A (2022). Personal Interview, October 13th.

Barros, R. V. [Happyforce Way]. (2022). *Liderzago humanista: aprendieno a liderar desde el ser* [Video].

Batouan, J.A. (7 November, 2022). Personal Interview.

Bayzakov, M. (2011). Gaining perspective on Uzbekistan value orientations: implications for expatriate managers. *Allied Academies International Conference Academy for Studies in International Business Proceedings, 11*(2), 1-6. http://www.proquest.com/scholarly-journals/gaining-perspective-on-uzbekistan-value/docview/912467847/se-2

Becker, T. H. (2004). *Doing Business in the New Latin America: A Guide to Cultures, Practices, and Opportunities.* Praeger.

Belize - Leadership (2022). Nations Encyclopaedia https://www.nationsencyclopedia.com/World-Leaders-2003/Belize-LEADERSHIP.html#ixzz7hgGiDCT1

Belize - share of economic sectors in gross domestic product 2018. (n.d.). Statista. https://www.statista.com/statistics/727205/share-of-economic-sectors-in-the-gdp-in-belize/

Bendong, L. (2022, November 23). *Teacher Lin Bendong: Why is leadership style important? What is effective management? How to build leadership?* [Video]. Bilibili. https://www.bilibili.com/video/BV1QY411o7bc/?spm_id_from=333.337.search-card.all.click

Benítez, L. (2014). Economic Impact of The Panamá Canal versus The Panamá Canal Railroad Company on the Liner Shipping Industry [MSc thesis]. Erasmus University Rotterdam.

Berendt, J., Panas, M., & Lorenc, V. (2018). Przywództwo oparte na empatii w systemowych zmianach w organizacji. *Coaching Review, 1*(10), 73-99.

Bhan, Z. (2022a, November 4). 28 young leaders graduate from Leadership Fiji. https://www.fijivillage.com/news/28-young-leaders-graduate-from-Leadership-Fiji-fr458x/

Biaka, F. H. (2020). Leadership Styles and Employee Performance in Cameroon: The Case of St. Veronica Medical Centre. *Open Journal of Leadership, 09*(4), 179–197. https://doi.org/10.4236/ojl.2020.94011

Bieberach Vanegas, A. M. (2004). Diferenciar los estilos de liderazgo en los equipos de trabajos en relación a los grupos de trabajos en una empresa de servicio al cliente en panamá. *Universidad de Panamá vicerrectoria de investigación y postgrado.*

Bloomberg Quicktake: Now. (2021, August 27). *Young Female Leader Breaks Stereotypes in Thailand's Auto Industry* [Video]. YouTube. https://www.youtube.com/watch?v=dxoegibit8g

Boia, L. (2001). Romania Borderland of Europe (J. C. Brown, Trans.). Reaktion Books. https://books.google.nl/books?hl=nl&lr=&id=zHTN-TQkd3cC&oi=fnd&pg=PA7& =false

Bordas, J. (2013). *The Power of Latino Leadership: Culture, Inclusion, and Contribution.* Macmillan Publishers.

Boscardi, A. (2022). Microsoft Teams interview. 10 November.

Bosma, N., Hill, S., Ionescu-Somers, A., Kelley, D., Guerrero, M., & Schott, T. (2021). *The Global Entrepreneurship Monitor (GEM) and its impact on entrepreneurship research 2020/2021 Report.* Global Entrepreneurship Research Association. https://www.gemconsortium.org/download@file

Botero, I. C., & Van Dyne, L. (2009). Employee Voice Behavior Interactive Effects of LMX and Power Distance in the United States and Colombia. *Management Communication Quarterly, 23*(1), 84–104. https://doi.org/10.1177/0893318909335415

Boubakary. (2015). The influence of the personal values of the leader on the growth of SMEs in Cameroon. *International Strategic Management Review*, 3(1–2), 15–23. https://doi.org/10.1016/j.ism.2015.09.002

Bourdieu P., (1998) *La domination masculine*, Paris, Seuil, coll. Liber, p.134

Brent, M. & Dent, F. (2012). *The Leader's Guide to Influence: How to Use Soft Skills to Get Hard Results.* Pearson UK.

Bretcha, A. (2021, June 28). Los orígenes del cooperativismo en Euskadi y Nafarroa, una historia de éxito. Deia. September 23, 2022, https://www.deia.eus/semana/2021/06/28/origenes-cooperativismo-euskadi-nafarroa-historia-1952143.html#:%7E:text=Fue%20a%20finales% 20del% 20siglo, cooperative% 20de% 20consumption% 20de% 20Euskadi

British Council. (2020, 21 October). #mycreativespark In Conversation with Entrepreneurs – Uzbekistan [Video.]. YouTube. https://www.youtube.com/watch?v=_DuA8ScZB-k

Brown, H. (2016). Post-Communist Poland and the European Union: Energy Policy and Relations with Russia. *The Polish Review, 61*(3), 85–98. DOI: 10.5406/polishreview.61.3.0085

Brown, J. L. (2016). Highways to Empire: The Inca Road System. *Civil Engineering*, 86(1), 08857024.

Brown, O., Paz-Aparicio, C., & Revilla, A. J. (2019). Leader's communication style, LMX and organizational commitment. *Leadership & Organization Development Journal,* 40(2), 230–258. https://doi.org/10.1108/lodj-03-2018-0129

Budrina, I. (2011, October 11). *Management culture in Romania: what does the boss say?* Romania Insider. https://www.romania-insider.com/management-culture-in-romania-what-does-the-boss-say

Building Literacy Leadership in Belize. (n.d.). Www.youtube.com. Retrieved October 28, 2022, from https://www.youtube.com/watch?v=7kx0xVgoujs

Busi, V. P. (1988). (2014). Multiculturalism in Kazakhstan: Evolution of a Multi-ethnic Society and the Progress of an Effective Intercultural Communication. http://dspace.unive.it/handle/10579/4142

Cameroon Professional Society. (2013, February 19). *CPS Congress 2012 -- Yves Bollanga - Leadership, From a Practical Perspective* [Video]. YouTube. https://www.youtube.com/watch?v=tWHP-RjplTM

Cameroon Professional Society. (2014, August 11). *Leadership Keynote by Joel Nana Kontchou* [Video]. YouTube. https://www.youtube.com/watch?v=FJiQSU1mzBU

Cardenas, M. C., Eagly, A., Salgado, E., Goode, W., Heller, L. I., Jauregui, K., Galarza Quirós, N., Gormaz, N., Bunse, S., Godoy, M.J., Rocha Sánchez, T.E., Navarro, M., Sosa, F., Aguilera, Y., Schulmeyer, M., Tanure, B., Naranjo, M., Soto, B.H., Darre, S. and Tungui, R. C. (2014) Latin American female business executives: an interesting surprise. Gender in Management: An International Journal 29(1), 11.

Cardoso, F. H., & Faletto, E. (1979). *Dependency and development in Latin America (Dependencia y desarrollo en América Latina, engl.).* Univ. Of California Pr.

Castaño, N., Sully de Luque, M. F., Wernsing, T., Ogliastri, E., Shemueli, R. G., Fuchs, R. M., & Robles-Flores, J. A. (2015). El Jefe: Differences in expected leadership behaviors across Latin American countries. *Journal of World Business, 50*(3), 584–597. https://doi.org/10.1016/j.jwb.2014.12.002

Castell, D. F. (2022). *TRASCIENDE: Principios de vida y liderazgo que impactan (Spanish Edition).*

Catana, D., Catana, A. G., Neal, M., & Finley, J. L. (2006). *Leadership authority and CEO motivations in Romania: Max Weber revisited.*

Cavia, B. (2005). Hacia una nueva cultura de la identidad y la política: Tendencias en la juventud vasca (Vol. 20). Gobierno Vasco, Departamento de Cultura, Viceconsejería de Cultura, Juventud y Deportes, Dirección de Juventud y Acción Comunitaria. Retrieved November 2022, https://www.euskadi.eus/gobierno-vasco

CCBS (2018). The Global Leadership Lookout. Comparative studies on leadership practices in eighteen countries. Retrieved November 2022.

CCBS Survey. (2017). Global Leadership Survey. In Qualtrics online: Amsterdam University of Applied Sciences.

CCBS Survey. (2019). Worldwide Leadership Survey. In Survey online: Amsterdam University of Applied Sciences.

CCBS Survey. (2022). Worldwide Leadership Survey. In Survey online: Amsterdam University of Applied Sciences.

Cei care schimbă jocul de Andreea Roşca şi Mona Dîrțu | Editura Publica. (n.d.). Publica.ro. Retrieved November 10, 2022, from https://www.publica.ro/mona-dirtu-andreea-rosca-cei-care-schimba-jocul.html

Central Asia-Caucasus Institute. (2021, 21 May). *CAMCA Forum Event: Uzbekistan's Emerging Private Business Development ft. Zafar Khashimov* [Video]. YouTube. https://www.youtube.com/watch?v=Nx9oHJIlqqc

Chaiprasit, W., & Rinthaisong, I. (2022). Assessing the dimension and quality of the compassionate leadership measurement model. Cogent Business &Amp; Management, 9(1). https://doi.org/10.1080/23311975.2022.2127190

Channel 5 Belize. (2022, 26 oktober). Global Leadership Summit. Www.YouTube.com. Retrieved October 28, https://www.youtube.com/watch?v=OZBM1dsYpwE

Chen, X. P., Eberly, M. B., Chiang, T. J., Farh, J. L., & Cheng, B. S. (2011). Affective Trust in Chinese Leaders. *Journal of Management, 40*(3), 796–819. https://doi.org/10.1177/0149206311410604

Cheng, B. S., Chou, L. F., Wu, T. Y., Huang, M. P., & Farh, J. L. (2004). Paternalistic leadership and subordinate responses: Establishing a leadership model in Chinese organizations. *Asian Journal of Social Psychology, 7*(1), 89–117. https://doi.org/10.1111/j.1467-839x.2004.00137.x

Cheville, L. R., Cheville, R. A. (1981). Festivals & Dances of Panamá. *Latin American Review* 2(1), p. 155-157.

Chhokar, J. S, Brodbeck, F. C., & House, R. J. (Eds.). (2008). Culture and Leadership Across the World: The GLOBE Book of In-Depth Studies of 25 Societies. Taylor & Francis Group

Chhokar, J. S., Brodbeck, F. C., & House, R. J. (2007). *Culture and Leadership Across the World.* Psychology Press. https://doi.org/10.4324/9780203936665

CNBC International TV. (2022, March 15). *Thai business leaders on balancing sustainability and commercial viability* [Video]. YouTube. https://www.youtube.com/watch?v=R2t8H_3LnKY

Cole, T.B. (2014). Crimson Autumn: Ural Tansykbaev. *JAMA: the Journal of the American Medical Association, 312*(15), 1496–1497. https://doi.org/10.1001/jama.2013.279783

Coleman, D. Y. (2013). *People. In Cameroon Country Review* (pp. 113–116).

Cooper, R. (2019). *CultureShock! Thailand: A survival guide to customs and etiquette*. Marshall Cavendish International Asia Pte Ltd.

Cordoba, G. F. (2022). The impact of the Panamá canal transfer on the Panamánian economy. *Economics Letters* 211. https://doi.org/10.1016/j.econlet.2021.110208

Cordoneanu, I. (2012). Cosmic Christianity in Mircea Eliade's Hermeneutics on "Mioriţa": The Possibility of a Cognitive Perspective on the "Sacred" in the Traditional Romanian Culture. *Procedia - Social and Behavioral Sciences, 63*(63), 129–135. ScienceDirect. https://doi.org/10.1016/j.sbspro.2012.10.020

Coventry, P. (2009). Australian National University: *State, society, and governance in Melanesia.* https://dpa.bellschool.anu.edu.au/sites/default/files/publications/attachments/2015-12/09_03_coventry_0.pdf

Cremer, D., & Tao, T. (2019, June 25). *Huawei's recipe for success: Empathic leadership*. Ifeng. https://ishare.ifeng.com/c/s/7nn6W8prGm1

D'Alessio, Fernando A. (2006). *The influence of personality, critical thinking, and emotional intelligence attributes in Peruvian managers' leadership*. [Thesis, University of Phoenix]. https://www.proquest.com/openview/fefc689c929fd72b593477d797f2be07/

Danish Kazakh Society. (2019). Introduction to Kazakhstan. Retrieved from http://kazakh.dk/eksempel3/ on 25 March 2019.

Dave Lavaki First Fighter. (2017, October 11). Leadership Fiji - The 15-year Journey [Video]. YouTube. https://www.youtube.com/watch?v=jmuQhto2trs

Daye, R. (2009). Poverty, Race Relations, and the Practices of International Business: A Study of Fiji. *Journal of Business Ethics*, 89(Suppl 2), 115–127. https://doi.org/10.1007/s10551-010-0370-z

De Jong, K. (2018, April 26). Work Culture in Spain. CareerProfessor.works. October 15, 2022, https://careerprofessor.works/work-culture-spain/

De La Cancela, V. (1986). A critical analysis of Puerto Rican Machismo: Implications for clinical practice. *Psychotherapy: theory, Research, Practice, Training*, 23 (2), 291.

Dearie, Linhart, C., Rafai, E., Nand, D., Morrell, S., & Taylor, R. (2021). Trends in mortality and life expectancy in Fiji over 20 years. BMC Public Health, 21(1), 1–1185. https://doi.org/10.1186/s12889-021-11186-w

Djamen, R., Georges, L., & Pernin, J. L. (2020, December 21). Understanding the Cultural Values at the Individual Level in Central Africa: A Test of the CVSCALE in Cameroon. *International Journal of Marketing and Social Policy, 2*(1), 28–41. https://doi.org/10.17501/23621044.2019.2105

Doga. (2019). *Vista de Consumo de café en el Paisaje Cultural Cafetero de Colombia (PCCC): el "mal consumidor" y el auge de los cafés especiales*. 131.90.33. https://201.131.90.33/index.php/historia/article/view/20931/16397

Donnelly, D., PhD. (2022, September 20). Thailand Business Culture: What You Need to Know. Horizons. 16 October 2022, from https://nhglobalpartners.com/thailand-business-culture/

Douglas, B. (1979). Rank, Power, Authority: A Reassessment of Traditional Leadership in South Pacific Societies. *Journal of Pacific History*. 14. 2-27. 10.1080/00223347908572362.\

Doyiso, D. W. (2022). Endurence Midinette Koumassol Dissake, Language and legal proceedings: Analyzing courtroom discourse in Cameroon. *Linguistique Et Langues Africaines*, 8(1). https://doi.org/10.4000/lla.1040

Drzewiecki, S., & Prokopowicz, P. (2022). Lider wystarczająco dobry. 12 lekcji autentycznego przywództwa na vasoczasy niepewności. Onepress.

Elvira, M. M., & Davila, A. (2005). Special research issue on human resource management in Latin America. *The International Journal of Human Resource Management*, 16(12), 2164–2172. https://doi.org/10.1080/09585190500358539

Elvira, M. M., & Davila, A. (Eds.). (2005). *Humanistic leadership: Lessons from Latin America, Journal of World Business.*

Eng, E. (2018). Global Leadership Reflection of Belize: Ya Da Fu We (Belizean Independence). International Center for Global Leadership. http://www.icglconferences.com/articles/global-leadership-reflection-belize-ya-da-fu-belizean-independence/Godfrey Mwakikagile. (2014). British Honduras to Belize : transformation of a nation. New Africa Press.

EPA - Encuesta de Población Activa de las Comunidades Autónomas 2022. (n.d.). Datosmacro.com. September 23, 2022, https://datosmacro.expansion.com/paro-epa/espana-comunidades-autonomas

ESAN. (2022). Liderazgo y cambio organizacional [Video]. Vimeo. *Liderazgo y cambio organizacional*

Escola Mobile. (2022, May 17). Turkusowe zarządzanie. Czy to już? [Video]. YouTube. https://www.youtube.com/watch?v=rMJRy0IDdPk&t=91s

Espacio360TV. (2013). *Baltazar Caravedo: 'El líder es un orientador, no el que manda'* [Video]. YouTube.

Eti-Tofinga, B., Douglas, H. and Singh, G. (2017), "*Influence of evolving culture on leadership: a study of Fijian cooperatives*", European Business Review, Vol. 29 No. 5, pp. 534-550. https://www.researchgate.net/publication/318127690_Influence_of_evolving_culture_on_leadership_a_study_of_Fijian_cooperatives

Europe-Uzbekistan Association (2020, March 27). Uzbek Review. *The Dialogue with EBRD President - Sir Suma Chakrabarti* [Video]. YouTube. https://www.youtube.com/watch?v=alq7R54ks20

Eyong, J. E. (2016, August 25). Indigenous African Leadership: Key differences from Anglo-centric thinking and writings. *Leadership, 13*(2), 133–153. https://doi.org/10.1177/1742715016663050

Eyong, J. E. (2019, April 3). Leadership for high performance in local councils in Cameroon and Nigeria: Examining deviant and concordant practices to the philosophy of Ubuntu. *Africa Journal of Management, 5*(2), 138–161. https://doi.org/10.1080/23322373.2019.1631030

Fang, R. (2020, March 27). Management lessons from Chinese business and philosophy [Video]. Bilibili. https://www.bilibili.com/video/BV1Q7411C7bo/

Fang, T. (2014). Understanding Chinese Culture and Communication: The Yin Yang Approach. *Global Leadership Practices*, 171–187. https://doi.org/10.1007/978-1-137-35001-5_10

Farrelly, T., A. & Nabobo Baba, U. (2014). Talanoa as empathic apprenticeship. *https://www.researchgate.net/publication/270912502_Talanoa_as_empathic_apprenticeship*

Fernández, N. (2015, September 14). ¿Cómo se ven los vascos a sí mismos? ¿Cómo les ven? El Correo. October 12, 2022, https://www.elcorreo.com/bizkaia/sociedad/201509/14/como-vascos-mismos-como-20150914193039.html

Ferreira, L. (2022). Google Meet interview. 6 October

Fiji Bureau of Statistics. (2022, March 31). Fiji's Gross Domestic Product (GDP) 2020. https://www.statsfiji.gov.fj/latest-releases/

Finn, V. (2019). Democracy in Croatia: From stagnant 1990s to rapid change 2000 2011. *International Political Science Review, 42*(2), 197–212.

Finney, M. (2008). *The Truth about Getting the Best from People*. FT Press.

Firth, S. (n.d.). Globalisation and Governance in the Pacific Islands. https://press.anu.edu.au/publications/series/state-society-and-governance-melanesia/globalisation-and-governance-pacific https://press-files.anu.edu.au/downloads/press/p55871/html/frames.php

Fofack, É. W., Fils, F. E., & Elong, F. X. (2019). *Cameroun, les dynamiques de construction du leadership en Afrique centrale: Regards croisés.* Editions L'Harmattan.

Fong, S. (2022). Any of us that have platforms, we need to open them to other leaders, global leaders, female leaders, young women coming up behind us. This is not a one generation, and it is going to solve this problem. It is going to take all of us to move forward in the world. https://www.linkedin.com/in/sharyne-fong-maicd-96857835/recent-activity/shares/

Forgha, N. G., & Mbella, M. E. (2016, February). The Implication of Female Labour Force Participation on Economic Growth in Cameroon. *European Centre for Research Training and Development UK*, *4*, 34–47. https://www.eajournals.org/journals/international-journal-of-development-and-economic-sustainability-ijdes/vol-4-issue-1-february-2016/the-implication-of-female-labour-force-participation-on-economic-growth-in-cameroon/

Franičević, V. (2008, February). Decent Work Country Report Croatia. University of Zagreb, Faculty of Economics.

Fu, R., & Guo, Q.-Y. (2018). The structure and characteristics of contemporary Chinese values: Based on a Survey of 2753 individuals. *Journal of Hunan University (social Science)*, 1, 142–148. In chinese

Fuerst-Bjeliš, B., & Glamuzina, N. (2021). *The Historical Geography of Croatia:Territorial Change and Cultural Landscapes (Historical Geography and Geosciences)* (1st ed. 2021). Springer.

Gao, J., Arnulf, J. K. & Henning, K. (2011). Western leadership development and Chinese managers: Exploring the need for contextualization. *Scandinavian Journal of Management*, *27*(1), 55–65. https://doi.org/10.1016/j.scaman.2010.11.007

Garcés, E. (2008). Colombian Women: The Struggle Out of Silence. In *Google Books*. Lexington Books. https://books.google.nl/books?hl=en&lr=&id=vSB1aTDOk2gC&oi=fnd&pg=PR1&dq=colombia+patriarchy&ots=5SF_jl36nH&sig=oY06iKuHulfDA9sF3P8Beo7CFrU#v=onepage&q=colombia%20patriarchy&f=false

Garcia Saucedo, K. (2022). Personal interview. 15 November.

Gębal, & Nawracka, M. J. (2021). From foreign language teaching methodology to comparative glottodidactics: The formation of the Polish didactics of languages and cultures in the light of the development of European didactic thought. *European Journal of Applied Linguistics*, 9(1), 89–114. DOI: 10.1515/eujal-2020-0026

Gierczak, A., & Grodecka, S. (2014). Empatia w Przywództwie: Kultura Organizacyjna Instytucji Edukacyjnej Oparta na Współodczuwaniu. *Modern Management Review*, *19*(21), 87-97. DOI: 10.7862/rz.2014.mmr.48

Giurchescu, A. (2019). Dance Aesthetics in Traditional Romanian Communities. *Yearbook for Traditional Music*, *35*(35), 163. Cambridge University Press. https://doi.org/10.2307/4149326

Globocnik Zunac, A. G. Z., Ercegovac, P. E., & Gutowski, M. G. (2022). Economic and Social Development (Book of Proceedings): 78th International

Goldberg, G. S., & Kremen, E. (1990*). The Feminization of Poverty: Only in America?* Greenwood Publishing.

Gollasch, S., Galil, B. S., & Cohen, A. N. (2006). Panamá Canal [E-book]. In Bridging Divides (1st ed., pp. 122–125). Springer Dordrecht.

Gorbaniuk, O., Jóźwik, B., & Mącik, R. (2013). Wyróżniki kultury organizacyjnej przedsiębiorstw eksportowych z województwa lubelskiego. *Przegląd Organizacji*, (5), 10-14.

Gronn, P. (1995), Greatness Re-Visited: The Current Obsession with Transformational Leadership, *Leading & Managing* 1(1): 14–27. 4 October 2022 from, Greatness re-visited: The current obsession with transformational leadership | Request PDF (researchgate.net)

Guluţă, M. C., & Rusu, C. (2019). *Leadership styles and managerial behavior in Romanian companies* (Vol. 13). https://www.infona.pl/resource/bwmeta1.element.baztech-a82c72fb-fc49-44cf-86a1-66d02f783983/content/partContents/508ab7d8-4156-38bc-9224-3f6713c20aba

Gurbanli, Z. (2020). Hofstede's Cultural Dimensions - Spain. Retrieved November 2022, https://www.researchgate.net/publication/357032937

Gutiérrez, J. C. (2022). *Memorias de un liderazgo conciliador*. Paidos Empresa Colombia.

Hamill, H. M. (1992). *Caudillos: Dictators in Spanish America (Revised)*. University of Okalahoma Press.

Hannerz, U., & Gingrich, A. (2017). Small countries: structures and sensibilities. University Of Pennsylvania Press.

Harrison, D. (2022). Working with the tourism industry: A case study from Fiji. *Social Responsibility*, 1(1-2), 249-70. https://www.researchgate.net/profile/David-Harrison-20/

Hassig, S. M., Quek, L., & Nevins, D. (2016). Religion. In Cultures of the world: Panamá (3rd ed., pp. 75–86). Cavendish Square.

Hauser, L. (2014). *workplace motivation in Romania: What are the main factors and their cultural background?* 1022. http://conferinta.management.ase.ro/archives/2014/pdf/100.pdf

Hernandez , H. G. (2022, november 3). Leadership in Colombia. (I. Ammy Driss, & T. Kloosterboer, Interviewers)

Hernández, J. A. C., & Bebbington, A. (2010). *Rural Territorial Development in the Midst of the Conflict.*

Hofstede Insights. (2017). *Peru.*

Hofstede Insights. (n.d.). *Country Comparison - Hofstede Insights*. Hofstede Insights. Retrieved October 12, 2022, from https://www.hofstede-insights.com/country-comparison/

Hofstede, G. (2001). *Culture's Consequences: Comparing Values, Behaviors, Institutions and Organizations Across Nations* (2nd ed.). Sage Publications, Inc.

Hofstede, G. (2013, August 21). Hierarchical Power Distance in Forty Countries (pp. 115-138). https://www.taylorfrancis.com/chapters/edit/10.4324/9780203370414-17/hierarchical-power-distance-forty-countries-geert-hofstede

Holmes, H., & Tangtongtavy, S. (1996). Working with the Thais: A guide to managing in Thailand. Bangkok: White Lotus.

House, R. J., Hanges, P. J., Javidan, M., Dorfman, P. W., & Gupta, V. (Eds.). (2004). Culture, leadership, and organizations: The GLOBE study of 62 societies. Sage publications.

House, R. J., Hanges, P. J., Javidan, M., Dorfman, P. W., & Gupta, V. (2004). *Culture, Leadership, and Organizations*: The GLOBE Study of 62 Societies (1st ed.). SAGE Publications, Inc.

Huang, Q., Davison, R. M., & Gu, J. (2010). The impact of trust, guanxi orientation and face on the intention of Chinese employees and managers to engage in peer-to-peer tacit and explicit knowledge sharing. *Information Systems Journal*, 21(6), 557–577. https://doi.org/10.1111/j.1365-2575.2010.00361.x

Huangfu, G., Jiang, D., & Zhang, G. (2013). From Organizational Commitment to Organizational Loyalty: The Concept and Structures of Chinese Organizational Loyalty. *Advances in Psychological Science*, 21(4), 711–720. https://doi.org/10.3724/sp.j.1042.2013.00711

Huţu, C. A. (2010). *Leading the change for quality enhancement: A Romanian cultural perspective*. Regent. https://www.regent.edu/acad/global/publications/ijls/new/vol5iss3/Hutu_4.pdf

Idiomas en el País Vasco. (n.d.). Mondragon Unibertsitatea. October 12, 2022, https://www.mondragon.edu/es/movilidad-internacional/guia-estudiante-internacional/idiomas-pais-vasco

IDWA (2014) Public Perceptions of Women in Leadership Fiji). https://iwda.org.au/assets/files/Public-Perceptions-of-Women-in-Leadership.pdf

Ilimkhanova, L., Perlenbetov, M., Tazhbayeva, S., Assylkhanova, M., Topanova, G., Sadvakassova, Z., Sveta, B., & Darkhanova, A. (2014). The Hierarchy of Value

INEI. (2021). Producto Bruto Interno por Sectores Económicos 1950 - 2021 (Valores a precios constantes de 2007) [Dataset]. *In Cuentas Nacionales Anuales* (Version 1). Instituto Nacional de Estadística e Informática.

James, T. (2006, August). Panamá Canal. In All locked up (4th ed., Vol. 17, pp. 16–21). IET.

Jansen, K. (2007) Thailand: The next NIC?, Journal of Contemporary Asia, 21:1, 13-30, https://www.tandfonline.com/doi/abs/10.1080/00472339180000031https://doi.org/10.1080/00472339180000031

José Manuel Gil. (2017, March 23). LID Editorial. https://www.lideditorial.com/autores/jose-manuel-gil

Juras, A. (2010). Traits, Skills, and Leadership Styles of Managers in Croatian Firms. *Sveuciliste u Splitu,* 15(2).

Kamp, B. (2017). Competitive strategies on behalf of international niche market leaders: evidence from the Basque Country. *Boletín de Estudios Económicos,* 72(221), 333. https://www.proquest.com/openview/698380da4b9fcdc42bc17586cdafc2fe/1?pq-origsite=gscholar&cbl=1536340

Kapusta, A., Wiluś, R. (2017). Geography of Tourism in Croatia. In: Widawski, K., Wyrzykowski, J. (eds) The Geography of Tourism of Central and Eastern European Countries. Springer, Cham. https://doi.org/10.1007/978-3-319-42205-3_4

Karibayeva, B., & Kunanbayeva, S. S. (2017). Power distance and verbal index in Kazakh business discourse. *International Journal of Speech Technology*, *20*(4), 779–785. https://doi.org/10.1007/s10772-017-9450-0

Kassymova, D., Kundakbayeva, Z., & Markus, U. (2012). Historical Dictionary of Kazakhstan. Scarecrow Press.

Ketch, A. (2021, March 6). *J'ai lu et je vous le recommande : MANAGEMENT PAR LE KONGOSSA*. Agenda Culturel Du Cameroun. https://www.agendaculturelducameroun.com/jai-lu-et-je-vous-le-recommande-management-par-le-kongossa/

King, P., & Wei, Z. (2014). Chinese and Western Leadership Models: A Literature Review. *Journal of Management Research*, 6(2), 1. https://doi.org/10.5296/jmr.v6i2.4927

Kiprop, V. (2019, 6 May). *What are the biggest industries in Uzbekistan?* WorldAtlas. https://www.worldatlas.com/articles/what-are-the-biggest-industries-in-uzbekistan.html

Klug, M. (2006). The Polish Market—Opportunities and Challenges for German Investors. *Market Entry Strategies in Eastern Europe in the Context of the European Union*, 83-102. DOI: 10.1007/978-3-8350-9334-8_5

Knecht, T. (2021). Sławomir Sowiński, Dobra nowina w czasach „dobrej zmiany". Kościół katolicki w sferze publicznej współczesnej Polski w latach 2015-2018. *Warszawskie Studia Teologiczne*, *34*(1), 232-238. DOI: 10.30439/WST.2021.1.14

Kohlhoffer-Mizser, C. (2020). Leader is the person who deals with conflict. Global answers in conflict management. *SHS Web of Conferences*, *74*, 06011. https://doi.org/10.1051/shsconf/20207406011

Kooyers, J. (2015). The United States and Spain: a comparison of cultural values and behaviors and their implications for the multicultural workplace. HonorsProjects.399

Kostić-Bobanović, M. & Bobanović, M. (2013). Research on Leadership: A Comparative Study in Croatia and Sweden. Economic Research *Ekonomska Istraživanja*, 26(sup1), 151–164.

Kowalik, A. (2021). Przegląd wartości organizacyjnych deklarowanych przez największe polskie firmy prywatne. *Kwartalnik Nauk o Przedsiębiorstwie*, *61*(4), 59-69.

Kretek, H., & Karczewski, L. (2018). *Biznes i zarządzanie a bezpieczeństwo w Polsce i na świecie.* Politechnika Opolska.

Kuepie, M., Dzossa, A., & Kelodjoue, S. (2013). Determinants of labor market gender inequalities in Cameroon, Senegal and Mali: the role of human capital and the fertility burden. *Explore LISER's Research Expertise*. October 16, 2022, from https://liser.elsevierpure.com/en/publications/determinants-of-labor-market-gender-inequalities-in-cameroon-sene-2

Kuras, A. (2022). Microsoft Team interview. 2 November.

La Croix Africa. (2020, June 10). *Données géographiques et identité religieuse au Cameroun.* September 23, 2022, from https://africa.la-croix.com/statistiques/cameroun/

Larrañaga, J. G. (2007). Prólogo a Folklore y Tradiciones, en la colección País Vasco. Ven y cuéntalo. October 12, 2022, https://core.ac.uk/download/11499492.pdf

Lasagabaster, D., & Huguet, Á. (2007). Multilingualism in European bilingual contexts. Language Use and Attitudes. Clevedon: Multilingual Matters. Retrieved November 2022, https://books.google.es/books?id=XDodTJ1B5AEC&printsec=frontcover&hl=es&source=gbs_ge_summary_r&cad=0#v=onepage&q&f=false

Leadership Fiji (n.d.). The Leadership Fiji initiative is aimed specifically at assisting our emerging leaders to cope with demands of the ever-changing world ["Info"].

Ledesma, A. (2022). Personal interview. 14 November.

Lenartowicz, T., & Johnson, J. P. (2002). Comparing managerial values in twelve Latin American countries: an exploratory study. *Management International Review*, 42(3).

Lewis, R. D. (2005). *When Cultures Collide, 3rd Edition: Leading Across Cultures (*3rd ed.). Nicholas Brealey Publishing.

Li, C. (2000). Confucianism and Feminist Concerns: Overcoming the Confucian "Gender Complex." *Journal of Chinese Philosophy*, 27(2), 187–199. https://doi.org/10.1111/0301-8121.00012

Li, C. H. V., & Sun, J. M. J. (2018). Chinese employees' leadership preferences and the relationship with power distance orientation and core self-evaluation. *Frontiers of Business Research in China, 12*(1). https://doi.org/10.1186/s11782-018-0027-9

Li, C.-L., & Carballo, N. A. (2018). When the East Meets the West: A Comparative Study of Belize's and Taiwan's Business Culture for Effective and Successful Business Communication and Opportunities in Belize. Proceedings of the 7th International Conference on Entrepreneurship and Business Management. https://doi.org/10.5220/0008489001130118

Li, H.-L. (2015). 'Ren Yi Li Zhi Xin': The modern value of Confucian moral education. *QILU Journal*, 5, 5–12. in Chinese

Li, M., Lu, Y., & Yang, F. (2018). Shaping the Religiosity of Chinese University Students: Science Education and Political Indoctrination. *Religions*, 9(10), 309. https://doi.org/10.3390/rel9100309

Li, X., Low, A., & Makhija, A. K. (2011). Career Concerns and the Busy Life of the Young CEO. *SSRN Electronic Journal*. https://doi.org/10.2139/ssrn.1761523

Littrell, R. F. (2011). Contemporary Sub-Saharan African Managerial Leadership: Some Recent Empirical Studies. *Asia Pacific Journal of Business and Management*, 2(1), 1179-626X. https://www.researchgate.net/publication/260080862_CONTEMPORARY_SUB-SAHARAN_AFRICAN_MANAGERIAL_LEADERSHIP_RESEARCH_SOME_RECENT_EMPIRICAL_STUDIES

Liu, Y.-L. (2010). Thirty years' research on 'ren yi li zhi xin.' *Henan Social Science*, 18(1), 187–190. in Chinese.

Londoño-Vega, P. (2002). *Religion, Society, and Culture in Colombia*. Clarendon Press. https://books.google.nl/books?hl=en&lr=&id=NxZREAAAQBAJ&oi=fnd&pg=PP3&dq=colombia+religion&ots=tOW8kXMML5&sig=mQZ1ul4UikiokAG4gCPsXa5B8tQ&redir_esc=y#v=onepage&q=colombia%20religion&f=false

López, A.(2022). Personal communication.

López, G. (2007, September). Tres generaciones de mejures con espíritu patriótico y universal. Tareas, 121-130.

López-Rodríguez, J., Faíña, A., & Manso, G. (2010). Sistemas de innovación regionales: el caso del País Vasco. Revista Galega de Economía, 19, 1-17.

Lupu, Dr. Prof. C. (2022, November 2). *Interview Prof. Dr. Lupu on How Romanians characterize leaders* (J. Imansoeradi & E. Beukers, Interviewers) [Personal communication].

Luthans, F., & Doh, J. P. (2012). International Management: Culture, Strategy, and Behavior. In *Google Books*. McGraw-Hill.

Madeleine Zúñiga, C. (2008). *La educación intercultural bilingüe: El caso peruano* (1a ed.). Buenos Aires: Fund. Laboratorio de Políticas Públicas.

Madinabeitia, M. (2021, November 22). Menos jefes, màs lìderes. El Diario Vasco, 22. October 2022, https://lectura.kioskoymas.com/el-diario-vasco/20211122

Mahadevan, R. (2009). The viability of Fiji's sugar industry. *Journal of Economic Studies*, 36(4), 309–325.

Mangubhai, F., & Mugler, F. (2003). The Language Situation in Fiji. *Current Issues in Language Planning*, 4(3-4), 367–459.

Manuel José Gil Vegas. (2021). Déjame trabajar por tus sueños. Retrived November 2022, https://books.google.nl/books/about/D%C3%A9jame_trabajar_por_tus_sue%C3%B1os.html?id=Dd9WEAAAQBAJ&redir_esc=y

Marriaga, M. M. M. (2016). *Power distance index: a problem in Colombia*. https://doi.org/10.13140/RG.2.1.1238.7600

Martín Molina Abogados y Economistas. (2018, February 24). Una lección de liderazgo empresarial, por Abel Valverde, Jefe de Sala del Restaurante Sant Celoni [Video]. YouTube. https://www.youtube.com/watch?v=djOKhNpCtdU

Martìnez De Luna, I. (2007). Euskal nortasuna eta kultura XXI. mendearen hasieran. Retrieved November 2022, https://www.eusko-ikaskuntza.eus/es/publicaciones/euskal-nortasuna-eta-kultura-xxi-mendearen-hasieran/art-14927/

Mary, M. E. M. T., & Ozturen, A. (2019). Sustainable Ethical Leadership and Employee Outcomes in the Hotel Industry in Cameroon. *Sustainability*, 11(8), 2245. https://doi.org/10.3390/su11082245

Mass Spectacle and Styles of Governmentality in Kazakhstan and Uzbekistan. (n.d.).

Máster de Emprendedores. (2019, October 17). Cómo ser un buen líder gestionando equipos en la empresa [Video]. YouTube. https://www.youtube.com/watch?v=SJNwgNPxnvE

Maximov, M. (2015). *2 Keys to Leadership - Maxim Maximov - Founder CNL TV* [Video]. YouTube. *https://www.youtube.com/watchv=JP7Zhf51qAY&list=LL&index=5&t=19s*

Maxwell Leadership Romania - YouTube. (2011, March). Www.youtube.com. https://www.youtube.com/@MaxwellLeadershipRomania

Maxwell, J. (2022). *Dezvoltarea leadership-ului şi a carierei | Maxwell Leadership*. Www.maxwellleadership.ro. https://www.maxwellleadership.ro

Mbah, F. J. A. (2018). Leadership Style and Performance of Small and Medium Size Enterprises in Cameroon. University of Younde II, Cameroon. https://www.academia.edu/36619070/Tittle_of_article_LEADERSHIP_STYLE_AND_PERFORMANCE_OF_SMALL_AND_MEDIUM_SIZE_ENTERPRISES_IN_CAMEROON

McIntosh, T. (2012). *Leadership Peruvian Style: How Peruvians Define and Practice Leadership (Illustrated)*. IUniverse.

Mekhum, W. (2020). The Influence of Personal Knowledge Management and Leadership Style on the Firms Performance: An Empirical Evidence from Thailand. *Systematic Review Pharmacy*, *11*(1), 382.

Meo-Sewabu, L. (2014). Cultural discernment as an ethics framework: An Indigenous Fijian approach. Asia Pacific Viewpoint, 55(3), 345-354.

Metz, D. (2019, September 13). Daniel Metz, CEO al NTT DATA Romania, despre dezvoltarea *propriei companii*. Daniel Metz; Daniel Metz. https://www.youtube.com/watch?v=tUy2yyuSFAQ

MFaktor. (2022, 11 November). https://t.me/s/mfaktoruz?q=Bu+kitob+siz+uchun+emas+

Miloloza, I. (2018). Analysis of the Leadership Style in Relation to the Characteristics of Croatian Enterprises. Interdisciplinary *Description of Complex Systems,* 16(2), 249–264.

Ministry of Education of People's Republic China. (n.d.). *中国语言概况 - 中华人民共和国教育部政府门户网站*. http://www.moe.gov.cn/s78/A18/s8357/moe_808/tnull_11132.html

Mittal, R., & Dorfman, P. W. (2012). Servant leadership across cultures.Journal of World Business. Retrieved November 2022, https://www.sciencedirect.com/science/article/abs/pii/S1090951612000107

Mjamo, C. W., & Achuo, E. D. (2021). Crude Oil Price and Real GDP Growth: An Application of ARDL Bounds Cointegration and Toda-Yamamoto Causality Tests. *Economics Bulletin*, 41(3), 1615–1626. https://EconPapers.repec.org/RePEc:ebl:ecbull:eb-21-00041

Mnich, J., & Walaszczyk, A. (2022). What characterises a good leader? A survey of organisational leaders in Poland. *Journal of Management and Financial Sciences*, (45), 81-91.

Moran, S. V., Abramson, N. R., & Moran, S. V. (2014). *Managing Cultural Differences*. Taylor & Francis.

Motivarea Ce pot face managerii şi cum. (2021, August 26). www.youtube.com; Radu Nechita. https://www.youtube.com/watch?v=9U5igW_Y91w

Mrówka, R. (2010). Przywództwo w organizacjach. Analiza najlepszych praktyk. Wolters Kluwer Polska.

Mukazhanova, K. (2012). A cross-cultural comparison of leadership choices: commonalities and differences among female leaders in the United States, Kazakhstan, and Sweden. 105.

Muminov, A.G., Nazarov, K., Xaynazarov, B., Polvonov, H. & Ktaybekov, S. (2020). Leading tendencies in the development of cultural and spiritual identity of the peoples of Uzbekistan. *International Journal of Psychosocial Rehabilitation, 24*(8), 5525–5538.

Mun, S. H. (2013). Printing press without copyright: a historical analysis of printing and publishing in Song, China. *Chinese Journal of Communication*, 6(1), https://doi.org/10.1080/17544750.2013.753497

Muratbekova-Touron, M. (2002). Working in Kazakhstan and Russia: Perception of French managers. *International Journal of Human Resource Management*, *13*(2), 213–231. https://doi.org/10.1080/09585190110102341

N Studios Fiji Multimedia Company. (2017, February 21). *Life of a CEO Water Authority of Fiji 2016 [Video].* YouTube. https://www.youtube.com/watch?v=wpYcD_jPMjA

Naciones Unidas. (2019). *Tiempo Total De Trabajo.*

Nanda, V. P. (1992). *Ethnic conflict in Fiji and international human rights law*. Cornell Int'l LJ, 25, 565.

Nasierowski, W., & Mikula, B. (1998). Culture Dimensions of Polish Managers: Hofstede's Indices. *Organization Studies, 19*(3), 495–509. DOI:10.1177/017084069801900306

Nayacakalou, R. R. (1976). Leadership in Fiji. Oxford University Press.

Nezhina, T. G., & Ibrayeva, A. R. (2013). Explaining the Role of Culture and Traditions in Functioning of Civil Society Organizations in Kazakhstan. *VOLUNTAS: International Journal of Voluntary and Nonprofit Organizations*, *24*(2), 335–358. https://doi.org/10.1007/s11266-011-9256-7

Njimanted, G. F., & Mukete, E. M. (2016). The implication of female labour participation on economic growth in Cameroon. *International Journal of Development and Sustainability*, *4*(1), 34–47.

Norton, R. (2015). The troubled quest for national political leadership in Fiji. The Round Table: The Commonwealth Journal of International Affairs, 104(2), pp. 13-22: https://doi.org/10.1080/00358533.2015.1017258

Novojenina, O. (2022). Personal interview. 11 and 22 November.

Nurhidayat, I., Pimpunchat, B., Noeiaghdam, S., & Fernández-Gámiz, U. (2022). Comparisons of SVM Kernels for Insurance Data Clustering. Emerging Science Journal, 6(4), 866-880. Retrieved November 27th, https://www.researchgate.net/profile/Samad-Noeiaghdam-2

Obiwuru, T. C., Okwu, A. T., Akpa, V. O., & Nwankere, I. A. (2012). Effects of leadership style on organizational performance: A survey of selected small-scale enterprises in IKOSIKETU Council development area of Lagos state, Nigeria. *Australian Journal of Business and Management Research*, *1*(7), 100–111. https://doi.org/10.52283/nswrca.ajbmr.20110107a11

OEC. (n.d.). *Colombia (COL) Exports, Imports, and Trade Partners*. Oec.world. Retrieved October 12, 2022, from https://oec.world/en/profile/country/col

Office of International Religious Freedom (2021, May 7). *2020 Report on International Religious Freedom: Uzbekistan.*

Ogliastri, E. (2007). Colombia: The human relations side of enterprise. In *Culture and Leadership across the world: The GLOBE Book of in-depth Studies of 25 Societies*. Mahwah.

Ojong, N. (2018). Informal borrowing sources and uses insights from the Northwest Region, Cameroon. *Third World Quarterly*, 40(9), 1730–1749. https://doi.org/10.1080/01436597.2018.1460201

Omazić, M.A., Slišković, T., Vlahov, R.D., Jelenc, L. (2018). Management and Leadership Development Needs: *The Case of Croatia*. In: Purg, D., Braček Lalić, A., Pope, J. (eds) Business and Society. Springer.

Orientations in Kazakhstan as the Basis of National Mentality. *Mediterranean Journal of Social Sciences*. (p. 3-6 vol. 5 no. 20) https://doi.org/10.5901/mjss.2014.v5n20p2641

Pakemoov, A. (2016). *Leadership Kazakhstan - interview - Alexander Pakemonov* [Video]. YouTube. *https://www.youtube.com/watch?v=KOV0Zjypc7o&list=LL&index=4&t=217s*

Panamá . (1996). Panamá . *Business American*, 117(11), 29.

Panov, S. (2012). *Interview met Muskie Alumnus uit Kazachstan Samat Panov* [Video]. YouTube. *https://www.youtube.com/watch?v=CiaBMuLVOrU&list=LL&index=4*

Parra, J. L. S. (2022). *José Luis Suárez Parra - Cómo influir en la estrategia de una firma de abogados como un nuevo socio.* Www.youtube.com; Young Partners Retreat Latinoamérica. https://www.youtube.com/watch?v=Oqwyw7BeSR4

Pascal Coppens. (2022, May 14). *Which leadership models are coming out of China? Decoding China's leadership models in business.* YouTube. https://www.youtube.com/watch?v=Lu-IvOKeftU

Persons, L (2022). Personal interview November 22nd

Pittaway, L., Rivera, O., & Murphy, A. (2005). Social identity and leadership in the basque region: a study of leadership development programmes. Journal of Leadership & Organizational Studies, 11(3), 17-29. https://www.researchgate.net/publication/242583752_Social_Identity_and_Leadership_in_the_Basque_Region_A_Study_of_Leadership_Development_Programmes

Polski Instytut Ekonomiczny. (2020), *Polska najszybciej rosnącą gospodarką Trójmorza.* https://pie.net.pl/polska-najszybciej-rosnaca-gospodarka-trojmorza/

Pop, C. (2016). Social classes in Romania. Methodology of inequalities. P RESA U NIVERSITAR Ă C LUJEAN Ă.

Popa, S. (n.d.). *Sorin Popa.* Www.facebook.com. Retrieved 2022, from https://www.facebook.com/popasorinnicolae

Poveda, V. (2016). *Etiquette and protocol and its incidence in the organization of events in charge of the secretaries (os) of the Eugenio Espejo Educational Unit of the Babahoyo Province of Los Ríos Canton* (Bachelor's thesis, Babahoyo: UTB, 2016).

Prasartruek, P. (2003), Population projection for Thailand, 2000-2025, Institute for population and social research mahidol university, https://kb.hsri.or.th/dspace/bitstream/handle/11228/1393/hs1084.pdf?sequence=2&isAllowed=y

R. Wolfsohn. (2021). T*hree Caudillos in Bolivia, Ecuador, and Peru.* In ResearchGate (doi:10.13140/RG.2.2.22596.35202)

*R*acolţa-Paina, N. D., & Irini, R. D. (2021, August). *Generation Z in the Workplace through the Lenses of Human Resource Professionals.* ResearchGate; Quality. https://www.researchgate.net/publication/352374489_Generation_Z_in_the_Workplace_through_the_Lenses_of_Human_Resource_Professionals_-_A_Qualitative_Study

Ralston, D. A., Egri, C. P., Stewart, S., Terpstra, R. H., & Kaicheng, Y. (1999). Doing Business in the 21st Century with the New Generation of Chinese Managers: A Study of Generational Shifts in Work Values in China. *Journal of International Business Studies, 30*(2), 415–427. https://doi.org/10.1057/palgrave.jibs.8490077

Ralston, D. A., Gustafson, D. J., Terpstra, R. H., & Holt, D. H. (1995). Pre-post Tiananmen square: Changing values of Chinese managers. *Asia Pacific Journal of Management, 12*(1), 1–20. https://doi.org/10.1007/bf01733968

Ramesh, S. (2012). China's Transition to a Knowledge Economy. *Journal of the Knowledge Economy*, 4(4), 473–491. https://doi.org/10.1007/s13132-012-0092-9

Rego, M. (2022, May 23). Las empresas vascas tienen por primera vez a más mujeres al frente. El Correo. October 12, 2022, https://www.elcorreo.com/alava/araba/empresas-vascas-tienen-por-primera-vez-a-mas-mujeres-al-frente-20220523110216-nt.html?ref=https://www.google.com/

Restrepo, C. (2020, July 8). *Charlas con Propósito: Liderazgo femenino en las organizaciones.* Www.youtube.com. https://youtu.be/S-HiBsBOtUs

Rhein, D. (2013) The workplace Challenge: Cross-cultural Leadership in Thailand, Mahidol University International College, October 4 from, (PDF) Supervisors' Perception of Instructional Supervision (researchgate.net)

Rivera, L. N. G. [EscuELAE]. (2017). *Liderazgo Social Efectivo* [Video]. YouTube.

Robles, F. Wiese, N. (2014). *Business in Emerging Latin America.*

Roessingh, C. (2007). Mennonite communities in Belize. International Journal of Business and Globalisation, 1(1), 107. https://doi.org/10.1504/ijbg.2007.013722

Romanian Business Leaders Summit. (n.d.). Romanian Business Leaders Summit. Retrieved December 5, 2022, from https://www.rbls.ro/

Romero, C., Paniagua-Zambrana, N. Y., & Bussmann, R. W. (2020). *Ethnobotany of Mountain Regions – Andes – Colombia and Ecuador. In Ethnobotany of Mountain Regions* (pp. 83–104). Springer. https://doi.org/10.1007/978-3-030-28933-1_3

Romero, E. J. (2004). Latin American leadership: El Patrón & El Líder Moderno. *Cross Cultural Management: An International Journal*, 11(3), 25–37. https://doi.org/10.1108/13527600410797828

Romero, E. J. (2004). Latin American leadership: El Patrón & El Líder Moderno. *Cross Cultural Management: An International Journal*, *11*(3), 25–37. https://doi.org/10.1108/13527600410797828

Rongińska, T. (2018). Główne składowe przywództwa: przegląd koncepcji. *Psychologiczne Zeszyty Naukowe*, (1), 163-180.

Rosca, A. (2022, November 29). The Vast&The Curious. https://www.andreearosca.ro/vast-curious/

Rosca, A. (n.d.). Andreea Rosca. Retrieved December 5, 2022, from https://www.linkedin.com/in/andreearosca/recent-activity/

Rosenlee, L. H. L. (2012). Confucianism and Women: A Philosophical Interpretation. *Amsterdam University Press.*

Saiti, A. (2020). Hierarchical Organizational Structure and Leadership. Oxford Research Encyclopedia of Education.

Salmon, W., & Gómez Menjívar, J. (2018). Tropical Tongues: Language Ideologies, Endangerment, and Minority Languages in Belize. Chapel Hill, NC: Institute for the Study of the Americas. https://doi.org/10.17615/d0cm-ad77

Satrusayang, C. (2015, January 15). Addicted to superstition: Thailand's 21st century mystics, Thailand's long-standing addiction to mystics, fortune tellers and superstition is alive, well, Bangkok Post, Retrieved from http://www.bangkokpost.com/print/457038/

School of Business and Management, Steyr Campus, Überwimmer, M., Füreder, R. & Schmidthaler, M. (2021). Proceedings CCBC 2022. In Cross Cultural Business Conference (Nr. 978-3-8440-8032–2)

Scientific Conference on Economic and Social Development. Univer B sity North, Koprivnica, Croatia.

Scroope, C. (2016). *Tai culture*. Cultural Atlas. 23 September 2022, from https://culturalatlas.sbs.com.au/thai-culture/thai-culture-greetings

Selvarajah, C., Meyer, D., & Donovan, J. (2013). Cultural context and its influence on managerial leadership in Thailand. Asia Pacific Business Review, 19(3), 356–380. 23 September 2022 from, https://doi-org.rps.hva.nl/10.1080/13602381.2012.714630

Sharipova, Z. & Usmonaliyeva, M. (2021). The current use of leadership styles. *Theoretical & Applied Science, 104,* 531-536. https://doi.org/10.15863/TAS.2021.12.104.52

Sharipova, Z. (2022). MS Teams interview. 22 November.

Shollenberger, T. (2014). Characterizing Ethical Decision-Making and Its Influences-Examining Higher Education Leaders in Poland. *Ethics in Progress*, *5*(2), 129-150. DOI: 10.14746/eip.2014.2.10

Sielski, J. (2020, December). Political leaders of Poland's transformation – in generational terms. *Annales Universitatis Mariae Curie-Sklodowska sectio M Balcaniensis et Carpathiensis, 5.* 9-27. DOI:10.17951/bc.2020.5.9-27

Sierra Restrepo, A. (2013). Actitudes y hábitos de consumo de café en Colombia: Tradición y bienestar. *Alimentos Hoy, 22*(28), 71-75. https://alimentoshoy.acta.org.co/index.php/hoy/article/view/157/151

Sigismond, H., & Fotso, R. S. (2021). Religion et comportement managerial : une analyse sur quelques PME au Cameroun. *Management & Sciences Sociales*, hal-03247166. https://hal.archives-ouvertes.fr/hal-03247166

Smith, M. L. (2020, June 20). Transformational Leadership in Higher Education in Panamá. Latitude Multidisciplinary Research Journal, 2(13), 39–40.

Soh, J. (2018). Management par le Kongossa (French Edition) (1st ed.). Living Books Publishing.

Song, L., Yao, Y., & Wang, X. (2012). Private Enterprise in China. *Australian National University Press.*

Soria, Karla, Honores, Guillermo, & Gutiérrez, Julián. (2016). Gender and Social Legitimacy of Entrepreneurship: Contribution to Entrepreneurial Intention in University Students from Chile and Colombia. Journal of technology management & innovation, 11(3), 67-76. https://dx.doi.org/10.4067/S0718-27242016000300008

Srića, V. (2020, March 30). Afterwork sa Srićom - LEADERSHIP kako postati vođa [Video]. YouTube.

Stachura, P. D. (2008). Review: Anita J. Prazmowska, A History of Poland, Palgrave Macmillan, 2004; 256 pp.; 0333972538, £47.50 (hbk), 0333972546, £15.99 (pbk). *European History Quarterly, 38*(1), 179–181. DOI: 10.1177/02656914080380010438

Stein & partner. (2020, September 21). *Transformational Leadership in Central Eastern Europe.* Www.youtube.com. https://www.youtube.com/watch?v=Q2k5GArWtH4&t=3061s

Stephens, D. B. (1981). Cultural Variation in Leadership Style: A Methodological Experiment in Comparing Managers in the U. S. and Peruvian Textile Industries. *Management International Review*, 21(3).

Stojcic, N. (2012). Two Decades of Croatian Transition: A Retrospective Analysis. *Southeast European Journal of Economics and Business*, 7(2), 63– 76. https://doi.org/10.2478/v10033-012-0015-5

Studentski Poduzetnički Inkubator. (2021, september 23). Leadership Marija Kalinić [Video]. YouTube.Energy Community. World Energy. Community/members/entry/Croatia

Sullivan, M. (2020). Panamá: An overview. Congressional Research Service.

Sully de Luqu e, M. F., & Arbaiza, L. A. (2005). The complexity of managing human resources in Peru. *The International Journal of Human Resource Management*, 16(12), 2237–2253. https://doi.org/10.1080/09585190500358661

Tarapuez Chamorro, Edwin. (2016). Las dimensiones culturales de Geert Hofstede y la intención emprendedora en estudiantes universitarios del departamento del Quindío (Colombia). Pensamiento & Gestión, (41), 60-90. Retrieved from http://www.scielo.org.co/scielo

TEDx Talks. (2018, December 11). Cómo motivar a los profesionales de tu empresa en 10 minutos | Alfonso Alcantara | TEDxLeon [Video]. YouTube. https://www.youtube.com/watch?v=OF_rEVrQHv

Teko, H. T., & Bapes, Y. B. B. (2010, September 29). Influence sociale et leadership dans la direction des personnes. *Sociologies*. https://doi.org/10.4000/sociologies.3204

Thai PBS World. (2020, June 15). *Leadership and "sav-ing face" in Thai society* [Video]. YouTube. https://www.youtube.com/watch?v=yOEIuBd0otk

Thailand 2021 international religious freedom report. (2022). In https://www.state.gov. United States Department of State Office of International Religious Freedom. https://www.state.gov/

Thompson, L.J. (2010). The global moral compass for business leaders. *Journal of Business Ethics*, 93, 15-32.

Thompson, O. (2022). Organisational Structure and Its Effects on Organisational Performance in Cameroon: The Case Of CDC. *Project House.* https://project-house.net/organisational-structure-and-its-effects-on-organisational-performance-in-cameroon-the-case-of-cdc/

Time News. (2022, August 19). The Basque Country registers its historical maximum of foreigners affiliated with Social Security. Time News. October 15, 2022, https://time.news/the-basque-country-registers-its-historical-maximum-of-foreigners-affiliated-with-social-security/

Ting-Toomey, S. (1988). Intercultural conflict styles. In Y. Kim & W. Gudykunst (Eds.), Theories in intercultural communication. Newbury Park, CA: Sage

Tomulić, A.M. & Grmuša, T. (2017). Empathy in working environment. *Media, culture and public relations, 8* (2), 194-205.

Torres , L. (2022, November 9). Leadership in Colombia. (I. Ammy Driss, & T. Kloosterboer, Interviewers)

Torres, L. E., Ruiz, C. E., Hamlin, B., & Velez-Calle, A. (2015). Perceived managerial and leadership effectiveness in Colombia. *European Journal of Training and Development*, *39*(3), 203–219. https://doi.org/10.1108/ejtd-08-2014-0062

Treviño, L.K., & Brown, M. (2004). Managing to be ethical: Debunking five business ethics myths. *Academy of Management Executive*, 18, 69-81.

Trompenaars, F., & Hampden-Turner, C. (1997). Riding the waves of culture: Understanding cultural diversity in business (2nd ed.). London: Nicholas-Brealey

Tsambou, A. D., & Ludwick, N. E. (2017). Caractéristiques Socioculturelles Du Manager Et Performance Des Pme Au Cameroun. *Revue Européenne Du Droit Social*, *1–34*, 90–116. https://www.ceeol.com/search/article-detail?id=478932

Turner, J. W. (1992). Ritual, Habitus, and Hierarchy in Fiji. Ethnology, 31(4), 291–302. https://doi.org/10.2307/3773421

Turner, R. (2018) Travel and tourism economic impact 2018 Belize

Tursunbaevich, B. B., Bulturbayevich, M. B., & Rahmat, A. (2021). The Impact of The Pandemic on The Economy of The Republic of Uzbekistan. *Aksara: Jurnal Ilmu Pendidikan Nonformal*, *7*(1), 161-168.

Twenge, J.M., Campbell, S.M., Hoffman, J.B. i Lance, C.E. (2010). Generational differences in work values: leisure and extrinsic values increasing, social and intrinsic values decreasing. *Journal of Management*, 36(5), 1117-1142.

Ukosakal, M. (2005). The significance of 'face' and politeness in social interaction as revealed through Thai 'face' idioms. In R. T. Lakoff & S. Ide (Eds.), Broadening the Horizon of Linguistic Politeness (pp. 117-128). John Benjamins Publishing Company, retrieved from http://digital.casalini.it/9789027294111

Universidad de Panamá , (2004). Universidad de Panamá Vicerrectoria De Investigacion Y Postgrado.

Urcola Consultoría. (n.d.).Nunca lo olvides, tú dependes de las personas que diriges | October 15, 2022, https://urcolaconsultores.net/nunca-lo-olvides-tu-dependes-de-las-personas-que-diriges/

Urziceanu, L, EMBA, CEC, ACC (n.d.). LinkedIn. Accessed 5 December 2022, from https://www.linkedin.com/in/liliana-urziceanu-emba-cec-acc-69294211/recent-activity/shares/

Valenta, M., & Gregurović, S. (2014). Ethnic groups and a dynamic of boundary making among co-ethnics: An experience from Croatian Istria.*Ethnicities*, *15*(3), 414-439. https://doi.org/10.1177/1468796814529551

Vanzie, M. (2022) Microsoft Teams interview. 23 November.

Vaughn, W. (n.d.). Characteristics of global Thai leaders [Docter of Education dissertation]. Pepperdine University

Vicente, E (2022). Personal Interview November 8th.

Vonk A. (7 November, 2022). Personal Interview.

Vora, D., & Kainzbauer, A. (2020). Humanistic leadership in Thailand: a mix of indigenous and global aspects using a cross-cultural perspective. *Cross Cultural & Strategic Management, 27(4),* https://doi.org/10.1108/CCSM-01-2020-0008

Votpusk. (2016). Государственные языки Казахстана. Retrieved from https://www.votpusk.ru/story/article.asp?ID=15759 on 31 March 2019.

Vrdoljak Raguz, I. (2017). Comparative research of dominant leadership styles in large enterprises in the Republic of Croatia.*W spółczesne Problemy Ekonomiczne*, 14, 79–87.

Wang, A. C. (2019). Developmental or Exploitative? How Chinese Leaders Integrate Authoritarianism and Benevolence to Cultivate Subordinates. *Academy of Management Discoveries*, 5(3), 291–313. https://doi.org/10.5465/amd.2018.0006

Wang, B. X., & Chee, H. (2011). Chinese Leadership. *Palgrave Macmillan*.

Wang, H., Han, X., & Li, J. (2020). Supervisor narcissism and employee performance: A moderated mediation model of affective organizational commitment and power distance orientation. *Basic and Applied Social Psychology*, 1–16. https://doi.org/10.1080/01973533.2020.1810042

Wang, J. (2011). Understanding managerial effectiveness: a Chinese perspective. *Journal of European Industrial Training*, 35(1), 6–23. https://doi.org/10.1108/03090591111095718

Wang, J., Wang, G. G., Ruona, W. E. A., & Rojewski, J. W. (2005). Confucian values and the implications for international HRD. *Human Resource Development International*, *8*(3), 311–326. https://doi.org/10.1080/13678860500143285

Warszewska-Makuch, M. (2019). Nierówności płci na rynku pracy: przegląd literatury. *Bezpieczeństwo Pracy: nauka i praktyka*, *9*. 15-19. DOI:10.5604/01.3001.0013.4544

Wengler, S., Fuereder, R., Ueberwimmer, M., & Hautamaki, P. (2021). *Sales organizations on the path of digitalization – A reflection from Germany, Finland, and Austria* (pp. 50–57).

Wheeler, C., Gallagher, J., McDonough, M. & Sookpokakit-Namfa, B. (1997), Improving SchoolCommunity Relations in Thailand, in W.K. Cummings & P.G. Altbach (eds), *The Educational Change in Thailand 205 Challenge of Eastern Asian Education: Implications for America* (State University of New York Press): 205–319.

Wilk, R., & Barbosa, L. (2013). Rice and Beans. Berg.

Winkler, R. (2013). Przywództwo i komunikacja w zespole projektowym. *Finanse, Rynki Finansowe, Ubezpieczenia*, *64*(1), 473-481.

Wirba, A. V. (2015). Leadership Style: School Perspective in Cameroon. *Education Research International*, 2015, 1–9. https://doi.org/10.1155/2015/439345

Witzel, M. (2004). Management: The Basics. Routledge.

Woods, J. C., Murzi, H., & Schuman, A. L. (2021). Effects of Uncertainty Avoidance and Country Culture on Perceptions of Power Distance in the Learning Process. *Conference: American Society for Engineering Education (ASEE) Annual Virtual Conference & Exposition, #34361*. https://www.researchgate.net/publication/354046507

Yannick, T. E. (2018, June). Cultural Aspect of Doing Business in Cameroon and Business Opportunities. *Centria University of Applied Sciences: Business Management*.

Yuan, L., Chia, R., & Gosling, J. (2022). Confucian Virtue Ethics and Ethical Leadership in Modern China. *Journal of Business Ethics*. https://doi.org/10.1007/s10551-021-05026-5

Zallo, R., & Ayuso, M. (Eds.). (2009). Conocer el País Vasco: viaje al interior de su cultura, historia, sociedad e instituciones. Servicio Central de Publicaciones del Gobierno Vasco.

Zhao, L. (2022). Uzbek for My Heart: Language Choice and Identity Negotiation in Multilingual Uzbekistan. *Security and Communication Networks*, *2022*, 1–8. https://doi.org/10.1155/2022/8220998

Zhu, J. (2022). WeChat video call interview. 24 November.

Zumitzavan, V (2022). Personal interview November 4th

Zùniga, Pozzi-Escot, Inez, Lopez, & Luiz Enrique. (1990). *Educación bilingüe intercultural: reflexiones y desafíos* (eds). Lima, Fomciencias.

英盛. (2022, November 22). *管理者领导力模型分享·领导需要掌握的技能 领导需要掌握的技能 领导风格与技能* [Video]. Bilibili. https://www.bilibili.com/video/BV1pd4y1t7r6/?spm_id_from=333.337.search-card.all.click

马云. (2018). *马云开挂夸女人：一家顶级公司应该女多男少* [Video]. 凤凰网科技. https://tech.ifeng.com/c/7fDkna6hYe0

黄, J. (2017). *Tea Ceremony, a new leadership style* [Video]. Youku. https://v.youku.com/v_show/id_XMzIzMDgzMTc2OA==.html?spm=a2h0c.8166622.PhoneSokuUgc_1.dtitle

黄景. (2022, October 13). 领导力的五种境界 · 看看你在哪一层？ [Video]. Bilibili.

www.ingramcontent.com/pod-product-compliance
Ingram Content Group UK Ltd.
Pitfield, Milton Keynes, MK11 3LW, UK
UKHW042010190726
13854UKWH00005B/2231